Urban Wildscapes

bout urban
ase derelict,
etation and
ustrial sites,
t lots and a
Frequently
ted and this

s, the book
meaning and
eir particular
, design and

diverse loca-
le from small
aginary wild-
including the
all kinds of
or landscape
capes to the

epartment of
the meanings
interested in
ciate Editor of

munication of
ations and as
an artist. He began working for a regional ~g~~~~~ ~~~~~~~~e in 2002 and left to set up Environment Room Ltd in 2005. After five years as Director, he moved on from the company and is now focusing on his artistic practices with the project *The Museum of Now*. The project incorporates photography, video, audio and physical installations, to raise questions about contemporary society.

Edited by Anna Jorgensen and Richard Keenan

Urban Wildscapes

Routledge
Taylor & Francis Group

LONDON AND NEW YORK

First published 2012
by Routledge
2 Park Square, Milton Park, Abingdon, Oxon OX14 4RN

Simultaneously published in the USA and Canada
by Routledge
711 Third Avenue, New York, NY 10017

Routledge is an imprint of the Taylor & Francis Group, an informa business

British Library Cataloguing in Publication Data
A catalogue record for this book is available from the British Library

Library of Congress Cataloging in Publication Data
Urban wildscapes/edited by Anna Jorgensen and Richard Keenan.
  p. cm.
  Includes bibliographical references and index.
  1. Urban ecology (Sociology) 2. Wilderness areas. 3. Vacant lands. 4. Abandoned buildings. I. Jorgensen, Anna. II. Keenan, Richard.
  HT241.U729 2011
  307.76–dc22

                                                                        2011002386

ISBN: 978-0-415-58105-9 (hbk)
ISBN: 978-0-415-58106-6 (pbk)
ISBN: 978-0-203-80754-5 (ebk)

Typeset in Frutiger
by Wearset Ltd, Boldon, Tyne and Wear
Printed and bound in Great Britain by Ashford Colour Press Ltd., Gosport, Hampshire

Contents

Notes on contributors

Chris Baines is an independent environmentalist and an award-winning broadcaster. He taught landscape design and management at postgraduate level until 1986. He was one of the founders of the UK's first urban wildlife trusts at the end of the 1970s and his book *How to Make a Wildlife Garden* (Frances Lincoln 1985) has been continuously in print for more than 25 years. He works with clients in the corporate sector and with central and local government and he is a national Vice President of the Royal Society of Wildlife Trusts. He works from home in inner-city Wolverhampton.

Jon Binnie is a Reader in Human Geography at Manchester Metropolitan University. His research interests focus on the urban and transnational politics of sexualities. He is the author of *The Globalization of Sexuality* (Sage 2004) and the co-author of *The Sexual Citizen: Queer Politics and Beyond* (Polity 2000) and *Pleasure Zones: Bodies, Cities, Spaces* (Syracuse University Press 2001). He is also the co-editor of *Cosmopolitan Urbanism* (Routledge 2005) and special issues of *Political Geography*, *Social and Cultural Geography* and *Environment and Planning A*.

Renée de Waal has worked since 2010 as a PhD researcher for the Landscape Architecture chair group of Wageningen University, focusing on renewable energy and landscape aesthetics. She graduated from Wageningen University in landscape architecture in 2009 and did both her internship and final thesis at the Internationale Bauausstellung (IBA) Fürst-Pückler-Land in Germany.

Arjen de Wit has worked as project manager for the Lusatian Lakeland for the Internationale Bauausstellung (IBA) Fürst-Pückler-Land in Germany since 2008. He graduated as a regional planner at Wageningen University in 2006 and subsequently worked as a researcher at Wageningen University for the chair groups Land Use Planning and Socio-spatial Analysis.

Nigel Dunnett is a Professor in Urban Horticulture in the Department of Landscape, and Director of the Green Roof Centre, at the University of Sheffield. His background lies within the fields of ecology, botany, horticulture, and garden and landscape design and his work integrates all these disciplines, with particular focus on green roofs, rain gardens, and naturalistic planting design. He developed the concept of 'Pictorial Meadows' and consults widely on naturalistic planting design, including for the London 2012 Olympic Park.

Tim Edensor teaches cultural geography at Manchester Metropolitan University. He is the author of *Tourists at the Taj* (Routledge 1998), *National Identity, Popular Culture and Everyday Life* (Berg 2002) and *Industrial Ruins: Space, Aesthetics and Materiality* (Berg 2005); as well as the editor of *Geographies of Rhythm* (Ashgate 2010), and co-editor of *Spaces of Vernacular Creativity* (Routledge 2009) and *Urban Theory Beyond the West: A World of Cities* (Routledge 2011). Tim has written extensively on national identity, tourism, industrial ruins, walking, driving, football cultures and urban materiality and is currently investigating landscapes of illumination.

Bethan Evans is a Lecturer in the Department of Geography and Centre for Medical Humanities at Durham University. She has published in journals such as *Transactions of the Institute of British Geographers, Antipode, Gender, Place and Culture, Geography Compass and Area*. Her research interests are in children's geographies, fat studies, embodiment and critical approaches to health. She is currently working on an Economic and Social Research Council project on the built environment in anti-obesity policy, and on a book entitled *Fat Bodies, Fat Spaces: Critical Geographies of Obesity* for the *Antipode* book series (Wiley).

Paul H. Gobster is Research Social Scientist with the United States Department of Agriculture Forest Service's Northern Research Station in Chicago, and the Editor of *Landscape and Urban Planning*. His current research examines people's perceptions of natural area restoration and management, the interface between aesthetic and ecological values in landscape, and the design and provision of urban green spaces to encourage healthy lifestyles.

Catherine Heatherington is reading for a PhD with the Department of Landscape at the University of Sheffield, whilst running her garden design practice in London. She loves the marshes and open skies of East Anglia, where she spent her childhood, and there are echoes of these muted landscapes in many of her gardens. Catherine's fascination with wildscapes and dereliction can also be traced to those early years, exploring abandoned waterside sites and the rotting hulks of boats near her home.

Maria Hellström Reimer is a visual artist with a PhD in landscape architecture, now holding a position as Professor in Design Theory in the School of Arts and Communication at Malmö University, Sweden. Her academic interests range from theoretical aesthetics and art activism to urban studies and design methodology. Current research includes the inter-disciplinary and arts-based project Land Use Poetics, an international collaboration around spatial practices, technologies and imaginaries. She is also affiliated with the Design Faculty at the Royal College of Technology, Stockholm and a member of the Swedish Research Council's Committee for Artistic Research.

Julian Holloway is a Senior Lecturer in Human Geography in the Division of Geography and Environmental Management at Manchester Metropolitan University. His research focuses upon the geographies of affect, embodiment and practice with particular attention given to religion, spirituality and the supernatural. He has published numerous articles related to these interests in journals such as *Environment and Planning A*, *Annals of the Association of American Geographers* and *Cultural Geographies*. He is also the co-editor (with Binnie, Millington and Young) of *Cosmopolitan Urbanism* (Routledge 2005).

Anna Jorgensen is a Lecturer in Landscape Architecture in the Department of Landscape at the University of Sheffield. Her research focuses on the meanings and benefits of urban green and open spaces, and she is especially interested in woodland and other urban 'wilderness' landscapes. She is an Associate Editor of *Landscape Research*.

Richard Keenan has spent the last nine years working on the communication of environmental and social issues both in marketing and communications and as an artist. He began working for a regional organization in Yorkshire in 2002 and left to set up Environment Room Ltd in 2005. After five years as Director, he moved on from the company and is now focusing on his artistic practices with the project *The Museum of Now*. The project incorporates photography, video, audio and physical installations, to raise questions about contemporary society.

Andreas Langer is an academically trained engineer and studied Landscape Planning at the Technical University of Berlin (1978–1984). He was a Research Assistant at the Institute of Ecology, Technical University of Berlin (1988–1992), specializing in the phytosociology of ruderal vegetation. Since 1992 he has been a partner in the planning office planland Planungsgruppe Landschaftsentwicklung with the main emphasis on landscape and environmental planning and landscape architecture.

Yichen Li holds an MA in Landscape Architecture from the Landscape Department of the University of Sheffield (2008–2010), in which he specialized in landscape planning and design, especially the regeneration of post-industrial landscapes. In 2010, as an assistant to the chief planner of the Shanghai Expo, he helped compile the publications entitled *Planning of Expo 2010 Shanghai China* and *Landscape of Expo 2010 Shanghai China*. He is currently an assistant landscape architect at Aedas Urban Design & Landscape Ltd, with the main emphasis on landscape design.

Lilli Lička is Head of the Institute of Landscape Architecture in the Department of Spatial, Landscape and Infrastructural Sciences at the University of Natural Resources and Applied Life Sciences in Vienna, Austria. She has worked in professional practice in the Netherlands, and since 1991 has had her own practice, koselička, together with Ursula Kose in Vienna (www.koselicka.at). Completed work includes projects in housing, historic landscapes and parks, gardens and the urban public realm.

Steve Millington is a Senior Lecturer in Human Geography at Manchester Metropolitan University. His research interests include football and place identity, place marketing and branding, and the relationship between light, place and society, including Christmas lights and Blackpool Illuminations. Steve has published widely in international journals including *Sociology* and *Environment and Planning A*. He is also co-editor of two edited collections, *Cosmopolitan Urbanism* (Routledge 2005) and *Spaces of Vernacular Creativity* (Routledge 2009). Steve is also a Fellow of the Institute of Place Management.

Helen Morse Palmer is a freelance artist (www.missmorsepalmer.com). She devises and performs regularly with Station House Opera and is an Associate Member of the Live Art Garden Initiative. She has collaborated with John Deller to form the Lookoutpost Artists Group. Since 2008 she has also worked part time as a Community Artist for Epping Forest District Council. She is an active participant and workshop leader for the Blue Museum of Small Objects Academy of Tea Trolley Dancing and holds a black belt in Kung Fu. Helen holds a first class honours degree in Fine Art from Reading University, and an MA in Fine Art from Central Saint Martins.

Katy Mugford believes that adventure, imagination and play are equally important for adults and children. She studied Art History at the University of York and Birkbeck College, London. She writes and paints.

Mattias Qviström holds an MSc (1998) and a PhD (2003) in Landscape Architecture, both from the Swedish University of Agricultural Sciences (SLU), with a dissertation on landscape theory and the materialization of modern ideas of time, speed and place within early twentieth-century road planning. He has been an Associate Professor in Landscape Planning in the Department of Landscape Architecture at SLU since 2008. From 2004 he has led several research projects on urbanization and landscape changes at the urban fringe, focusing on the interplay between spatial planning and everyday life. His current research combines landscape and planning history in studies of urban sprawl and peri-urban landscapes.

Ian D. Rotherham, environmental geographer, ecologist and landscape historian, is a Reader in Tourism and Environmental Change, Professor of Environmental Geography, and International Research Coordinator at Sheffield Hallam University. He is an international authority on urban ecology and environmental history. He has researched and written extensively on the history and ecology of Yorkshire landscapes, and on urban and riverine ecologies and histories. His particular fascination is the transformation, often beyond recognition, of ancient landscapes by human activity. Ian's work on this landscape change in relation to people and flooding has been very widely reported. He also writes and broadcasts on environmental issues.

Dougal Sheridan is a Lecturer in Architecture at the University of Ulster, a member of the Building Initiative Research Group (www.buildinginitiative.org), and Principle of LID Architecture (www.lid-architecture.net). His research publications focus on critical theory in relation to the appropriation of urban space, and publications and awards in practice relate to the use of landscape concepts and strategies in architecture and urbanism.

Marian Tylecote was born in South Africa where she studied Fine Art before moving to England. She taught art and worked as a designer (mainly in advertising and textiles) before gaining a BSc in Landscape Design and Ecology in the Department of Landscape at the University of Sheffield, and thereafter an MA in Landscape Research and Planning at the same institution. She specializes in the application of ecology in designed urban landscapes (both in teaching and research) and is reading for a PhD focusing on ruderal perennial vegetation and competitive grassland.

Catharine Ward Thompson is a Research Professor of Landscape Architecture at Edinburgh College of Art and the University of Edinburgh. She is Director of OPENspace – the research centre for inclusive access to outdoor environments – based at Edinburgh College of Art and Heriot-Watt University and directs the College's Landscape Architecture PhD programme. She leads a multidisciplinary research consortium entitled I'DGO (Inclusive Design for Getting Outdoors), which focuses on quality of life for older people, in collaboration with the Universities of Salford, Warwick, Heriot-Watt and Edinburgh. She is a Fellow of the Landscape Institute and an Advisory Group member of SPARColl (the Scottish Physical Activity Research Collaboration) led by the University of Strathclyde.

Christopher Woodward is an art historian whose interest in ruins began when working at Sir John Soane's Museum. He was Director of the Holburne Museum of Art, Bath, until 2005, and is currently Director of the Garden Museum in London. His book *In Ruins* (Chatto & Windus 2001) was shortlisted for the Rhys Prize for young writers; it has subsequently been published in America, China, Japan and Italy. The chapter in this book reflects his new interest in the ruins of modern cities – and, in particular, the new cult of the ruin in the United States.

Foreword

The wild side of town

Chris Baines

HALF A CENTURY OF LANDSCAPE CHANGE

I was born in inner-city Sheffield soon after the end of the war, in a terraced house surrounded by bomb-sites and building sites. When I was three, my family moved to a village on the edge of town, where the fields were still relatively rich in wildlife, but where new housing estates were already beginning to blanket the landscape. As a student I moved to rural Kent and experienced the new agro-chemical revolution at first hand, and I have spent my working life in the thick of urban Britain.

In those sixty-odd years I have seen a striking role reversal in the relationship between the land and its wildlife. Whilst much of Britain's farming countryside has become sterile and relatively lifeless, Britain's urban landscapes have grown wilder and greener. As a child, if I wanted to hear skylarks I would walk out into the farmers' fields beyond the edge of town. Now they have become a rural rarity, but skylarks are a familiar feature of the post-industrial grasslands in the Black Country, Merseyside, South Yorkshire and most of the UK's other conurbations.

Until quite recently the UK's mainstream nature conservation movement focused almost all of its efforts on the battle to stem the tide of habitat loss in the rural countryside. Surviving landscape fragments were plucked from the advancing tide of industrialized farming and forestry, to be preserved as small islands of excellence. This strategy did help to protect some species, but it also made nature very exclusive and it helped to speed up the disintegration of the wider landscape.

By contrast, whilst Britain's rural countryside was being increasingly denatured, the urban landscape was becoming richer. The decline of heavy industry, the downscaling of the railway network and the closure of the coal mines left an extensive legacy of urban wasteland where benign neglect resulted in a wildscape of great complexity – popular as an informal playground and ideal for many of the wild plants and animals that were finding it increasingly difficult to survive in the new agricultural landscapes. This network of relatively scruffy urban wasteland has become the perfect complement to the more manicured public parks, playing fields and recreation grounds that form the official green space network in our towns.

URBAN ECOSYSTEMS

Figure F.1
A wild edge in the amenity green space surrounding social housing at Norfolk Park forms part of Sheffield's wider urban ecosystem (photograph: Richard Keenan, 2009)

The scrubby woodland of the railway sidings or the canal-side bramble banks may be more obviously 'wild'. Nevertheless, the broad sweeps of grassland, the mature trees and the ornamental flower borders of more formal parks and public open spaces also contribute to the intricate mosaic of different habitats that make up the urban ecosystem. It is the diversity of interconnected habitats that makes urban areas so valuable for nature conservation.

The ecological quality of urban wild Britain has only very recently been recognized by the conservation establishment, although Sheffield University, through the work of the late Oliver Gilbert and others, has been in the vanguard of research and awareness raising for much longer than most. Now, at last, there seems to be a realization that urban wild spaces are really very significant in the UK.

The urban landscape has become critically important for a whole range of species. For example, goldfinches (*Carduelis carduelis*), which were once almost exclusively farmland birds, are now quite common visitors to garden bird feeders. They have learned to supplement their natural food of wasteland weed seeds with more exotic sunflower hearts. The urban landscape has also become the most likely place to see wild poppies (*Papaver rhoeas* L.), because whilst there is very little weedy disturbed ground in the farming countryside, disturbance is an inherent feature of urban areas. Migrant painted lady butterflies (*Vanessa cardui*), arriving from North Africa, will feed on urban wasteland thistle flowers and then move over the garden fence to exploit *Buddleia* blossom. Urban hedgehogs (*Erinaceus europaeus*) may be at greater risk from traffic, but they are less likely to fall prey to badgers (*Meles meles*), and the urban supply of food, from garden slugs to cat food, makes this a relatively supportive environment.

Although there are occasional very large wild spaces in the heart of town it is the integrity of the whole mosaic of different contributing elements in the landscape that really makes the difference (Figure F.1). That ecological continuity is important at every scale from the tight network of suburban gardens, to the road, railway and river corridors that cross whole conurbations. Relatively small urban sites can provide critical stepping stones for birds and insects in transit, particularly when the sites are linked together. For instance, swallows (*Hirundo rustica*) on migration will roost in reed beds each night. Big rural reed beds have a vital role to play, but small urban reed beds greatly increase the chance of successful migration. What is more, as climate change leads plants and animals to shift their comfort zone, this ecological continuity of the urban green space network will help to make territorial adaptation more achievable.

MULTIFUNCTIONAL URBAN GREEN SPACE

Urban wild space is clearly important for wildlife and for casual recreation, but it has other important roles to play in response to climate change. For example, more frequent rain storms and flash floods are predicted and wild spaces can provide the temporary holding ground for storm water run-off. Whilst roosting swallows and breeding newts (*Triturus* sp.) are important, so is the need to reduce the impact of flash flooding. This kind of multifunctional role for landscape is at last beginning to be taken seriously. In the context of heavily developed urban Britain we need to make use of issues such as surface water management to help in justifying the retention of wild informal open spaces. Urban wild space needs to be managed for the role that it can play in more sustainable environmental protection.

This is not easy territory for politicians or policymakers. These landscapes are regarded in a variety of conflicting ways – as storm water management facilities, swallow roosts, development sites and places to dump stolen cars. As a consequence, urban wild space tends to end up in the 'too hard to manage' category. Most of it survives by default and is managed through benign neglect. Local authorities rarely have a positive strategy for managing the entire mosaic of publicly owned, privately owned, temporary and permanent wild open spaces. Official open spaces will increasingly be enhanced by professional rangers and educational facilities. By contrast, whilst the informal landscape over the fence may have much more potential, its management seems very rarely to be taken seriously.

PEOPLE IN THE LANDSCAPE

The social management of urban wild space is really crucial, but it is undoubtedly also very challenging. As a youngster, I would happily disappear at eight in the morning and turn up again at four in the afternoon, covered in mud. That kind of free-range childhood is very rare today. In the 1970s and 1980s a number of us were working in the wild spaces of Brixton, Deptford and other inner-city neighbourhoods, introducing groups of children to nature on their doorstep. We had great times together, and all learned a great deal, but such informal and unregulated access by children to wild urban spaces would be out of the question today. Intellectually, most people agree that our children deserve more natural stimulation in their lives, and we know that urban wild space can provide it. Nevertheless, with every week that goes by there seems to be another good reason why rational parents choose to keep their kids inside. There is an urgent need for more creative management of dynamic landscapes close to home.

Urban wild space has a valuable role to play in tackling some of the great problems of today. Access to nature, environmental protection, healthy living, safer neighbourhoods – they can all be achieved in part through a more positive approach to urban green space management. In the chapters that follow, a number of experienced academics and practitioners share their enthusiasm for urban wild space. Together they make a powerfully persuasive case for taking this resource more seriously. If we do, then future generations of wildlife and people will have every reason to be grateful.

Introduction

Anna Jorgensen

'Urban wildscapes' are one of many 'scapes' that are currently being used to highlight and promote particular landscape qualities, functions and experiences. The name 'urban wildscape' suggests something specific, and the conference organized by the Department of Landscape at Sheffield University in 2007,[1] from which the idea for this book emerged, focused on:

> urban spaces where natural as opposed to human agency appears to be shaping the land, especially where there is spontaneous growth of vegetation through natural succession. Such wildscapes can exist at different scales, from cracks in the pavement, to much more extensive urban landscapes, including woodland, unused allotments, river corridors and derelict or brownfield sites.

> (Jorgensen 2008: 4) (Figure I.1)

However, both the scope and scale of the 'urban wildscapes' under consideration in this book has broadened considerably. Dougal Sheridan defines them as 'any area, space, or building where the city's normal forces of control have not shaped how we perceive, use, and occupy them' (Chapter 15 in this book: p. 201; 2007: 98). Here the 'normal forces of control' include planning policy,

Figure I.1
Miniature wildscape at the edge of the pavement in Sheffield, UK (photograph: Marian Tylecote, 2007)

building regulation, the normal commissioning process for the built environment, policing, surveillance and the ways in which places are contextualized within the official cultural narratives of the city (Chapter 15 in this book). The subject matter of this book ranges in scale from the small planting design interventions described by Marian Tylecote and Nigel Dunnett to the vast wastelands created in the aftermath of the brown coal mining operations in Lusatia, German Democratic Republic that are the subject of the chapter by Renée de Waal and Arjen de Wit. It includes 'untouched' wildscapes, planning and design interventions within these sites, as well as a wider discussion of how wildscape qualities may inform the planning, design and management of the urban environment more generally. Whilst vegetation is a crucial element within many of the landscapes described in this book, it is not necessarily the defining characteristic of all of them, and the book covers a range of soft and hard places. A fundamental aim of the book is to demonstrate that there is no dichotomy of regulated and wild urban places: rather there is a continuum ranging from 'wilderness' to apparently ordered spaces, with different levels of wildness existing at multiple different scales at each locality. In this sense wildscape can be seen as an idea, a way of thinking about urban space, rather than a closed category that can be spatially located.

The book itself is divided up into three parts. Part 1 contains a series of contributions exploring theoretical aspects of urban wildscapes; Part 2 consists of a collection of international case studies describing different interventions in urban wildscapes; the chapters in Part 3 describe the implications for landscape architectural and urban design practice, both in relation to derelict and post-successional wildscape sites and to the wider urban environment.

In Part 1, Christopher Woodward explores the aesthetics and iconography of the ruin in the twentieth and twenty-first centuries; Paul H. Gobster examines the natural history of the city of Chicago, and the future role of wildscapes within urban areas; and Catharine Ward Thompson describes the social history of parks and wildscapes, focusing on their value as environments for children and young people. Tim Edensor, Bethan Evans, Julian Holloway, Steve Millington and Jon Binnie question the teleological and normative orderings of the life course and the city that banish playful activities to childhood and wild spaces; and Katy Mugford contrasts the depiction of wildscapes in children's fiction as fertile ground for the development of life skills, with their real-life image as a threat to children and young people.

The case studies in Part 2 begin with Renée de Waal and Arjen de Wit's account of the different strategies being used to rehabilitate the landscape aftermath of the opencast brown coal mining in Lusatia, formerly in the German Democratic Republic and now part of a reunified Germany; Yichen Li describes the ambitious measures taken to preserve and enhance an urban wetland, as part of the development of a former wildscape site for the 2010 Shanghai World Expo; and Maria Hellström Reimer asks what the idea of the 'commons', as exemplified by the self-proclaimed free state of Christiania in Copenhagen,

Denmark, has to offer in the context of contemporary urban planning and design. Ian D. Rotherham traces the historical development of the River Don, a linear urban wildscape, and outlines its future potential within the city of Sheffield, UK; Marian Tylecote and Nigel Dunnett introduce their experiments in supplementing and enhancing ruderal vegetation in the context of a new district park on a former wildscape site in Sheffield, UK; and Andreas Langer describes the creation of the Nature-Park Südgelände, on a former freight railway yard in Berlin, Germany. Concluding Part 2, Helen Morse Palmer recounts the use of Sydenham Hill Wood in South London as the venue for a series of outdoor art events inspired by the woodland.

Part 3 moves the discussion towards a consideration of how the theory and case studies (and others like them) can be used to inform landscape architectural practice, both in relation to the treatment of urban wildscapes, and to the planning and design of the urban public realm more generally. Catherine Heatherington explores four different ways of writing and reading narratives in the landscape, and illustrates these approaches with projects involving derelict and post-industrial sites; and Mattias Qviström demonstrates the limitations of the tools and terminologies of landscape architectural and planning practice in relation to urban wildscapes, using Gyllin's Garden, on the outskirts of Malmö, Sweden, as an example. Dougal Sheridan shows how spatial, temporal and material planning and design strategies can be developed from a theoretical understanding of wildscapes, using examples from his own practice across a range of urban sites in Ireland; and finally, Anna Jorgensen and Lilli Lička show how qualities inherent in urban wildscapes can form the basis for design approaches within the wider urban landscape, drawing on projects from Lička's design practice in Vienna.

What are the common threads running through this consideration of such a diverse selection of landscapes and approaches to landscape architectural theory and practice, and why is it relevant to combine a discussion of these issues in one book at the present time? This introduction will explore these themes and issues in relation to the contributions in this book and their wider context.

Explicit or implicit in many of the chapters is a desire to understand and re-interpret the aesthetics of urban wildscapes. Here, the emphasis is not on the formal or visual qualities of these landscapes but rather on their functional characteristics and the value systems that give them their meaning. What are these landscapes, why do they evoke such contradictory responses, why do they matter now and how can they be revisioned in the towns and cities of the future? As Christopher Woodward points out in Chapter 1, what was formerly counter-cultural urban decay, has in some respects become mainstream, informing disparate cultural productions ranging from the music and fashion industries to architectural and landscape practice. The idea of using industrial ruins as a structural motif in landscape architecture dates back at least to Gas Works Park in Seattle, USA, opened to the public in 1975, and designed by the American landscape architect Richard Haag. A more recent example, widely thought of as representing landscape architectural best practice in the re-use of former industrial sites, is the Landschaftpark in Duisburg, Germany, designed by Peter Latz in 1991 (described in more detail by Catherine Heatherington in Chapter 13 of this book).

Yet despite this partial acceptance of the derelict in some contexts there is still a fundamental and long-standing uneasiness surrounding many derelict sites and the buildings and structures they contain. Whilst the ruins of ancient buildings have been used in landscape, art and literature as emblems celebrating the greatness of past civilizations, or as vehicles for sentimental reflections concerning *vanitas*, the vanity of human endeavour (Woodward 2002), at their most basic, ruins have always signified the death, disaster or misfortune that befell their previous occupants (Jorgensen and Tylecote 2007). Furthermore, to many, the ruins that form part of derelict urban sites are too new, too ubiquitous, too extensive or too closely bound up with economic collapse, war or natural disaster to evoke the same feelings of awe or pleasurable melancholy (Roth 1997: 20) (Figure I.2).

In the opening chapter of this book Christopher Woodward uses Detroit as a prime example of the global phenomenon of the shrinking city[2] to kick start an exploration of the visual iconography and the multiple meanings that underlie our conflicted relationship with ruins, industrial and otherwise, exploring many of the previously mentioned themes, including the question of whether there is a straightforward divergence of opinion between 'insiders' and 'outsiders' as to the fate of industrial ruins and their physical and social infrastructures. In Chapter 6, Renée de Waal and Arjen de Wit describe how residents of Lusatia in the former Democratic Republic of Germany, when confronted with the aftermath of opencast brown coal mining, opted for radical landscape remediation in contrast

Figure I.2
Hotel Jugoslavija in the Novi Beograd district of Belgrade in Serbia, which was badly damaged in the 1999 NATO (North Atlantic Treaty Organisation) bombings; like many public buildings in Belgrade the hotel is dilapidated, testifying to the country's recent troubled history and lack of resources for investment in public infrastructure. The ubiquity and recent history of urban decay in some parts of Belgrade gives it a more sombre set of meanings compared with its equivalent in, for example, the UK (photograph: Anna Jorgensen, 2010)

to a development proposal that would have retained the dramatic landscape created by the mining operations.

As Woodward (2002) and others have pointed out, nature in ruins also has an ambivalent role (Jorgensen and Tylecote 2007). On one hand it has a kind of picturesque effect, softening and decorating ruined buildings and structures; on the other it signifies the presence of the natural processes that progressively *destroy* those buildings and structures, what Janowitz (1990: 108) calls 'a frightening reversion to matter'.

Historically, many Western cultures have tended at various times to maintain highly dichotomized visions of nature and culture (Plumwood 1993). During the period of colonization of the so-called 'New World' these visions were used to justify the annexation of 'wilderness' or *terra nullius* by European settlers for their own exploitation and use. The continued existence of primordial wilderness was depicted as morally reprehensible, and abandoning land that had been settled was said to be even more dishonourable (Jorgensen and Tylecote 2007). Later, during the nineteenth century, as pristine wilderness became relatively scarce, it was rehabilitated as a recreational and spiritual resource, and subsequently given legal protection as natural park or nature reserve. Paradoxically, whilst pristine wilderness rose in status, land that had been built upon or cultivated and then abandoned was considered to have been allowed to revert to wilderness, and retained the negative connotations of the original *terra nullius*. Such land is still often referred to as wasteland, defined by the *Oxford English Dictionary* as 'land (esp. that which is surrounded by developed land) not used or unfit for cultivation or building and allowed to run wild' (1989). Just as the premodern terra *nullius* was regarded as a void awaiting colonization and exploitation, so contemporary wasteland is frequently regarded as a nonentity, fit for nothing but improvement or development; and as with the old *terra nullius*, it is often shown as literally blank space on maps and plans (Doron 2007).

In many contemporary urban wildscapes the derelict buildings and structures are embedded in extensive landscapes of natural succession composed of urban pioneer vegetation communities, mixtures of natives and exotics, frequently forming dense thickets of woody species, described by Schama as 'scraggly, misshapen good-for-nothing growths of willow and bog alder, and white birch' (1996: 178). These Frankensteinian assemblages do not conform to any comfortable landscape stereotypes, in terms of their species selection, spatial organization or productivity. On the contrary, they seem to confound accepted boundaries between nature and culture (Figure I.3).

Paul H. Gobster's account of the natural history of Chicago's wildscapes or 'unnatural places' in Chapter 2 is particularly interesting in relation to such dichotomous ideas of nature (wilderness) and culture, bearing in mind that the colonization of North America's 'wilderness' took place in relatively recent history. As Gobster describes, the idea of an urban nature that is a response to a unique set of conditions created by humans over time has yet to become established in the US. He gives, as one example, the book entitled *A Natural History of the*

Figure I.3
Buddleia exhuberantly spills over the boundary of a derelict site in Sheffield (photograph: Marian Tylecote, 2007)

Chicago Region (Greenberg 2008). It seems that this book focuses on the native ecosystems of the region as they were before the city of Chicago was built, and that wildscapes are not mentioned except as a threat to those ecosystems. Thus, as Gobster points out, 'the appreciation we come away with for the *region* of Chicago is one that has no *city* of Chicago in it' (Chapter 2 in this book: p. 33). If this assertion seems a trifle exaggerated one has only to read about the restoration work at Montrose Point, Chicago, where mainly native plant species were used to create a series of established wildland habitats on a pre-existing wildscape, or about Chicago's weed ordinances, which class spontaneous wild urban vegetation as a public nuisance, for which landowners can be fined. Is the memory of primordial wilderness too recent and too threatening in the US collective unconscious to make urban wild spaces and their hybrid ecologies a viable landscape approach there? Gobster argues otherwise, but is clearly operating in a different and more challenging cultural context as regards re-visioning urban wildscapes.

The case study presented by Andreas Langer in Chapter 11, the Nature-Park Südgelände, presents a radically different view, in which the ruderal plant communities found in a post-successional abandoned freight railway yard in Berlin, Germany, formed the whole basis for the masterplanning of a new urban green space, the Nature-Park. The creation of the Nature-Park was supported by local residents, who encouraged the authorities to carry out an ecological survey that ultimately revealed the site to be one of the most biodiverse localities in the city. Validation of these ruderal plant communities that succeeded to the site is encapsulated by Langer in a phrase from the chapter title, 'pure urban nature'. In the Südgelände, urban nature is no longer seen as contaminated.

A different but equally radical approach to the revalidation of ruderal vegetation is set out by Marian Tylecote and Nigel Dunnett in Chapter 10, in the description of their work with tall herb vegetation, as part of the gradual transformation of Manor Fields Park from a wildscape to a new district park in a socially deprived area of Sheffield. One of the overriding aims informing the park's development is to retain its wildscape characteristics, whilst providing enhanced access and facilities to encourage existing and new users to develop a more positive relationship with the site. The chapter describes experiments in enhancing the existing tall herb vegetation by the addition of non-native herbaceous perennial species, with the aim of adding colour and prolonging the flowering season.

Another radical way of working with existing nature within a wildscape is presented by Yichen Li in Chapter 7. He describes how, as part of the development of the World Expo 2010, Shanghai, China, a decision had to be made as to the appropriate way of protecting the Houtan wetland, part of a post-industrial site south of the Huangpu River, which was to be transformed into the new Houtan Wetland Park. The design team devised an ambitious strategy of creating an entirely new wetland alongside the existing one, together with a riverside walk running the entire length of the two wetlands. As Catherine Heatherington points out in Chapter 13, the conservation of pre-existing wildscape features is still unusual in the UK and the approach currently being taken on the development site for the 2012 London Olympics is one of *tabula rasa*.

As Christopher Woodward concludes in Chapter 1, ruins challenge us to re-imagine the world. One of the imaginative leaps this challenge presents us with is to move beyond the boundaries of individual wildscape sites, and to think instead of a network of wildscape opportunities on a landscape scale. In Chapter 9, Ian D. Rotherham puts the launch of the River Don Catchment Trust in 2010 – to realize the potential of 'a linear urban wildscape' in providing multiple ecosystem services including wildlife habitat and flood regulation – in its historical context. The historical trajectory of the River Don, from vast wetland, to canalized and contaminated sewer, to recovering wildscape is typical of many urban rivers. Likewise in Chapter 6 Renée de Waal and Arjen de Wit describe the strategy for rehabilitating the former brown coal sites of Lusatia by creating a new regional-scale lake system.

Just as the abandonment of urban sites creates opportunities for pioneer vegetation to move in and colonize their unused spaces, so it creates a vacuum that attracts human pioneers to occupy and use the space in ways that are not possible within the more regulated and ordered parts of the city. As Edensor (2005) and others (Schneekloth 2007) have described, urban wildscapes are used for an enormous range of activities, ranging from the illicit to the respectable, including drug-taking, sexual encounters and prostitution, joy-riding, dumping unwanted stolen goods, fly-tipping, rough sleeping, lighting fires, impromptu buying and selling of goods, squatting, play and exploration, building shelters and dens (Figure I.4), tagging, gathering fruits and other objects, observing

Figure I.4
Makeshift shelter in the
Rivelin Valley, Sheffield
(photograph: Anna
Jorgensen, 2007)

nature, guerilla gardening, taking short cuts and walking the dog. In the same way as abandoned and derelict sites are frequently shown as empty space on maps and plans, so many of the less salubrious activities that take place in them are overlooked. In what Doron (2003) calls 'the void that does not exist' the actions of the socially invisible are ignored.

To say that wildscapes enable a range of uses that are not possible in most urban areas is, however, understating it: wildscapes do more than this. For some people, being in a space in which there is a complete absence of surveillance, regulation and frequently, other people, is a highly psychologically liberating experience in which the individual is free to be whatever they want to be: whether that be meditative, playful, sexually active, or whatever they are able to imagine (Doron 2007; Schneekloth 2007); and to engage with and modify their environment in ways that are not possible in other public open spaces. In Chapter 12, Helen Morse Palmer describes how Sydenham Hill Wood in London became a venue for a series of annual art events, in which the artists, freed from the constraints of showing in more conventional settings, were inspired to work in new ways, exploring diverse themes relating both to the past and present uses of the wood, and wider issues concerning the interrelationship between nature and culture.

For many people, the illegal or illicit activities that sometimes take place in wildscapes are seen as very threatening, so that they are effectively excluded from them. For these people, wildscapes are synonymous with these activities. Yet, as Catharine Ward Thompson comprehensively describes in Chapter 3, wildscapes are in many respects the ideal locations for children and young people to play or hang out in, providing numerous developmental and social benefits. For children, they are ideal play spaces, having the right combination of 'water and/or dirt, trees, bushes, and tall grass, variable topography, animal life, "loose parts", i.e. things to build with and "found" resources such as berries or fruits' (Hart 1982: 5) (Figure I.5); whilst for young people they offer both privacy and space in which to socialize and to try out new identities and behaviours. However, as Ward Thompson describes in her chapter, because of the perceived risks inherent in wildscapes, many children and young people are prevented from using them by their parents and carers, or are themselves reluctant to do so given their negative image and having had no previous positive experience of wildscape environments.

Ward Thompson places the whole question of children and young people and their relationship with wildscapes in the historical and social context of the origins of urban park and open space development, demonstrating that these places were generally intended to have a civilizing and improving impact on their users, and were not seen as wilderness-like environments for physically challenging or adventurous activity, or as an appropriate settings for horse-play or risqué behaviour. She shows how these early ideas about appropriate behaviour in public green space have been supplemented by fears concerning the presence of young people in public space, and how these and other barriers have served to limit the range of opportunities open to them.

In Chapter 5, Katy Mugford maps out the role of wildscapes in children's literature as imaginary settings for their personal development, focusing especially on themes of independence, responsibility, negotiating risk and emotional maturity; as well as the acquisition of physical skills, ranging from 'survival' skills such as swimming, to crafts normally reserved for adults, such as motor mechanics. She also explores the paradoxes inherent in the ways in which today's adults and parents recognize that wildscapes are in many respects the ideal setting for childhood development, having experienced wildscapes themselves, but feel compelled to restrict their own children's access to them.

An idea that is touched upon by Mugford, but taken up more centrally in Chapter 4 by Edensor *et al.*, is the way in which the worlds of the child and the adult are distinguished, both in terms of the activities that are deemed to be appropriate at each stage in the life course, and the ways in which these childish and adult activities are spatially located (and separated). Edensor *et al.* examine ruins as a locale for all types of playful activity, whilst critiquing a number of theoretical approaches that see play solely as childish, instrumental or purposeless behaviour, maintaining that play and playful actions are integral to many aspects of childhood and adulthood, and exposing the illusory nature of the rigid separation between activities associated with work or leisure. They identify ruins as 'exemplary realms' for an investigation of the playful potential of urban space more generally (Chapter 4 in this book: p. 65). Mugford also cites Cloke and Jones (2005), who point out that instead of making places 'safer' for children, hyperseparated notions of childhood and adulthood have a tendency to do the opposite, by removing the checks and balances that might prevent both childish excess and adult abuse.

Figure I.5
Children playing in rough
vegetation in the Nature
Playground in
Valbyparken,
Copenhagen, designed
by Helle Nebelong
(photograph: Anna
Jorgensen, 2008)

A distinguishing feature of the playful and other human activities that take place in wildscapes is their interaction with their surroundings. In most public urban spaces users are not permitted to change the physical fabric and the manner of using the space is heavily constrained by an array of social norms and legal instruments. In most urban green spaces even activities such as picking flowers and fruits or pitching tents are forbidden, or at least discouraged. In more extensive wildscapes users are free to interact with and modify the site in numerous ways such as harvesting vegetation or other materials, building structures, or indulging in acts of wanton destruction. For many people living in highly ordered urban environments the opportunities to experience the world in this way are few and far between, outside of private gardens, or remote wilderness areas. Furthermore, the absence of state-sponsored regulation in wildscapes creates opportunities for new forms of social organization ranging from the temporary co-operation needed to build a den or a raft to the complex long-term social structures that are needed to sustain the vast slum of Dharavi in Mumbai – where 80 per cent of the city's plastic waste is said to be recycled (Channel 4 2010) – or informal markets such as Izmailovo Market, Moscow (Russia), Istanbul Topkapi (Turkey) and Arizona Market in Brčko (the Balkans) (Mörtenböck and Mooshammer 2007).

In Chapter 8, Maria Hellström Reimer contrasts the Danish free state of Christiania, another self-organized squatter settlement, which has persisted in the centre of Copenhagen since the first unauthorized occupants made the former military barracks their home in 1971, with current officially-sanctioned trends in urban place-making. She uses the idea of the 'commons' to highlight Christiania's ability to manage its resources collectively, for the benefit of the community, whilst providing a space in which individuals are free to deviate, demonstrating its relevance as a socially reflexive approach to the contemporary production of urban space (Figure I.6).

Figure I.6
One of the main public open spaces in the Danish free state of Christiania, Copenhagen (for more information about Christiania, see Chapter 8 in this book) (photograph: Anna Jorgensen, 2010)

The question of how wildscapes can inform urban planning and design is addressed in different ways in most of the chapters in this book, and is the main focus of Part Three. Although earlier versions of the wildscape-inspired approaches to urban planning and design advocated in the book have been popular in the past – for example in the ecological approach to planning and design in the UK during the 1970s and early 1980s (Tregay and Gustavsson 1983) – they have fallen out of favour in the decades since. Whilst there is currently a great deal of interest in alternative approaches to landscape production based on what may loosely be termed urban wildscapes, there is a marked lack of theory and practice in this area. When I originally gave the paper on which Chapter 16 (the final chapter in Part Three of this book) is based, at the 'Landscape – Great Idea!' conference held in Vienna in April 2009, some members of the audience responded by asserting that the characteristics of wildscape are not replicable, that wildscapes develop spontaneously and can exist only in relation to the normative urban landscape, and that the moment we try to recreate, or even just preserve them, their special qualities are destroyed.

One of these special qualities is the 'layeredness' of wildscapes: the way in which they contain evidence of previous uses that become progressively obscured by subsequent uses and by the anthropogenic vegetation that quickly invades the abandoned or disused site, progressively decontextualizing the objects and surfaces it covers. In Chapter 13, Catherine Heatherington investigates different ways of responding to these 'buried narratives', concluding that a purely symbolic approach that utilizes objects or structures to tie the meaning of the site to a particular stage in its history is of limited value, turning the landscape into a riddle that is quickly solved. Such an approach does indeed tend to destroy the special qualities of the wildscape. On the other hand, approaches that seek to utilize the *processes* at work in wildscape, such as natural succession or atrophy, create a more dynamic landscape, whose meanings are both more complex and more fluid. Heatherington continues by suggesting that a 'relational' approach to the site goes one step further by not only utilizing wildscape processes but also connecting those processes spatially with the wider landscape, and temporally with the site's past and future.

In Chapter 14, Mattias Qviström suggests that planning policy and the architectonic spatial concepts commonly employed in landscape architecture are both significant barriers to the perpetuation of wildscapes, using Gyllin's Garden, a former plant nursery on the outskirts of Malmö, Sweden, as an example. Closed down in the 1970s, the nursery site became overgrown and was appropriated as a wildscape by local residents; but is now being transformed into a 'nature-park' and housing. Qviström describes the difficulties inherent in planning wildscapes, given that they are not formally recognized in planning instruments; and the shortcomings inherent in a masterplanning approach which emphasizes formal or spatial relationships when dealing with a wildscape.

In Chapter 15, Dougal Sheridan also addresses the need for appropriate planning typologies and mechanisms, and design approaches, when dealing with wildscape sites. In this chapter he explains how his previous study of the occupation and use of abandoned buildings in Berlin, Germany, has informed his urban design practice, effectively linking a comprehensive theoretical analysis of wildscape properties and processes to a series of strategies for intervention in the urban public realm. The chapter is illustrated with examples of completed projects in Dublin, Republic of Ireland, ranging from a small intervention in an extensive wildscape, to programmes and designs for two urban public open spaces with less overtly wildscape characteristics. Working with process, and, by implication, temporality, is key to many of the approaches he describes, whether it is by using a small intervention to facilitate wider changes, employing a programme of public involvement to determine the future of an existing public open space or creating a temporary public square with shipping containers in the docklands of post-credit crunch Dublin.

The final chapter, by Anna Jorgensen and Lilli Lička, adopts a similar approach to that of Dougal Sheridan, by making connections between specific wildscape characteristics and examples of ways in which these characteristics may be articulated in the design of public open spaces, drawn from Lička's practice in Vienna, but with more of an emphasis on the formal and/or spatial qualities of the projects under consideration. The chapter contrasts these wildscape qualities with the landscape characteristics inherent in contemporary trends in urban landscape design, focusing especially on a comparison of the efficacy of these qualities and characteristics as an expression of place and local identity.

At the beginning of this introduction it was suggested that wildscape is not just a spatial designation but a way of thinking about urban space; and the chapters in this book illustrate the diverse ways in which it can contribute not only to the theorizing of urban spaces and places, but also to their planning, design and management. As the examples referred to in this book demonstrate, landscapes that embody wildscape processes and qualities have the potential to be socially engaging if not socially-generated, expressive of their locality, low in resource inputs and may also constitute one of the ways in which green infrastructure, providing a suite of ecosystem services, may be retrofitted into urban areas. Urbanism currently has the task of responding to huge challenges including climate change, resource depletion, social division and an uncertain future for local, national and global economies. Paradoxically, it seems that urban wildscape is a useful nexus for ways of responding to these challenges.

NOTES

1 Background information on the book and conference can be found at www.urbanwildscapes.org
2 Shrinking cities are cities that are in the process of becoming depopulated as a result of economic, political and social processes such as de-industrialization, post-socialism and suburbanization with the result that large parts of the city become derelict. www.shrinkingcities.com/index.php?L=1.

REFERENCES

Channel 4 (2010) *Slumming It.* Online: www.channel4.com/4homes/on-tv/kevin-mccloud-slumming-it/ (accessed 10 January 2011).
Cloke, P. and Jones, O. (2005) 'Unclaimed territory: childhood and disordered space(s)', *Social and Cultural Geography*, 6(3): 311–333.
Doron, G. M. (2003) 'The void that does not exist', in Institut für Architekturtheorie der TU Wien und Österreichische Gesellschaft für Architektur (eds) *UmBau 20: Morality and Architecture. Architektur und Gesellschaft*, Vienna: Verlag edition selene.
—— (2007) 'Dead zones, outdoor rooms and the architecture of transgression', in K. A. Franck and Q. Stevens (eds) *Loose Space*, London: Routledge.
Edensor, T. (2005) *Industrial Ruins: Space, Aesthetics and Materiality*, Oxford: Berg.
Greenberg, J. (2008) *A Natural History of the Chicago Region*, Chicago: University of Chicago Press.
Hart, R. A. (1982) 'Wildlands for children: consideration of the value of natural environments in landscape planning', *Childhood City Quarterly*, 9(2): 3–7.
Janowitz, A. (1990) *England's Ruins*, London: Blackwell.
Jorgensen, A. (2008) 'Introduction', in A. Jorgensen and R. Keenan (eds) *Urban Wildscapes Ebook*. Online: www.urbanwildscapes.org.uk (accessed 10 January 2011).
Jorgensen, A. and Tylecote, M. (2007) 'Ambivalent landscapes: wilderness in the urban interstices', *Landscape Research*, 32(4): 443–462.
Mörtenböck, P. and Mooshammer, H. (2007) 'Trading indeterminacy: informal markets in Europe', *Field*, 1: 73–87. Online: www.field-journal.org (accessed 5 January 2009).
The Oxford English Dictionary (1989) Oxford: Oxford University Press.
Plumwood, V. (1993) *Feminism and the Mastery of Nature*, London: Routledge.

Roth, M. S. (1997) 'Irresistible decay: ruins reclaimed', in M. S. Roth, C. Lyons and C. Merewether (eds) *Irresistible Decay*, Los Angeles, CA: The Getty Research Institute.

Schama, S. (1996) *Landscape and Memory*, London: Fontana.

Schneekloth, L. H. (2007) 'Unruly and robust: an abandoned industrial river', in K. Franck and Q. Stevens (eds) *Loose Space*, London: Routledge.

Sheridan, D. (2007) 'Berlin's indeterminate territories: the space of subculture in the city', *Field Journal*, 1: 97–119. Online: www.fieldjournal.org/index.php?page=2007-volume-1 (accessed 1 May 2010).

Tregay, R. and Gustavsson, R. (1983) *Oakwood's New Landscape: Designing for Nature in the Residential Environment*, Stad och land Rapport nr 15, Alnarp, Sweden: Sveriges Lantbruksuniversitet and Warrington and Runcorn Development Corporation.

Woodward, C. (2002) *In Ruins*, London: Vintage.

PART 1

THEORIZING WILDSCAPES

Chapter 1: Learning from Detroit or 'the wrong kind of ruins'

Christopher Woodward

'You've got to go to Detroit', said a man in the audience. I was speaking about ruins at the Clark Institute of Art in Massachusetts, USA, in conjunction with their exhibition of Old Master's drawings of the ruins of ancient Rome. I'd been told that several times: if you like ruins so much, go to Detroit.

The schedule took me to friends at the Museum of Fine Arts in Boston but I changed the ticket, and flew to Detroit. The taxi passed empty brick mansions and rows of wooden houses, then derelict Modernist factories and Art Deco skyscrapers. 'Why are you here?' asked the driver. I explained that I'd come to the USA to lecture on the beauty and inspiration of ruins, and we talked about Rome – and Detroit. He shook his head: 'These are the wrong kind of ruins'.

In my book *In Ruins* (2001) I tried to understand the process by which ruins – the result of bombs, fires, natural disaster, poverty, abandonment – can become places which are beautiful, uplifting, and even comfortable. What makes old stones and charred bricks feel alive?

Firstly, by the fact of its incompleteness, a ruined structure compels the viewer to supply the missing pieces from their own imagination. Our response is creative, and personal. The reality of a ruin is subjective; put another way, when we write about ruins we cannot escape writing about ourselves. Rose Macaulay's classic *Pleasure of Ruins* (1953) is presented as an anthology of other travellers' experiences but it is also an undeclared autobiography. She chose to write about ruins alive with birds, vines, or noisy peasants as an expression of her own rebirth as a Christian after the nihilism expressed in her novel, *The World My Wilderness* (1950), in which the bomb sites of London are the backdrop to the lives of a generation brutalized by the war.

Secondly, a ruin represents a contest between people and nature. We watch a battle between the ambitions of the builder and the processes of nature – with nature expressed, above all, by spontaneous vegetation. And, stepping back, we might enjoy ruins integrated into a landscape – whether by design, as in the incorporation of abbeys into eighteenth-century gardens, such as Fountains Abbey in Yorkshire, UK, or by chance, as in the gardens of Ninfa, Italy, 'discovered' by romantic travellers in the late nineteenth century. At the same time, vegetation has an ambivalent role: from the 1920s until recent times it was perceived as a destructive threat by state archaeology.

Thirdly, juxtaposition. A Christian chapel built inside the Colosseum, or a shepherd's hut erected from the rubble of an emperor's tomb: the dramatic juxtaposition suggests a narrative of change over time. These changes become causes for reflection. Such juxtapositions also suspend, or reverse, normal assumptions of time, and progress; eighteenth-century travellers to Rome were highly conscious that they were treading in the dust of a civilization more magnificent than Paris or London but, nevertheless, in fragments.

We can suggest a formula, therefore, in which these elements of incompleteness, nature, and juxtaposition combine to transform a pile of broken or burned materials into a place of beauty and inspiration. It explains why we climb to a castle on a cliff-top with a picnic basket, or linger in a temple above a Mediterranean seashore. But does it apply to Detroit?

The urban ruins of the twentieth and twenty-first centuries pose a new aesthetic challenge and, I shall argue, writers, artists, planners and designers are at the very beginning of formulating a convincing response. It is a new challenge, most obviously, because for millions of urban dwellers, modern ruins are on our doorstep, staring us in the eye each morning. They are embedded in buildings, traffic, asphalt and chain-link fence, and not in nature, time is not suspended as it might be in a site that is isolated or elusive.

More profoundly, destruction is of a different speed and scale. Bombs flatten cities more quickly than soldiers slaughter citizens with pikes and bayonets. Above all, the nature of the economy means that we construct more, and bigger, buildings more quickly than ever before – and abandon them more quickly than ever before.

Detroit's population halved over two decades but the most extreme cases of urban shrinkage are in China. Yumen in Gansu province was built for oil under Chairman Mao's rule; but the oil has stopped, and the bureaucracy relocated to a new city. An English journalist described a city with no jobs, and flats to be bought for US$280 (Graham-Harrison 2008); of 118 towns built by Mao to extract natural resources, 18 are 'classified as resource-exhausted' by the Asian Development Bank. What will happen to a concrete and steel city with no jobs, few children, and too many cigarettes?

In the last two decades urban decay has become photogenic and fashionable: it is popular with a new generation of artists, particularly young photographers[1]; it is even counter-culture chic, as in the eponymous range of cosmetics. However, there is a mismatch between the aesthetic response and the reality of urban decline. It is an aesthetic challenge of a new order. How can we integrate modern ruins with our current ideas of what cities should look like, and accept dereliction as an integral element of the modern city?

*****

In twentieth-century USA, artists, writers, and film-makers have created the most powerful images of future destruction since England, France and Germany in the

Romantic age, whether of nuclear war (the shattered Statue of Liberty at the conclusion of Franklin J. Shaffner's *Planet of the Apes* (1968)) or of ecological collapse (Cormac McCarthy's *The Road* (2006)).

The prophetic fantasies of destruction have not come true, with the exceptions of Chernobyl, 9/11 and Hurricane Katrina. What *has* happened instead is the ruination of cities by economic and social change. Detroit is the most extreme example. According to the US census its population declined from 1.85 million in 1950 to 911,000 by 2003, a reduction of more than 50 per cent. No city has depopulated so quickly during peacetime since Rome in the century and a half subsequent to its capture by the Goths. And, visually, Detroit is the most dramatic example of modern times because of the ambition and wealth with which it was built: Art Deco skyscrapers with mosaic glittering in their vaulted lobbies, such as the Book Building; factories that rose as luminous, vast cathedrals of mass production; the concrete columns of Albert Kahn's work are as muscular and determined as the arcades of Karnak. The Book Building is empty; the cathedral glass is shattered; Kahn's Post Office is burned, a forest self-seeded in the ashes. These are the last great ruins of Western civilization (Figure 1.1).

Figure 1.1
Abandoned mansions in Brush Park, Detroit. When Brush Park was built at the end of the nineteenth century it was the most exclusive residential neighbourhood in the city (photograph: Christopher Woodward, 2006)

The city is also a case study of the possibilities created by dereliction, from urban farming to new aesthetics.

*****

All I knew about Detroit was based on the photographs of Camillo Jose Vergara; perhaps the best-known depicts a car park inside the flaking, opulent interior of a cinema. Born in Chile, Vergara came to study engineering at the University of Notre Dame at South Bend, Indiana, USA, in the late 1960s. An article in *Time* magazine led him to the slums of Gary, Indiana: 'With my eyes smarting from the smoke of the steel works, I saw people gambling and drinking' (Vergara 1999: 23). He has revisited Gary a hundred times in the four decades since: 'Now the city is ruined, but the air is clean' (Vergara 1999: 23). It was the beginning of a photographic exploration of the US rust belt which he presents as a political and sociological project: he visits and revisits to record changes in the built and social environment.

In addition, Vergara argues that ruins are integral to the story of the USA, and – in contrast to the sanitized narrative of unblemished progress exemplified by their Smithsonian Institution – should be accepted as national heritage. In 1995 he proposed that a section of downtown Detroit become a wildlife park, an 'American Acropolis' for the study of skyscrapers:

> We could transform nearly 100 troubled buildings into a grand national historic park of play and wonder, an Urban Monument Valley … Midwestern prairie would be allowed to invade from the north. Trees, vines, and wildflowers would grow on roofs and out of windows; goats and wild animals – squirrels, possums, bats, owls, ravens, snakes and insects – would live in the empty behemoths, adding their calls, hoots and screeches to the smell of rotten leaves and animal droppings.
>
> (Vergara 1995)

My expectations of Detroit were as much defined by Vergara's imagery as eighteenth-century Grand Tourists' expectations of Rome by Piranesi's engravings. I shared a taxi from the airport with a man on business, who got out at a blue glass hotel. If I am honest, I was disappointed by the commercial bustle. The riverside has been regenerated: circular benches and steps set against mown grass decorated with silver hoops of abstract sculpture. In the Guardian building, a restored Art Deco masterpiece, you can buy sepia-tinted photographs of 1930s swish, but there are no pictures of ruins available. Outside a woman in a suit climbs into her SUV, locks the door, and rounds the corner with a firm turn of the wheel.

But walk ten minutes and Vergara's Detroit begins. It is midday but there are no people inside or outside (Detroit is, *inter alia*, the easiest city in the world in which to find a parking space). My two-and-a-bit days were bewildering. At one point I was so depressed by the dereliction that I walked back to the small island of commercial activity. After miles of cracked concrete, leafless ivy, and congealed litter it was reassuring to see new plastic tables in McDonalds, window-cleaners, doors that opened, and to breathe the new, shiny smell of fresh paperbacks in Borders.

Nevertheless, the ruins are exhilarating. In the Book Building I snuck past the security guard. One of six elevators worked. As it ground its way up thirty-six empty storeys I lost all sense of whether I was rising, or falling. I was too scared to climb into the Central Station by myself but returned the next day with a friend. A thin voice rang out from a high window: 'Want a tour?'. Sean charges US$10 for a tour of the Central Station and Post Office. Seventeen years old, he is an 'urban explorer', one of six or seven – his estimate – active in the city. The tour begins in the Central Station vestibule (like Grand Central Station in New York designed by the architects Carrere and Hastings as an echo of the Baths of Caracalla in Rome). Sean narrates a natural history of the urban ruin. First, the water and electricity are turned off. For a while there will be a security guard. Next come the robbers, many of whom are junkies. They steal the copper, and any ornaments that can be sold. After that, the vandals. In Grand Central they have smashed the marble cladding in the corridors just for the thrill. Finally, the graffiti artists and the urban explorers arrive. And, last of all, I wonder, the tourists?

Later, we descend into the basement, and by the light of a torch cross a frozen pool to climb on to an old conveyor belt, which took the mail, underground, to the Post Office across the street, a Modernist structure by Albert Kahn. Hands and knees pattering on the frayed fabric you climb up the belt on to the third floor. The tour was timed so that we emerged at sunset (Figure 1.2). The building, put to new use as the Book Depository for the City's Public Schools, had (been?) burned and the low sun illuminated piles of charred paper, and

Figure 1.2
The author with two urban explorers and (centre back) the writer M. T. Anderson in Detroit Central Post Office, designed by Albert Kahn in the 1920s (photograph: Christopher Woodward, 2006)

books. I stepped onto the top of a mound of molten metal, a metre high. 'Staples', said Sean drily. And my friend Tobin was standing on a small hill of melted sellotape. A section of the roof had collapsed and trees had self-seeded and grown through the void. In one corner of the roof water had collected into a pond, and a fringe of reeds had grown at its edge (Figure 1.3).

The happiest surprise in Detroit was the ebullience of nature. I have never seen so many birds in a city: not pigeons – who leave with the people – but birds that flutter and chirp on traffic lights, and in the tilting porches of the empty houses. The lights change but there is no traffic, and the only sound but for the birdsong was the creak of a bicycle ridden round and round by an old, seemingly homeless, black man.

*****

My friend (a writer) and I stalked through the prairie grass. 'When Detroit was built America was a place of production', he observed. 'Now it's a country of consumers. Detroit symbolizes that'.

The city has symbolized the fortunes of the USA to an accelerated degree, from the invention of the production line in the Model T age to the Second World War – when a quarter of the tanks that liberated Europe were made here – to the race riots of 1968 and white flight in the 1970s. Since the credit crunch – alleged to have started in sub-prime Detroit – it has been featured as the place to buy a house for US$5. It's a one-stop shop for TV journalists who want a dramatic backdrop to a punch-line.

In the spring of 2010, Julien Temple's *Requiem for Detroit* was broadcast on BBC4, and at a public symposium at the London School of Economics (LSE) Cities Programme. At the end, a panel of four academics flanked a High School Principal

Figure 1.3
The rooftop at Detroit Central Post Office (photograph: Christopher Woodward, 2006)

from the city, Yalik Makini. What's the lesson of Detroit? To one, it symbolized the risk of over-dependence on a single industry; London – and he paused to look at the audience – is over-dependent on the financial sector. What has happened is that Detroit has become a sandpit for urban theorists across the world. In the USA it is the epicentre of self-doubt, a place for the nation to navel-gaze.

* * * * *

The makers of *Requiem for Detroit* chose a happy ending: the new phenomenon of urban farming. Young white men and old black women see orchards beside empty freeways as a vision of redemption for a ruined city. It is an alternative vision to the investment in conference centres and automobile museums which has characterized the city's public policy. 'Let the future begin!' cried one city mayor, as an Art Deco department store was blown up. But it didn't. The future has gone somewhere else.

Figure 1.4
Vacant lot, Detroit. There are over 60,000 vacant lots in the city, some of which are available for purchase for as little as US$50 (photograph: Christopher Woodward, 2006)

The film coincided with a story in *Fortune* magazine in which a financial speculator named Michael Hantz announced an investment of millions of dollars in urban farming in Detroit (Whitford 2009). He is said to be buying up land in the city: 40 out of 139 square miles of the city is abandoned (I was quoted US$200 to buy a lot – US$50 to residents) (Figure 1.4). The Hantz Farms website

promises to 'reintroduce Detroiters to the beauty of nature', returning the site to its roots as farmland (Hantz Farms 2010). Malik Yakini expressed disquiet at the distance between the spontaneous reality of her school project and Hantz's media-led images of commercialized urban agriculture. But how many urban farmers are there in Detroit? 'Five or six hundred' suggested Malik at the LSE. On my visit I could not find a single cultivated plot in twelve miles' walk. But it is a vast city.

Whether it is five hundred or not – and evidently the number mattered less to Malik than the actuality of the kids in her project, milking goats and planting up old tyres – the impact on Detroit belies the image presented by the film. In general, I would argue, the degree of curiosity about urban farming – the *zeitgeist* of 2009 – represents a growing ambivalence about the artificiality of the modern city. In the context of Detroit it also represents something else: the divide between external perception and internal reality is much greater than in a functional city. Creatively, this is liberating; socially, it is more problematic.

*****

The sociologist Alice Mah has developed the concept of 'proximity' to understand this divide: she has argued that our aesthetic or emotional reaction to ruins is defined by our distance from the actual event of the dereliction. This 'proximity' can be measured in terms of time, physical distance, or wealth.

Mah's (2010) UK case study was Walker, a ship-building district in Newcastle, whose population declined from 13,035 in 1971 to half that thirty years later. It is the most deprived neighbourhood in the city. Her interviews revealed a diversity of individual perspectives. A shop steward fighting the closure of Swan Hunter, the last shipyard, described its structures as 'the cathedrals of the working class', and questioned a service economy in which we 'all sell each other baskets and jam' (Mah 2010: 404). By contrast, a family that had moved away and set up a successful mini-cab firm were happy to leave industry behind; it was exhausting, dangerous, and smelly. Her conclusion is that our perspective on an urban ruin is defined by how rich we are, where we live, and whether we were directly involved in the activity and the trauma of its ending. This is not just a question of aesthetics. At the time of her research Newcastle City Council wished to knock down the 1920s and 1930s terraced housing and build 'Walker Riverside'. The hostile reaction showed the strength of social and familial networks that were invisible to the outsider, whether town-planner, politician, or artist.

Mah (2009) encountered the same phenomenon in her US case study: the Highland district of Niagara Falls, New York, whose population declined from 120,000 to 50,000 when the chemical plants closed. Residents who stayed built homes they would never sell, and extensions that would never return the investment. The jobs would not come back, they knew, but the strength of family, street, and church gave a valuable sense of belonging. It is a second lesson in how aesthetic judgments can mislead us.

When urban decay does have a chance to answer back, it does not say what we expect.

*****

In the short length of Broadway Market (my neighbourhood in Hackney, London, UK) you can buy adhesive patches of fake rust which can be stuck onto bicycles, postcards of dereliction chic – such as a one-armed teddy bear lolling on a sofa in a backyard – and in the photography store there are books about the derelict High Line railway in New York, and shut-down oil wells and petrol stations. When did industrial decay become so photogenic?

According to Alexander Page (personal communication May 2010), a photographer friend who shares the interest, photography of ruins is as old as the medium itself: ruins are picturesque, owing to the drama of silhouette, and the exaggerated contrasts of light and shade. By the 1860s there was a circle of photographers specializing in ruins in Rome who met at the Caffè Greco. In 1935, Walker Evans photographed the 'luminous dilapidation' of the slumbering antebellum mansions of the US Deep South (Mora and Hill 2004: 122). The next year he and the writer James Agee documented the poor families of Hale County, Alabama, USA, in *Let Us Now Praise Famous Men* (1941). In that project, observes Page, Evans was the first to 'aestheticize the cracked floor board, the newspaper wall paper, and the ramshackle street'. Rural abandonment continued as a potent theme in US art, with the family homestead presented as a heroic but ultimately transient presence in the landscape. In 1961, William Christenberry photographed a creaking wooden house known as The Old Psalmist's Building; he returned year after year, and the sequence of pictures over two decades documents its obliteration by a kudzu vine. William Eggleston and Robert Adams are two other great photographers with a similar interest in human presence in the landscape of the US south and west. However, this imagery of rural abandonment responds to a different set of issues.

A second genre is the celebration of industry – as in Charles Sheeler's heroic images of factories in motion in the 1930s – and a third is the genre of social reportage in the 1950s and 1960s by 'the concerned photographer', such as Eugene Smith. But, as Page notes, 'these are portraits of the social dereliction of the inner city focused very much on individual human tragedy and not an aesthetic of dereliction'.

The first artists to represent industrial architecture in the consciousness of its transience were Bernd and Hilla Becher. Bernd grew up in Siegen, Germany, a small town in the Ruhr in which 'grime spread through the town centre' (Liesbrock 2010: 6). As an art student in the 1950s he began to draw an industrial plant being dismantled; he took up his camera because it was demolished too quickly for a pencil to record. Their first book was published in 1970: *Anonymous Sculptures and a Typology of Technical Constructions*.

In the Bechers' industrial landscapes it is impossible to tell whether the factory is redundant or not. That, too, is a decision: the Bechers were photographing for the future:

While the zeitgeist was fixed on the future and did not want to read the writing on the wall, they sensed in the present … the imminent end. Their pictures have an unmistakeable mood. There is no evidence of the grime and noise that constantly enveloped the facilities. The coal mines and iron works of the Ruhr are depicted as silent monuments to an epoch which is definitively at an end…

(Liesbrock 2010)

In 1966 they came to Britain on a British Council Fellowship and their photographic documentation of industry and coal mines represents the first project of its kind in the UK.

The next year Robert Smithson undertook the journey recorded in his photographic essay, 'A tour of the monuments of Passaic, New Jersey' (1967), in which he wrestled with the significance of the detritus of modern construction – and, as noted, Vergara arrived in Michigan. In the early 1970s a colony of radical artists in the Bronx led by Gordon Matta-Clark made the dereliction and disorientation of the depopulated inner city the basis of a body of site-specific work. In less than a decade urban decay had become established as a subject for artists to respond to.

*****

As noted above, juxtaposition was an important element in the historical experience of ruin, whether visual – as in the washing hung up to dry between the columns of Roman temples – or aural; Edward Gibbon tells us that he was inspired to write The *History of the Decline and Fall of the Roman Empire* (1776–1789) by the *sound* of monks singing vespers in what had been the Temple of Jupiter. However, modern ruin imagery places an ever greater reliance upon juxtaposition. Vergara is a master, as in the automobiles parked in the theatre, or his shots of the extinguished neon signs and cars that once dazzled with promise; to him, ironic juxtaposition presents an alternative to the official narrative of progress (Vergara 1999: 209). A stunning image is the wrecked grand piano in a hotel vestibule, newly-published in Andrew Moore's *Detroit Disassembled* (2010).

The aesthetic challenge of urban decay is greater when the element of juxtaposition is not present. In East London this happens if you travel east of the Lea Valley. Along the route of the A13 the Eurostar high-speed train is visible gleaming through Rainham Marshes, and in Dagenham water towers with the iconic letters 'Ford' loom above a *Buddleia* forest. Click, and click. These are the only two 'picturesque' moments between the urban drama of Hackney and the countryside of Essex, in which sheep graze below the wooden tower of a Saxon village church.

The French landscape architect Gilles Clement has argued that we must establish a new value for the zones which fall between the aesthetic categories of city and country. To Clement, the value of this 'Tiers Paysage' or Third Landscape is ecological not visual: a brownfield site 'is no longer a place abandoned to rubbish and weeds, but becomes a sort of reservoir or "biological time capsule" for the future' (Clement *et al.* 2006: 92). The challenge, however, *is* visual: we must see an ecological value in what is – but for six weeks of flowering – an expanse of weeds and brambles.

In Lille, France, he designed the Île Derborence (designed 1991–95): debris excavated for the new Eurostar railway station has been piled up and clad in white concrete. It is an island in a flat, grassy park, and the white walls are cliff-like enough for us to imagine the squawk of seagulls. The plan of the island is identical to the shape of a particular island in the South Seas; the plants on top are spontaneous and self-seeding, and the only visitor is a botanist who climbs a ladder once a year to record what has grown.

Île Derborence is a synthesis of sculpture, myth, and ecology and a glimpse of genius. Its impact does not depend on an immediate visual juxtaposition; the island is on the other side of the world, and the connection is between a ground-plan and a shape drawn on a map. Clement challenges us to abandon all precon-ceptions and think ourselves *inside* nature. He has moved the aesthetic challenge several paces further forward.

So, Clement replaced Vergara in my knapsack as I walked from Hackney to Essex, determined to jettison my own aesthetic education and discover a new and ecological beauty in the underpasses and old railway lines. But that desire leaked away with each mile of concrete, poverty, and carelessness. Echoing in my head was a line somewhere in Richard Mabey's work, in which he notes that nature does not have a purpose or an agenda with which to go forward or back. 'Nature just *is*'. Between the A12 and the M25 poverty just is. Dereliction just is. I went home, and got the car.

*****

Just across the M25 there is a 'Third Landscape' with is neither urban nor rural: The Plotlands of Laindon, Essex. The story is told in *Arcadia for All: The Legacy of a Makeshift Landscape* by the late Colin Ward and Dennis Hardy (1984). After the decline in agriculture in the late nineteenth century, entrepreneurs sold off small plots to Londoners to build weekend retreats, or summer homes. By the 1930s over 8,000 had been built at Laindon on a grid of grass streets, a mix of converted railway carriages and 'chalets' self-built with salvaged material. It was a self-made community in which the absence of sewers, electricity and made-up roads was balanced by independence, neighbourliness, nature – and, above all, the escape from London's East End. The Plotlands can be seen as a new sponta-neous landscape which struck a balance between man and nature, self-sufficiency and communality.

After the Second World War the Plotlands posed a challenge to the state's values of planning, order, and hygiene and, at bottom, to the mentality of gov-ernment control. The self-built community at Laindon was demolished, and the Brave New World of Basildon built over the 75 miles of grass roads.[2] Arcadia hap-pened here. But we knocked it down, and built Basildon. Today 'The Basildon

Health Walk' crosses the site. In 2009, 18.1 per cent of children in Basildon were obese.[3] In the Plotlands children ran, gardened, cooked, and told stories by the light of gas lamps.

It is easy to romanticize their vanished life but there is no doubt that aesthetically – and ecologically – the Plotlands has become a happy ruin. It is a self-seeded wood with signs to 'First Avenue' and 'Sans Souci', in which from time to time you encounter a pair of gateposts, or a tin bath. Flowers planted by the Plotlanders continue to bloom. Architects and conservationists enjoy quoting Christopher Wren's lapidary dictum 'All architecture should aspire towards the eternal'; the audience will always nod. But – as shadows stole over the grass streets of Laindon – for the first time I questioned that assumption. Should that continue to be the ideal in a century that will be judged by its relationship with the environment? Why should new buildings last for ever? The plotlanders hammered together old planks, and corrugated iron, at exactly the same time as the Auto-Pharaohs of Detroit erected their most monumental factories and skyscrapers. Laindon is a less troublesome ruin than Detroit. Should we build cities with a return to wilderness built into their design DNA?

* * * * *

The most powerful statement of architectural ephemerality in modern times is a further two hundred miles to the east: the Eco-Cathedral built at Mildam, the Netherlands, by Louis Le Roy (1924–). Le Roy is an artist and environmentalist, and in the 1970s he bought a piece of open farmland on which he began to assemble a sculptural form from discarded building materials: bricks, concrete drainage pipes, old gravestones. It is very beautiful, reminiscent of a Mayan city lost in the jungle (Figure 1.5). Le Roy will be buried here, and intends the structure to be left to nature.

The Eco-Cathedral is a provocation, not a solution. It rises out of the same landscape as Jacob van Ruisdael's painting, *The Jewish Cemetery* (1654). It is intended to challenge the vanity of humanity, telling us that whatever we build – a pompous tomb, a great stone structure – is but dust in the eyes of God. Ruin is inevitable; nature is divine. In 1926 the picture was donated to the Detroit Institute of Fine Arts by Julius H. Haass (1869–1931), a banker, art collector and philanthropist. No one imagined that, one day, the Institute would be surrounded by ruins.

Detroit, like Rome, was built as if it would last for ever. Indeed, according to Sean the urban explorer, the railway station is still standing only because it was so well-built that it could not be blown-up. Will we ever build a Detroit again? And if not, what alternatives do we have?

* * * * *

Property developers have a clear-eyed view of posterity. According to John Ritblatt, Chairman and Chief Executive of British Land until 2006, a building repays its investment if it stands up for thirty years (personal communication May 2010).

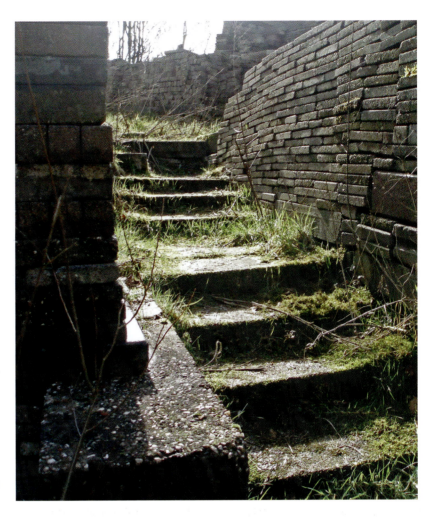

Figure 1.5
The Eco-Cathedral built
by Louis Le Roy at
Mildam, the Netherlands
(photograph: Christopher
Woodward, 2006)

Anything after that is a bonus. Few other people have reconciled this reality with their ideal of architecture.

An exception is the artist Ed Ruscha, who has taken as his subject the new commercial architecture of California. He is not troubled by the reality that a structure is designed to have five or six tenants in its thirty-year life, so is designed to be as anonymous and as flexible as possible. In 2005, Ruscha was commissioned to represent the United States at the Venice Biennale. His subject was 'The Course of Empire', in response to the series of paintings (1833–1836) in which Thomas Cole (1801–1848), a young US artist who had travelled to Rome, presented an allegory of the rise and fall of an empire as an implicit warning to the young nation.

Ruscha re-visited sites in Los Angeles which he had painted in 1992 in his *Blue Collar* series: a garage, a factory, a telephone booth, and so on. By 2005, the factory has become a fast-food joint; a silver birch grows where the telephone booth stood. Questioned, Ruscha answered:

Deterioration is an ongoing thing, and it could be viewed negatively, of course. But it's kind of awesome to imagine that everything has to go through its life cycle and to visualize everything that might encompass and to know that nothing lasts. There are people who imagine how the world goes and that things actually get better. We certainly live that way, don't we? I don't view things quite that way.

(De Salvo and Norden 2005: 31)

Ruscha – and you must imagine that paragraph spoken in his gravelly, quiet, deadpan voice – is content to imagine a future in which architecture is flexible, shiny, and ephemeral.

*****

Interest in ruins is much higher than at any point in the 15 years since I began my research. Why? Urban decay has coincided with the rise in environmental awareness, and a ruin is a metaphor for our relationship with nature. To adjust to this new reality will require a seismic shift in our aesthetic traditions.

But such shifts do happen. In the early eighteenth century the Picturesque movement 'claimed' wild nature for the artist and traveller. In the decade after 1965, a handful of artists transformed perceptions of industrial architecture. Today, I believe, art is more powerfully inspired by ruin than at any time since the eighteenth century. In the single field of American photography there is Robert Adams, William Christenberry, William Eggleston, Andrew Moore, Robert Polidori, and Camillo Jose Vergara. It is a magnificent line-up.

In the UK the excitement – to the ruinist, that is – is that ruins have again become 'relevant'. In the eighteenth century the ruins of Rome were as much about the future as about the past; would London – the new Rome – be a victim of the same vices and tyrannies? At home, the ruins of monasteries divided Catholic from Protestant, and the fate of castles divided Whigs from Tories as they continued to debate the rights of Crown and Parliament. Today, however, these ruins are consigned to a picture postcard past. In consequence of a new age of dereliction, however, modern ruins are, again, becoming as aggressive, divisive, and challenging as in the eighteenth century.

One of my photographs of Detroit shows a vast asphalt desert, flat and featureless but for tall, hazy grasses growing between the cracks of what was once a car park (Figure 1.6). The next picture on the disc shows a row of new wooden houses, with spotless paint, and families sitting on the steps; inside children are doing homework, and the oven is hot. The audience cannot guess but the photographs were taken from exactly same point; you just have to turn 180 degrees and face the opposite side of the avenue. Ruins help us to choose our future.

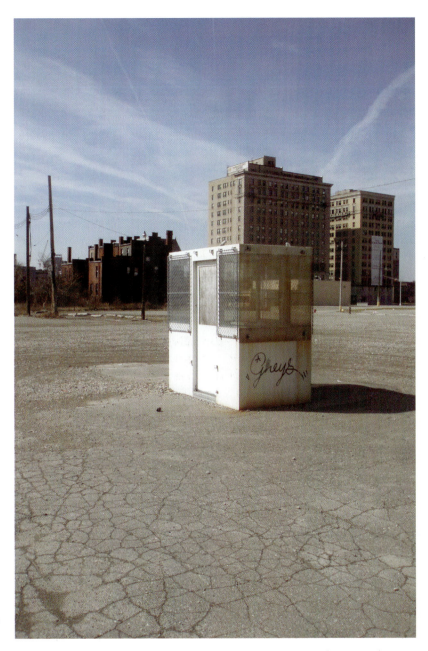

Figure 1.6
Vacant lot, Detroit
(photograph: Christopher
Woodward, 2006)

NOTES

1 See, for example, the powerful pictures of abandoned lunatic asylums by Amelie Riis on
   her website www.urbandecay.org.uk.
2 One house has been preserved as a museum in a zone handed over to the Essex Wildlife
   Trust as a nature reserve.
3 The *Basildon Recorder*, 30 March 2010, citing an increase from 16.8 per cent reported
   to the east of England by the Child Measurement Programme.

REFERENCES

Agee, J. and Evans, W. (1941) *Let Us Now Praise Famous Men*, Boston MA: Houghton Mifflin.

Becher, B. and Becher, H. (1970) *Anonymous Sculptures and a Typology of Technical Constructions*, Dusseldorf: Eugen Michel Art Press.

Clement, G., Rahm, P. and Borani, G. (2006) *Environ(ne)ment: Approaches for Tomorrow*, Milan: Skira.

De Salvo, D. and Norden, L. (2005) Essay in *Ed Ruscha: Course of Empire*, Ostfildern: Hatje Kantz.

Gibbon, E. (1776–1789) *The History of the Decline and Fall of the Roman Empire*, London: Strahan & Cadell.

Graham-Harrison, E. (2008) *The New York Times*, 17 April 2008.

Hantz Farms. Online: www.hantzfarmsdetroit.com (accessed 20 April 2011).

Liesbrock, H. (ed.) (2010) *Bernd and Hilla Becher: Coal Mines and Steel Mills*, Munich: Schirmer/Mosel.

Macaulay, R. (1950) *The World My Wilderness*, London: Collins.

—— (1953) *Pleasure of Ruins*, London: Weidenfeld & Nicolson.

Mah, A. (2009) 'Devastation but also home: place attachment in areas of industrial decline', *Home Cultures*, 6(3): 288–310.

—— (2010) 'Memory, uncertainty and industrial ruination: Walker Riverside, Newcastle upon Tyne', *International Journal of Urban and Regional Research*, 34(2): 398–413.

McCarthy, C. (2006) *The Road*, New York: Random House.

Moore, A. (2010) *Detroit Disassembled*, Akron OH: Damiani.

Mora, G. and Hill, J. T. (2004) *Walker Evans: The Hungry Eye*, London: Thames & Hudson.

Shaffner, F. J. (1968) *Planet of the Apes*, Twentieth Century Fox.

Smithson, R. (1967 [1996]) 'A tour of the monuments of Passaic, New Jersey', in: J. Flam (ed.) *Robert Smithson: The Collected Writings*, Berkeley: University of California Press.

Temple, J. (2010) *Requiem for Detroit*, London: BBC.

Vergara, C. J. (1995) 'Downtown Detroit: "American acropolis" or vacant land – what to do with the world's largest concentration of pre-depression skyscrapers', *Metropolis*, April 1995.

—— (1999) *American Ruins*, New York: Monacelli Press.

Ward, C. and Hardy, D. (1984) *Arcadia for All: The Legacy of a Makeshift Landscape*, London: Mansell.

Whitford, D. (2009) 'Can farming save Detroit?' *Fortune*, 29 December 2009.

Woodward, C. (2001) *In Ruins*, London: Chatto & Windus.

Chapter 2: Appreciating urban wildscapes

Towards a natural history of unnatural places

Paul H. Gobster

The ecosystems of a given place reflect the response of living organisms to their environment (Bradshaw 2003). Woodlands can become wetlands with too much moisture and grasslands with too little; increases in elevation can turn a deciduous forest into a coniferous one; and fire and other disturbances can set back a climax community to its early stages of ecological succession. The sum total of these environmental influences results in a place's biodiversity, and while the study and description of these processes and their expression in the living landscape is usually considered the business of the ecological sciences, humanistic narratives that construct the unique ecological stories of a place in order to build appreciation and support for ecosystem protection might more appropriately fall into the domain of natural history.

The recent book, *A Natural History of the Chicago Region*, provides a good example. Written as a 'seventeen-year labour of love' by nature writer and long-time local conservationist Joel Greenberg (2008), the 595-page book tells an engaging story about the native ecosystems and species of the region. Using thick description of people connecting to place over time, Greenberg details the character and history of the prairies, savannas, forests, and other ecosystems, flora, and fauna indigenous to the Chicago region; describes their beauty and utility; and in chronicling their decline, builds a compelling case for their restoration. But while Greenberg's natural history goes far to develop an understanding and appreciation of the native ecosystems of the region as they once existed, his approach to natural history gives little insight into how the forces of the human environment and its legacy of settlement and urbanization have worked to shape the living landscapes that now dominate the region. Wildscapes, complexes of spontaneous 'ruderal' (hardy or weedy pioneer) vegetation that colonize disturbed urban sites, as detailed by the various authors in this book, are not recognized in Greenberg's nomenclature except as threats to the native landscapes he identifies, and thus the appreciation we come away with for the *region* of Chicago is one that has no *city* of Chicago in it. This approach may work when read as a strictly historical narrative, but even for those who are focused on protecting and restoring native landscapes it offers little guidance for moving forward in the light of the radically changed soil, temperature, surface water, and other conditions that now occur.

The young field of urban ecology offers clues to how a more robust natural history of urban regions might be constructed, a natural history that recognizes wildscapes as the living landscape's response to environmental conditions common in cities. Urban ecologists make little differentiation as to whether a given condition or process is of human or natural origin, and with much of the early work in the field coming from Europe, the long history of dense human settlement there makes distinctions such as 'native biodiversity' less meaningful (Del Tredici 2010). Adopting this same perspective in writing the natural history of urban places could, I believe, lead to a better understanding of wildscapes as legitimate green space types for protection, use, and appreciation. In this chapter I highlight four major types of human-created green spaces in the Chicago region and present a brief case study example of each, focusing on their wildscape components as found within the City of Chicago. These landscapes differ from the ecosystems described by Greenberg, yet my intent is to examine them in a similar way as particular land types having evolved communities of flora and fauna that are worthy of deeper understanding and appreciation. Being neither a natural historian nor an urban ecologist severely limits the insights I can bring to such an endeavour, yet by drawing on previous research and personal observation, my aims are to outline the beginnings of a framework within the scope of this chapter and highlight the potential of such an approach for further scholarly attention.

METROPOLIS'S NATURE: FOUR CHICAGO WILDSCAPES

Although Greenberg's book provides the initial impetus for writing a natural history of Chicago wildscapes, it is environmental historian William Cronon's *Nature's Metropolis: Chicago and the Great West* (1991) that helps place wildscapes within the broader understanding of the relationships between people and ecosystems. Cronon's interregional analysis describes how Chicago as a city grew and prospered as a result of its location at a biotic crossroads, and the ecosystem diversity described and venerated by Greenberg is shown by Cronon to be the root cause for its growth. Pine forests to the north provided a ready supply of lumber for building, prairies to the west forage for cattle, and the Mississippi and Great Lakes waterways a means to ready access and transport. Once connected by canals and then railways, Chicago became the great machine for processing the raw materials of nature and transferring them to eastern population centres for consumption.

But just as Chicago stands as exemplar of the city as created by nature, so, too, does it reveal how nature is then created by the city, albeit a nature that reflects the city's distinctly human image and purpose. Thus, the broad scale patterns and processes discussed in Cronon's interregional analysis are taken down in scale to the major types of green spaces within the city perceived and used by people on an everyday basis. In Chicago, this includes dedicated parkland and other purposefully designed public green spaces, green edges along water and land transportation corridors, small-scale patches of undesignated green space in neighbourhood residential and commercial areas, and medium- to large-scale patches of post-industrial land. In the sections that follow, I describe the evolution and existence of wildscapes within each of these four green space types and provide a case study example of how such spaces have been dealt with by the people who interact with them. By considering these spaces as the response of living organisms to their human dominated environment, I then suggest how we might develop a better appreciation for wildscapes in addressing particular issues and problems.

FILLED-IN NATURE: WILDSCAPING THE LAKEFRONT PARKS

While the rich intersection of land and water resources had long made the Chicago region a strategic place for people, large-scale settlement of what is now the City of Chicago did not come until there was extensive modification of the flat, marshy landscape. French explorers who visited the area in 1673 found villages of Illinois and Miami Indian tribes along the upland ridges and hills of the region, but subsequent waves of fur trappers and military looked to the low-lying land between the Chicago and Des Plaines Rivers as their focus for settlement. When Indian lands were ceded to the US in 1833, plans to build a canal connecting these rivers and linking the Great Lakes and Mississippi watersheds fuelled rampant real estate speculation near the present location of downtown Chicago. Land improvement for commerce and residence were the foremost goals in building the city, but the commissioners charged with drawing up plans for the canal inserted a small note on their map that would in later years be instrumental in protecting the shoreline of Lake Michigan as Chicago's greatest natural asset: 'Public Ground – A Common to Remain Forever Open, Clear, and Free of Any Buildings, or Other Obstruction Whatever' (Wille 1972: 23).

The city grew rapidly from its incorporation in 1837, and by the early 1860s density and related problems experienced by its 100,000 residents compelled civic leaders to lobby for the development of public parks as 'the lungs of the city'. A cemetery just north of the city was moved from its low-lying shoreland location and in its place rose Lincoln Park, a 24-hectare naturalistic playground for Chicago's rich and poor alike. The park was instantly popular, and the dredge and fill construction techniques that transformed its natural wetlands into ponds for boating and fishing and uplands for pathways, lawns, and shade trees were soon replicated in many large landscape parks and smaller neighbourhood parks across the city. Landfill played a major role in creation of the lakefront park system that now lines 87 per cent of the city's 48-kilometre shoreline. Beginning with the tragedy of the Great Chicago Fire of 1871, which levelled much of the city of 300,000 residents, debris pushed into the lake created a bounty of new land, and two decades later civic leader Montgomery Ward was successful in using the 'Forever Open, Clear, and Free' argument to establish Grant Park in this space. The idea of a public lakefront and creating 'free land' from landfill upon which to build it soon took hold, and between 1890 and 1950 as the city grew from 1 million to 3.6 million residents, massive construction projects barged sand and sediments from the Indiana Shoals south of the city and dredged a series of harbours to build a nearly seamless string of parkland more than 1200 hectares in extent (Chicago Park District 1995).

While most of this lakefront parkland is manicured green space with facilities that accommodate the diverse recreational interests of its 65 million annual visitors, awareness of its value as an urban natural area grew in large part due to a wildscape that emerged following a change in park land use. A 50-hectare portion of Lincoln Park called the Montrose Extension was developed during the 1930s from extensive breakwater construction, landfill, and dredging for harbour development (Figure 2.1). The outermost 5 hectares of the addition extends more than 1 kilometre into the lake and forms a promontory called Montrose Point. Originally designed in a naturalistic style for passive park use, the point was taken over by the Army soon after its development for use as a World War II radar station and further developed during the Cold War as a Nike Missile base complete with barracks and underground missile silos. The site was finally vacated during the 1970s, and without plans or funding to address this change in land use, Montrose Point became a wildscape dominated by Eurasian grasses and forbs, with its only distinguishing feature being a remnant fence line dominated by Japanese honeysuckle (*Lonicera japonica*) that once separated the Army barracks from the park proper. Now receiving little human use, the remote extension became a natural resting place for migrating birds, and when some 200 different bird species were found to be using the area in and around the fence line birders dubbed it the 'Magic Hedge' (Gobster 2001) (Figure 2.2).

Figure 2.1
A 50-hectare portion of Lincoln Park called the Montrose Extension was developed during the 1930s from extensive breakwater construction, landfill, and dredging for harbour development (photograph: Chicago Park District, 1934)

Figure 2.2
From top: The so-called 'Magic Hedge' on Montrose Point (photograph: Paul H. Gobster, 1991); wildscape buffer between the ecologically managed natural area and the mown and manicured park proper on Montrose Point (photograph: Paul H. Gobster, 2010)

Efforts by birders during the 1980s and early 1990s to protect and enhance the Magic Hedge resulted in the designation of a no-mow zone to discourage active recreation and increase grassland bird habitat, in essence encouraging the evolution of the site as a wildscape. Learning from this serendipitous 'natural experiment' (Gross 2010), park planners, civic organizations, and bird groups and other nature enthusiasts began to work toward the formal designation of Montrose Point and other suitable sites within Lincoln Park and other lakefront parks as migratory bird habitat. As a by-product of a park-wide framework plan, a site master planning process was initiated during the late 1990s with broad stakeholder participation. While many of the participating groups agreed on keeping

Montrose Point wild and for the birds, its ambiguous history as submerged land, historic designed park, army base, and successful wildscape raised many questions about which nature should be expressed in the plan. The nature that was negotiated for the site attempted to reconcile the existing wildscape values of the site (particularly the honeysuckle hedge) with other ecological and historic design ones, and today the site is managed by park district staff and volunteers as a natural area based on the original design theme but using a palette of primarily native plants that maximize food and cover for birds in a diverse assemblage of grassland, wetland, woodland, savanna, and dune habitats. While the current management philosophy of the site is more akin to ecological restoration where natives are emphasized and ruderal non-natives discouraged, in recent years a strip of unmanaged grasses and forbs has been left to grow along the outer edge of the site to provide a wildscape buffer between the ecologically managed natural area and the mown and manicured park proper (Figure 2.2).

It is in this transitional zone between managed areas where a potential future for park wildscapes lies. Natural areas fill an important need as bird habitat, and while habitat creation that uses native plants may be an appropriate choice if it can be adequately maintained, the designated purpose and fragility of such sites often restricts more active recreational uses from occurring. For example, there are no places in Lincoln Park where children can actively explore nature in their own, unsupervised way – picking flowers, digging holes, building forts, and other creative play activities that would be inappropriate in both restored and manicured park settings. Providing wildscape transitional zones in such places may foster such opportunities while at the same time create habitat buffers and lower park maintenance budgets in ways that do not seem as though park managers are shirking their maintenance duties. In other cases where restoration management is difficult to accomplish because of harsh site conditions, lack of funds, or lack of volunteer assistance, it may be that unmanaged or lightly managed wildscapes could by themselves provide sufficient habitat, just as Montrose Point originally did prior to restoration activity.

ELEVATED NATURE: WILDSCAPES ALONG RAPID TRANSIT CORRIDORS

One key to a successful and livable large city is its transportation network, and Chicago's birth in the 1830s not only positioned it for development of a diverse set of corridors filling various transportation needs, but left a legacy of linear green space that today provides important natural and recreational values throughout the metropolitan region. The same canal development effort mentioned above that led to protection of the downtown lakefront as green space also became recognized in its own right in 1984 with US National Park Service designation of the Illinois and Michigan Canal as the country's first National Heritage Corridor (Harris 1998). Use of the canal was short-lived but critical in making the city a hub of commerce, and when railroad development began in 1848 the importance of

Chicago would grow immensely. Within two decades key regional lines converged in the city, and in 1869 completion of a transcontinental route placed Chicago at the centre of an Atlantic-to-Pacific trade route (Condit 1973). Alongside these long-distance routes came a variety of city, inter-urban, and regional commuter train lines, and some of the corridors remaining from outmoded lines have since become the backbone of a vibrant 1600-kilometre regional recreational trail system, including the Illinois Prairie Path, which in 1963 became one of the country's first rail-trails (Chicago Metropolitan Agency for Planning 2010). Finally, while the flat landscape of the region lent itself easily to development of a dense grid of residential and arterial streets, forward-looking park and city planners such as Dwight Perkins and Daniel Burnham also developed a system of parkways and boulevards that continues to provide important green space and pleasurable driving environments for residents (Chicago Department of Planning 1989).

Among the various transportation corridors, the local and metropolitan rapid transit rail lines stand out in the Chicago landscape, not just because of their raised elevation – 4 metres or higher above the flat topography – but also because of the wild ruderal vegetation that commonly populates their narrow, steeply sloping embankments. Often fenced off at the bottom to minimize the hazards of trespass, these strips of land are not only difficult to maintain but also challenging environments in which to grow vegetation.

For the past 25 years I have lived in the City of Chicago near one such rail line, casually observing the nature of this green space for a few kilometres to either side of my house as well as participating in a neighbourhood greening project that stretches 150 metres or so along the embankment closest to our residential block. Originally built by the Chicago and Milwaukee Railroad in 1855 to link these two cities by passenger rail, the Lakeshore Line (now called the Union Pacific North line and run by Metra, the regional rail authority) was instrumental in the development of Chicago's wealthy North Shore suburbs, as it provided swift access between the gritty, bustling city and what was widely viewed as a peaceful, lakeshore paradise (Ebner 1988).

While many of the suburban municipalities have groomed the Metra line through their community with mown banks and ornamental trees and flowers, on the elevated and fenced off Chicago portion with which I am familiar, it is the rail authority that takes official responsibility for management. Their concern however, has tended to be more focused on vegetation clearance than landscaping, and they periodically cut back areas of heavy tree growth and spray with herbicides so that corridor sight lines are maintained to meet safety standards (Randall 1997). This generally has resulted in a patchwork of wild exotic and native ruderal vegetation along the corridor (Figure 2.3). Along a southerly section a linear savanna of large cottonwood trees (*Populus detoides*) presides over an embankment dominated by grasses such as tall fescue (*Lolium arundinacea*) and quackgrass (*Elymus repens*). Further north, single young silver maple (*Acer saccharinum*) and box elder (*Acer negundo*) trees have sprung up on a stretch with a diverse ground cover of grasses interspersed with visually dominant

Figure 2.3
Two sections of the steeply sloping embankment of the Metra rapid transit rail line: after clearance by the rail authority (top), and with overgrowth of ruderal vegetation (photographs: Paul H. Gobster, 2010)

flowers such as evening primrose (*Oenothera biennis*), Ohio spiderwort (*Tradescantia ohiensis*), and common mullein (*Verbascum thapus*). Just north of there a dense stand of young tree-of-heaven (*Ailanthus altissima*) has taken hold, obscuring most ground cover vegetation save for a thick growth of field bindweed (*Convolvulus arvensis*) that covers the fence. There are also notable differences in vegetation as a function of their position along the slope of the embankment, with carpets of primitive, herbicide-resistant horsetails (*Equisetum sp.*) growing out of the rocks closest to the rails and trees and a greater variety of flowering plants near street grade where the slope is gentler and soils are deeper.

While some of these wildscape variants may be more aesthetically successful than others, it has been my impression that most residents who live near the corridor generally do not perceive any of them as ideally attractive. And perhaps in response to the general neglect for its management by an official body, a number of individuals and neighbourhood groups along the corridor have taken on sections as community greening projects. As a participant observer in the project on my own block, I have heard others involved say they feel the grasses are too dominant and messy looking and the forbs too inconspicuous and weedy. And although some participants acknowledge that these wild volunteer plants may do a good job holding down the soil on the steep slope and require no maintenance, they feel compelled to remove large clumps of them to plant ornamental flowers and shrubs, including those that may require watering, a difficult proposition given that there is no supply on site. As amateur gardeners and prairie enthusiasts, my spouse and I have, over the years, attempted to sway the group towards more sustainable solutions, working within the pre-existing matrix of wild urban plants and incorporating a combination of hardy ornamentals such as day lilies (*Hemerocallis sp.*), hollyhocks (*Alcea sp.*) and showy natives such as cup plant (*Silphium perfoliatum*) and butterflyweed (*Asclepias tuberosa*). By using these plants and other 'cues to care' such as signage, and exposing an attractive limestone terrace wall that is part of the original embankment (Nassauer 1995), I believe that there may be a happy middle ground between an unmaintained wildscape and one with some human intervention. Part of this intervention is aimed at protecting the balance and diversity that can exist in the humanized wildscape by keeping invasives like bindweed and tree of heaven from taking over, but no doubt a major part of it is the act of gardening itself and the benefits it yields for individuals and communities.

IN-BETWEEN NATURE: WILDSCAPE FRAGMENTS IN DENSE URBAN NEIGHBOURHOODS

In densely developed cities like Chicago, neighbourhood public green space is often at a premium, and even if nearby parks do exist, their access and use by some groups such as young children and older adults can be constrained by busy streets, crime, or other concerns. At the same time, there may often be an abundance of small, isolated patches or edges of unmanaged green space that exist between the boundaries of different land ownerships or land uses, and while these wildscape fragments are usually seen as a burden to those who own them, they could provide substantial value if made available as semi-public, community-managed open space.

Such has been the case with another neighbourhood greening project I have been involved in, the aim of which has been to make better use of the small green spaces that exist on our block at the margins between residential and municipal property. The neighbourhood is in the Rogers Park community area on the city's Far North Side, and homes on the block were built between 1914 and 1918 as part of the city's rapid expansion to its northern border with suburban Evanston. The southern alley of the block shared a property line with a Chicago

Railways Streetcar Depot, which housed electric streetcars from 1901 until 1957, when its then owner Chicago Transit Authority switched to all-bus transportation (Samors *et al.* 2001). In the early 1970s the property was redeveloped as a sanitation district ward yard and district police station, with an access road and parking lot abutting the alley. To separate the ward yard, the sanitation district erected a chain link fence and on the residential side of it built a 1 × 120-metre planter and filled it with arborvitae trees (*Thuja occidentalis*). The police district simply fenced their property, but on either end of the parking lot left two small green spaces, one 20 × 20 metres for a tall communications tower, and a smaller 10 × 10 metre patch for unknown purposes.

The conditions under which these spaces evolved are typical of many urban wildscape fragments, which they had become when I first observed them in the late 1980s. The narrow width and sun and wind exposure of the alley planter made it difficult for the arborvitae to survive, and where they had died they were replaced by volunteer trees such as box elder (*A. negundo*), white mulberry (*Morus alba*), and Siberian elm (*Ulmus pumila*). Its ambiguous ownership status seemingly absolved landowners on either side of the fence from management responsibility, and such discoveries as piles of road salt spilled from the district side and motor oil and construction debris deposited on the residential side suggested that the planter had become a miniature 'tragedy of the commons' (Hardin 1968). The two patches of ground at the back of the police station parking lot did not fare much better. Being far removed from the rest of the site's green spaces significantly reduced attention by the grounds crew, and the drifts of discarded styrofoam coffee cups and doughnut bags accumulated along the fence lines and corners only helped reinforce the beat-cop stereotype.

A spring 1989 neighbourhood 'cleaning and greening' effort helped to raise awareness and appreciation for these small green spaces and their value to those on the block and the larger community. Momentum for action was bolstered by a 1990 open space assessment that found the Rogers Park area to have among the lowest amount of per capita open space in the city, which helped the project secure a small grant to improve these small areas as community-managed open spaces. New trees and shrubs were planted along the length of the planter, along with flowers purchased or dug from neighbours' backyards. Working with the police station's office of neighbourhood relations, project participants relocated the fence surrounding the two patches of police property so that it closed off the parking lot and opened into the alley. The larger patch surrounding the tower was filled with new topsoil to start a community vegetable garden and the smaller patch was planted with ornamental crab trees (*Malus sp.*), lilacs (*Syringa sp.*), and annual and perennial flowers for a community flower garden. Subsequent plans at the community and city levels identified the value and usefulness of small spaces such as these in filling open space and recreation needs in dense areas of the city, and in 1995 the neighbourhood greening effort was designated as a city model demonstration project exemplifying 'public–private partnerships for landscape management and programming' (City of Chicago 1998: 116) (Figure 2.4).

Figure 2.4
The community flower garden in 1989, 1993 and 2010 respectively (photographs: Paul H. Gobster)

The last fifteen years have been an evolving lesson in what sustainability means, both ecologically and socially, and has implications for how wildscapes can best fit into small urban spaces. Ecologically, these small sites are very challenging and even with soil modification plant selection is critical. Apart from the vegetable garden, many of the plants put in during the early years of management were not robust enough, particularly the flowers, to survive under minimal management, and over time we have resorted to hardier species of trees and shrubs and selected flowers such as day lilies, hollyhocks, and cup plants that mass and can take dry conditions. We have also been more accepting of volunteer trees and other spontaneous wild plants, and where appropriate incorporate them into the landscape. Socially, however, the tolerance level for these species is quite low and in the context of these small spaces the need for neatness, colour, and familiarity still prevails. This lesson was reinforced in early 2010 when we discovered that a new fence had been erected, blocking the access to the community flower garden from the alley side. Prior to this, in recent years the trees and vines on this small site had shaded out many of the flowering understorey plants, and it had become a secret garden of sorts for neighbourhood children who would climb the trees, swing, and build forts. The police district's neighbourhood relations department, however, had a very different sense of aesthetics, and felt it was too messy and neglected. Ironically, now in the absence of use and maintenance, wild urban vegetation has quickly reclaimed the site, and except for the planted trees the patch today looks much like it did when first appropriated by the block in the early 1990s.

RECOVERED NATURE: WILDSCAPES IN LARGE VACATED AREAS

While the search for green space fragments continues in parts of cities like Chicago's Rogers Park community area where density remains high, many cities when looked at as a whole are experiencing de-densification and attempting to deal with the reality of large amounts of vacant land. This is particularly true of older cities with economies based on heavy industry, and as national and global economies shift production of raw materials and finished goods to other locations, a cascade of abandonment across industrial, commercial, and residential land uses has resulted in large areas of highly disturbed and often contaminated open space. These brownfields are the most visible manifestation of what has been called the 'shrinking cities' phenomenon, and what happens to these lands and the role of wildscapes in their reinvention has become an international topic in urban planning and landscape management (Rink and Kabisch 2009).

The Calumet Region of Southeast Chicago and Northwest Indiana provides a good case study example of how wildscapes can fill short- and long-term needs in the ecological recovery of extensive brownfield areas. Prior to development, this area along the southern shore of Lake Michigan was an ecologically rich mosaic of lake, wetland, prairie, and dune ecosystems with more than 1,300 species of plants. While its bountiful fish and wildlife were highly regarded by early Indian and European settlers, as the city grew its water and railway system made Calumet the logical centre for industrial development and the wetlands a convenient place for waste disposal. By the 1880s Calumet had gained status as a steel making centre, and as giant steel plants and their associated company towns prospered they attracted additional industry and manufacturing for chemicals, cement, and other products. Industrial waste from these operations, particularly the rocky mineral 'slag' from which the iron for steel making was extracted, was dumped into nearby wetlands, and the region also became a major landfill site for municipal waste (National Park Service 1998).

By the late 1970s the US steel industry had severely declined, causing many industrial concerns to vacate the Calumet region. Today, slag deposits cover more than 15,000 hectares of the region to a depth of 2–20 metres, and in Chicago alone more than 300 hectares of landfill tower over the otherwise flat landscape. But significant remnant natural areas still exist, providing habitat for endangered black-crowned night herons (*Nycticorax nycticorax*), yellow-headed blackbirds (*Xanthocephalus xanthocephalus*), and other native plant and animal species (Figure 2.5), and reconceiving the region as a zone for ecological and economic revitalization has been the focus of two plans focused on the City of Chicago portion of Calumet. In the *Calumet Open Space Reserve Plan* (Chicago Department of Planning and Development 2005), 600 hectares of existing public open

Figure 2.5
Snowy egrets (*Egretta thula*) scattering in wetland with landfill in the background, Calumet region of Chicago (photograph: US Forest Service, 2008)

space will form the core of a 2,000-hectare reserve, with new lands to be acquired for open space preservation, recreation, and reclamation, the last category of which will protect open space character while maintaining functions related to waste treatment or energy. A second plan, the *Calumet Ecological Management Strategy* (Chicago Department of Environment 2002) develops strategies for addressing management goals for ecologically significant sites.

While they may not be explicit about it, the plans offer examples of the important roles that wildscape vegetation can play in rehabilitating the more severely disturbed and damaged lands of the Calumet region. A landfill adjacent to a key wetland has been listed as a US Environmental Protection Agency 'Superfund' site because its toxic contents are leaching into the groundwater, and scientists are exploring the use of fast-growing cottonwood (*Populus sp.*) and willow (*Salix sp.*) trees to remove contaminants in a process called phytoremediation. Along the edge of another key marsh, the aggressive common reed (*Phragmites australis*) has firmly established itself, but wildlife ecologists recognize its value as nesting structure for one of the state's largest rookeries of black crowned night herons, and are hesitant to recommend removal until suitable alternatives are established. Finally, in a number of areas, steel slag was poured in molten form onto the landscape, and after many decades the only vegetation capable of colonizing the near impenetrable surface has been low growing weedy ruderals. In each of these cases, it is recognized that wildscape vegetation can provide a useful environmental service, and often free of charge. For brownfield sites such as these, the social-aesthetic considerations are outweighed by functional ones, and the large scale of the landscape may permit a greater use of wildscape vegetation as short- and even long-term management solutions (Westphal *et al.* 2010).

CONCLUSION

In this chapter I have outlined how a natural history approach can help us understand the genesis and evolution of urban wildscapes. Using case study examples in the City of Chicago, I have identified four major human-created green space types and discussed the place of wild urban vegetation within them. Surely there are additional types that could be discerned, and in some cities certain types may be more important than others. But as a way to think about the place of wildscapes in the context of other green spaces, I believe the examples usefully describe the range of conditions that can exist and illustrate how wildscapes can be better understood and appreciated.

In park settings such as the lakefront example, wildscapes might provide a useful transition zone between formally managed natural and manicured areas and offer a unique, low-maintenance setting for active nature exploration activities, which neither type of managed area now provides. In corridor settings such as the elevated rail example, wildscapes provide a low-maintenance solution to linear sites that are ecologically and economically difficult to manage, and aesthetic acceptability might be increased by varying the structure of vegetation along segments of the route as well as engaging community groups to embellish visible neighbourhood zones with showy plantings and other indicators of stewardship. Extensive use of wild urban vegetation faces the biggest social hurdles on small, open-space fragments in densely populated neighbourhood settings, but judicious incorporation and management of volunteer trees and other plants along with the planting of hardy, low-maintenance native and horticultural varieties can help to mainstream their acceptance. And in large-scale brownfield areas, justifying the functional and economic benefits of wild urban plants may help to offset the perceived costs of their aggressive, 'otherness' qualities, especially when considered as temporary solutions.

By thinking about wild urban vegetation as the living landscape's response to the often harsh conditions provided by human-created open spaces, we may gain a stronger ecological and economic appreciation for their utility as sustainable solutions to urban green space planning and management. Moving from these perspectives to a social and aesthetic appreciation is a more difficult task, and in cities like Chicago where weed ordinances[1] still take a largely negative position on unmanaged, spontaneous vegetation, there are also formidable technical and policy hurdles to overcome. But by understanding wildscapes from a natural history approach and considering the various contexts in which they are perceived and experienced, it may be possible to work toward a greater appreciation in this realm as well.

NOTE

1 Like many US cities, Chicago has an ordinance aimed at minimizing untended weedy vegetation, and declares that any weeds taller than 10 inches (25 cm) are considered a public nuisance, for which owners can be fined from US$100–300. In recent years, the city has attempted to clarify the distinction between unmanaged weeds and managed native vegetation, but as written, the guidelines still put spontaneous wild urban vegetation in the category of a public nuisance.

REFERENCES

Bradshaw, A. D. (2003) 'Natural ecosystems in cities: a model for ecosystems and cities', in A. R. Berkowitz, C. H. Nilon and K. S. Hollweg (eds) *Understanding Urban Ecosystems: A New Frontier in Science and Education*, New York: Springer.

Chicago Department of Environment (2002) *Calumet Area Ecological Management Strategy*, Chicago: Chicago Department of Environment.

Chicago Department of Planning (1989) *Life along the Boulevards: Using Chicago's Historic Boulevards as Catalysts for Neighborhood Revitalization*, Chicago: Chicago Department of Planning.

Chicago Department of Planning and Development (2005) *Calumet Open Space Reserve Plan*, Chicago: Chicago Department of Planning and Development.

Chicago Metropolitan Agency for Planning (2010) *Northeastern Illinois Regional Greenways and Trails Plan: 2009 Update*, Chicago: CMAP.

Chicago Park District (1995) *Lincoln Park Framework Plan: A Plan for Management and Restoration*, Chicago: Chicago Park District.

City of Chicago (1998) *Cityspace: An Open Space Plan for Chicago*, Chicago: City of Chicago.

Condit, C. W. (1973) *Chicago 1910–1929: Building, Planning, and Urban Technology*, Chicago: University of Chicago Press.

Cronon, W. (1991) *Nature's Metropolis: Chicago and the Great West*, New York: W. W. Norton.

Del Tredici, P. (2010) *Wild Urban Plants of the Northeast: A Field Guide*, Ithaca, NY: Cornell University Press.

Ebner, M. H. (1988) *Creating Chicago's North Shore: A Suburban History*, Chicago: University of Chicago Press.

Gobster, P. H. (2001) 'Visions of nature: compatibility and conflict in urban park restoration', *Landscape and Urban Planning*, 56: 35–51.

Greenberg, J. (2008) *A Natural History of the Chicago Region*, Chicago: University of Chicago Press.

Gross, M. (2010) *Ignorance and Surprise: Science, Society, and Ecological Design*, Cambridge, MA: MIT Press.

Hardin, G. (1968) 'The tragedy of the commons', *Science*, 162: 1243–1248.

Harris, E. (1998) *Prairie Passage: The Illinois and Michigan Canal Corridor*, Chicago: University of Illinois Press.

Nassauer, J. I. (1995) 'Messy ecosystems, orderly frames', *Landscape Journal*, 14: 161–170.

National Park Service (1998) *Calumet Ecological Park Feasibility Study*, Omaha, NE: National Park Service Midwest Region.

Randall, W. (1997) 'Northwest suburbs fear losing beauty along tracks', *Chicago Tribune*, October 9: B-1.

Rink, D. and Kabisch, S. (2009) 'Introduction: the ecology of shrinkage', *Nature+Culture*, 4: 223–230.

Samors, N., Doyle, M. J., Lewin, M. and Williams, M. (2001) *Chicago's Far North Side: An Illustrated History of Rogers Park and West Ridge*, Chicago: Rogers Park/West Ridge Historical Society.

Westphal, L. M., Gobster, P. H. and Gross, M. (2010) 'Models for renaturing cities: a transatlantic view', in M. Hall (ed.) *Restoration and History: The Search for a Usable Environmental Past*, New York: Routledge.

Wille, L. (1972) *Forever Open, Clear, and Free: The Struggle for Chicago's Lakefront*, Chicago: University of Chicago Press.

Chapter 3: Places to be wild in nature

Catharine Ward Thompson

Throughout the history of urban civilizations, there has been recognition of the need for engagement with the natural world: the therapeutic walk through a garden or park and the multisensory delights of singing birds, flowering plants and shade trees, the flow of watercourses, the tug of wind and rain or the pattern of clouds and sunlight, marking the changing seasons of the year. Romantic notions of the wider countryside, the rural and the uncultivated landscape, embraced both the delights and the terrors of wild nature. What such ideas had in common was the concept of something unconstrained by the strictures of built form or cultivated plot, where the complex patterns and unpredictability of the natural world offered surprise and delight (to paraphrase Alexander Pope, 1731), risk and possibly the thrill of danger (a version of Burke's 1757 'sublime' landscape), (Burke 2008); but also relief for the mind as well as recreation for the body (Ward Thompson 2011). These themes recur as urbanization has gathered momentum and the vast majority of Western populations now live in towns or cities and lead urban lifestyles.

The response to this in terms of urban planning and landscape design has been to provide urban parks, recreation grounds or sports fields, where people could engage with some form of natural environment and the opportunity for physical exercise. The first public parks of Europe and North America were developed in the nineteenth century and were consciously designed to be the antithesis of the urban condition (Ward Thompson 1998), offering a sense of freedom and escape associated with a richly planted environment that usually combined semi-natural woodland, water and meadow, 'affording the most agreeable contrast to the confinement, bustle and monotonous street-division of the city' (F. L. Olmsted, quoted in Schuyler 1986: 85). Recreation or sports grounds, often developed in the early decades of the twentieth century, were usually conceptually and practically rather different, with an emphasis on functional design rather than naturalistic aesthetics.

The nineteenth-century vision of nature was, however, in many ways different from our twenty-first-century view, informed as it is by ecological science and concepts of biodiversity. In planning and designing New York City's Central Park, Olmsted and Vaux were emulating Joseph Paxton's Birkenhead Park in the UK.

They were creating an idealized naturalistic landscape that drew on a vision of the forest plant communities of the Adirondack and Appalachian mountains of the USA but also the managed versions of parkland and pastoral scenery that 'Capability' Brown had so successfully incorporated into the designs of his many eighteenth-century English landscapes (Ward Thompson 1998). Thus, the concept of the large urban park was to provide a modified or tamed simulacrum of 'wild', or at least semi-natural, landscapes, but one where behaviour was imagined to be anything but wild. American landscape designer Andrew Jackson Downing felt that European parks fostered 'social freedom, and an easy and agreeable intercourse of all classes', qualities 'worth imitating in our more professedly democratic country' (Schuyler 1986: 65). Park planners saw the virtue of such mingling as providing an opportunity for moral and behavioural refinement, where the 'labouring classes' would benefit from the example of their social superiors. Both Downing and Olmsted saw parks as places for moral and intellectual reform, where the poor would receive 'an education to refinement and taste and the mental and moral capital of gentlemen' (Schuyler 1986: 66): the hope was that 'rough corners' of character and behaviour might be smoothed through the educative, aesthetic, and social influences of park use (Schuyler 1986: 65–66).

In Britain, the provision of parks was also about character formation and citizenship (Worpole 2007). A decade after Victoria Park was created in the 1830s in London's East End, it attracted the following, approving note:

> Many a man whom I was accustomed to see passing the Sunday in utter idleness, smoking at his door in his shirt sleeves, unwashed and unshaven, now dresses himself as neatly and cleanly as he is able, and with his wife or children is seen walking in the park on the Sunday evening.
>
> (Alston 1847)

The intention in creating urban parks in the nineteenth century was thus to create a setting that would promote 'civilized' behaviour and encourage conformity to expected types of use: children to play in appropriately designated playgrounds; adults to promenade or ride (or drive carriages, if they were wealthy enough to own one), and (particularly latterly) to engage in games such as tennis or cricket. Yet some of the key early urban parks, especially in North America, were large enough to accommodate woodland, wildlife, and greater informality of use, as were many common lands in and around urban areas in Britain, such as London's Hampstead Heath. The opportunity for wilder, freer kinds of uses was always welcome to many but then, as now, subject to disapproval and attempts at constraint by those in authority (see for example, Bartlett 1852). The original inhabitants of the Central Park site in New York (many of them African American ex-slaves) were treated as squatters, and evicted as the site was developed. Early laws regulating park use imposed severe restrictions on drinking, picnicking, music-playing, dancing, gambling, and other entertainments which were, for many people, the cultural norm (Rosenzweig and Blackmar 1994). Ironically, it was exactly these kinds of entertainments that were so popular among all strands of society (including royalty) in London's much-visited Vauxhall Gardens for two centuries from 1661; but, by the time the gardens were closed in 1859, the proprietors were complaining that the magistrates continually banned their most popular attractions as either too dangerous, or too disruptive for the newly-respectable neighbourhood of Kennington (Coke 2005) (Figure 3.1).

No doubt there was demand for a range of other uses, too, often adventurous and risky, but also mundane uses by those on the margins of society for whom comparatively wild or unregulated places were the only possible locations for their day-to-day activities. And while society has always been concerned about illegal or undesirable activities lurking in the interstices of the urban fabric, it appears to be a constant of urban living that there are those who need such places, whether it is for sleeping rough, informally cultivating plots, repairing and recycling equipment and materials, bartering goods or simply hanging out with friends away from the mainstream. This seems as likely to be true in the twenty-first century as it was in the nineteenth. So which places offer the flexibility and freedom needed for such kinds of use? Not formally designated urban parks, it would seem. As many urban parks underwent restoration or renewal in the late twentieth and early twenty-first century, a recurring theme has been the need for managers to control behaviour and use.

Many 1980s and 1990s preservation initiatives for large, historic, North American urban parks identified a range of unacceptable uses: not only anti-social activities that might be illegal or disturb other users but also activities such as mountain biking and excessive trampling that were seen as problems for plant regeneration, erosion and storm water management. The nineteenth-century language of behavioural 'rough corners' that might be smoothed through park use seems unacceptably patronizing today but the principles of social education are very much alive in many park plans and promotional material (Cramer 1993; Ward Thompson 1998). Recent guidance for the British context from CABE Space highlights 'the relative importance of certain norms of behaviour' (CABE Space 2004: 87) and promotes 'Decent parks? Decent behaviour? The link between the quality of parks and user behaviour' (CABE Space 2005).

Contemporary writing about anti-social behaviour, and the kinds of open space use and users deemed anti-social, has many dimensions, but a common theme is its bias against teenagers and young people. The presence of teenagers in recreational places is disliked by many adults and considered likely to 'cause trouble' (Tucker and Matthews 2001). Indeed, 'the very presence of groups of preadolescents or adolescents in a public place is apparently considered a potential threat to public order' (Cahill 1990: 339) (Figure 3.2). Often, unacceptable activities reflect the behaviour of older teenagers trying to establish their self-identity and a desire for territory of their own, which conflicts with notions of ownership, control and responsibility expressed by managers and other persons in authority, or by the community as a whole. And while such behaviour may be perceived as a threat to safety by other groups, what are described as anti-social activities may be merely symptoms of the main issues that fuel this behaviour –

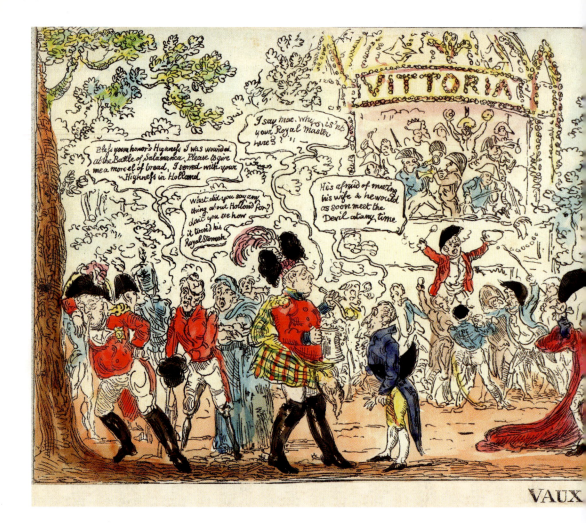

boredom, deprivation and poverty of opportunity, for example (Bell *et al.* 2003; Natural England 2010).

This is a complex issue since, even among teenagers, the presence or behaviour of one group can be threatening to another; but where *are* the places where young people can legitimately explore the limits of the world into which they are growing? The evidence available from talking to young people – mostly teenagers – is that they feel the lack of opportunities for free and adventurous activity, and landscapes that might allow this to happen. They seek places to gather with friends, or to be largely solitary, which allow them the space to explore and challenge boundaries (in every sense) as they go through adolescence and approach adulthood (Natural England 2010). They seek places to test their physical skills, to take risks and learn about the way their bodies react with the environment, to be boisterous and sometimes destructive as well as to be quiet and contemplative (Bell *et al.* 2003; Ward Thompson *et al.* 2004) (Figure 3.3). Most of all, they seek places to interact with friends but also to meet

Figure 3.1
Vauxhall Fete: engraving by George Cruikshank, published by *Town Talk* in 1813. A satirical depiction of the antics at the 'Vittoria Fete' held at Vauxhall Gardens to celebrate the achievements of Field Marshal the Marquis of Wellington

Figure 3.2
Teenagers gathering in public green space in the new town of Peterlee, UK (photograph: Anna Jorgensen, 2007)

new people, to develop a sense of their own identity as well as to engage with, and react to, the society of their peers.

Yet, despite these needs and desires, it is very hard to find places in the urban realm where teenagers are tolerated, engaging with each other and the world in this way, particularly where the activity is free and informal rather than part of structured activity (such as organized sports), or where payment and age restrictions apply (such as clubs). Indeed, the idea of a place that might encourage teenagers to gather informally has become anathema – a byword for all that is undesirable in planning or designing public space. The only kinds of places where such things are tolerated, by and large, are the informal, often naturally regenerated wastelands of derelict sites, abandoned gaps in the urban structure – the urban wildscapes of this book's title theme (Figure 3.4). As Baines (1999) and others have argued (for example Hart 1979; Halseth and Doddridge 2000), such places can play a vital role in childhood and adolescence, particularly for those living in poverty and deprivation. Such 'found' spaces often serve people's needs (and a wide range of needs) in ways that designed spaces cannot (Ward Thompson 2002). These flexible, 'loose-fit' places can often provide important places of escape for people with troubled childhoods, as well as for age groups or social or ethnic groups not welcome in conventional, well-supervised parks (Ward Thompson 2002; Natural England 2010).

Figure 3.3
Perching boy in Manor Fields Park, Sheffield (for more information about this park, see Chapter 10 in this book) (photograph: Marian Tylecote, 2010)

Running counter to this theme is the considerable amount of work and literature on 'wilderness' experience: on taking young people to comparatively remote countryside areas and encouraging physically as well as emotionally challenging activities. Such organized wilderness activities are greatly appreciated and enjoyed by many young people, offering opportunities not readily available to families living in urban poverty and deprivation, and with ultimate benefits that include physical development, emotional and mental health and wellbeing, and social development (Barrett and Greenaway 1995; Natural England 2010). Yet, despite the numerous benefits of organized outdoor activities in wild and remote places, it appears that unstructured, and often unsupervised, play is the principal means by which children and young people engage with nature and enjoy multiple benefits from their outdoor experience (Cole-Hamilton *et al.* 2001; Natural England 2010). In addition, mental health and well-being benefits from play in natural settings during childhood appear to be long-term and can contribute to emotional stability in young adulthood. For example, 'woodland and forests can provide certain therapeutic qualities that a young adult may use to alleviate stress and mental health problems' (Bingley and Milligan 2004: 74). Indeed, if tolerated by site managers, the extensive and flexible physical environment provided by large, accessible woodlands offers a free resource for a range of exploratory, rebellious and risk-taking behaviour, which might otherwise be considered anti-social or abuse of the environment (Bell *et al.* 2003).

So how much access do young people in urban environments have to 'wild' nature and the opportunities they need for healthy development? Do they want

Figure 3.4
Boys constructing skateboard ramps in one of the main thoroughfares in the Danish free state of Christiania, Copenhagen (for more information about Christiania, see Chapter 8 in this book) (photograph: Anna Jorgensen, 2010)

to get outside into urban wildscapes and, if so, how much freedom do they have to do so? Louv (2005) and Cooper (2005) have suggested that today's young people suffer from 'nature deficit disorder'. They describe the kind of society that we live in now as suffering from 'cultural autism', where a real, physical, sensual, direct bodily engagement with the natural world is replaced by a secondary, vicarious, distorted experience, usually only dual-sensory (vision and sound) and often one-way, derived from television and other electronic media. There may be considerable knowledge about the environment but often it is only indirectly learnt, very much a mediated experience. Even when people are actually outdoors in the real and natural world, the IT-based habits of texting, talking or seeking information, or listening to music, mean that they are not necessarily engaging with whatever there is out there, and this is particularly true of young people.

A report on outdoor recreation demand in England by Henley Centre HeadlightVision (2005) underlines how lifestyles have changed: increasingly urban, increasingly sedentary, increasingly technology-led. In consequence, the places where most young people are likely to be seeking engagement with nature will be urban, and they may need to provide a different 'nature' from the wilderness areas of interest to nature conservation bodies. In the urban context, 'wildscapes' are likely to be messy, perhaps dangerous, and contain unpredictable elements and structures but may well be more attractive to teenagers because of their flexibility than the tidy, managed landscape of the conventional urban park. Even for younger children, environments that allow for making and breaking things, that tolerate the building of dens and their destruction, or simply digging the ground and playing with water, are hugely attractive (Ward Thompson 2007; Natural England 2010) (Figure 3.5). Cole-Hamilton *et al.* (2001), Louv (2005), Gill (2007)

Figure 3.5
Den in Coldfall Wood, Muswell Hill, London (photograph: Marian Tylecote, 2007)

and others have shown how important such experience is as part of childhood development but one that seems increasingly difficult to access in today's society. We live in a risk-averse culture and this has had a huge impact on the freedom children and young people have to access urban wildscapes.

Every time we pick up a newspaper or see a news report on television, we are likely to be confronted by information about accidents, crimes, dangers to the security and safety of people like ourselves and our children, reported in vivid detail and often repeated over days and weeks if there is a particularly high profile case. It is no wonder that this proliferation of (often sensationalist) information has made people more cautious about the freedom they can countenance for their own children. However much support there is, on the part of parents and educationalists as well as child development experts, for children and young people to have freedom and to be given the opportunities to learn from experience, there remains a need to overcome fears.

In research on wild adventure space for young people by OPENspace (Natural England 2010), all kinds of different fears were identified: fears of accidents, racist assault, physical assault, moral injury, strangers, other children and teenagers, and fear of accidents in an environment where it is difficult to get help. All of these are real fears, some more justifiable than others in terms of statistics, and they all inform how people behave. But young people also told us that they like going to risky and dangerous places, places where they can have fun, have excitement, where they can take risks and make dares with their friends. One of the key questions is: how much risk should be tolerated, and how much happens that responsible adults do not (or need not) know about? We talked to teenagers who said that they liked being away from adult supervision, the challenge of getting into places and being chased by security guards, exploring abandoned buildings, discovering what is inside and what can be 'smashed up'. Even the younger teenagers, and perhaps the less bravado-filled ones, talked about liking a bit of risk: 'It makes it more interesting, you don't know what's going to happen' (Natural England 2010: 17). But many young people, especially those entering their teenage years and in the early stages of adolescence, also identified the importance of feeling safe, of having a place of their own where they felt secure. There is often an ambivalence to adult oversight: a preference for some adult help to be available if needed but a strong desire for freedom from adult influence or constraint: 'where you can relax and feel free', '...where you can do what you want' (Natural England 2010: 17).

The Forestry Commission has attempted to develop a methodology to help land managers take a more sympathetic approach to risk management in relation to young people's use of open space. They suggest it is important to look at opportunity costs as a way of balancing the risk management equation, so that the costs of missed developmental opportunities are also considered. Forest Schools and other initiatives are part of an attempt to tolerate a greater diversity of woodland use in the spirit of supporting healthy risk and adventure (Gill 2006). Writing on his role working with the Adventure Activities Licensing Authority,

Bailie (2005) claims that, by constraining young people's access to adventure, 'we have already condemned an entire generation to a life of awful quality and shocking brevity': a strong statement from someone in an authority charged with licensing adventure activities, underlining how important it is that society adopts a different attitude to risk.

OPENspace focus groups with young people have helped illustrate the issues. Many deprived young people recognize the need for something 'to keep you out of trouble' and a breathing space away from family or peer pressures (Natural England 2010: 18). One focus group with young people on the largest public housing estate in Europe (in Northumbria, UK) told us about family environments that are cramped, noisy, stressful and difficult, and said they wanted a place to get away, a respite. They also want a place that offers 'risk and challenge', a place that 'inspires you to do things', as well as one that offers a level of freedom, including freedom from external pressures (Natural England 2010: 17).

What makes this so hard to achieve? Current attitudes to risk and a general antipathy towards young people in public places (as identified earlier) are some of the key barriers to young people enjoying urban wildscapes and the potential benefits they offer. However, socio-spatial deprivation is also a key issue: middle class teenagers often have much readier access to outdoor adventure space than those living in urban poverty (Natural England 2010). As one youth said: 'teenagers don't really want to be on the streets, they want to be somewhere with their friends where there is no one to tell them to get off', yet for many disadvantaged young people there is nowhere else to go (Natural England 2010: 18). Despite a desire for freedom, more than one focus group told us they also like activities organized by youth workers; clearly some structured or facilitated use of outdoor space is important as well, partly perhaps because it legitimizes such use. Young people know that society does not welcome them and that ASBOs (Anti-Social Behaviour Orders) are often a threat to their free use of outdoor places. Without somewhere to go, or youth workers to legitimize activities, there is little alternative for such young people but to hang out in the street with their friends, and yet the public do not like this, almost regardless of what young people are actually doing (Figure 3.6). This socio-spatial exclusion may be exacerbated by ASBOs or similar legal measures that constrain young people back into the very homes whose stresses and tensions have often contributed to their problems in the first place. Not surprisingly, it can become a vicious circle. Lack of adequate resources such as support staff, quality space and management of that space, lack of transport, and, in particular, a lack of places that are readily accessible on foot, create considerable barriers for many young people. In addition, a number of societal pressures, and fears and scepticism on the part of both parents and youth, reinforce negative perceptions of urban wild space and its use (Natural England 2010).

Concerns about risk, referred to earlier, including fear of other teenagers, are also self-imposed by young people. It seems to be a constant that different

Figure 3.6
Skateboarders in public
open space in Vienna
(photograph: Anna
Jorgensen, 2010)

age and social groups within youth society present problems for each other. Perhaps this is to some extent unavoidable but it underlines how the needs, desires and perceptions of young people, individually and in their social groups, are in a state of flux; given this fact, access to diverse and flexible wild space within the urban fabric offers a better chance of meeting needs and providing alternatives. Young people also told us about the difficulties and restrictions they face through lack of transport, funds, and even just confidence. A focus group with young people from disadvantaged backgrounds in North Cheltenham illustrated how, even when one or more members of the group had a driving licence and some level of access to private transport, they did not appear to feel confident about going out into the surrounding countryside and having a good time on their own. Perhaps this needs more money than they have access to, but also way-finding and organizational skills that they lack. It may also reflect limitations on earlier childhood experiences in natural settings. Instead, they relied on the youth workers to help them organize such activities, which they clearly enjoyed (Natural England 2010).

Our research with adults in urban central Scotland and the English East Midlands has underlined the importance of childhood experience in adult patterns of use and enjoyment of outdoor, wild places. The evidence points, in particular, to the possibility that a lack of experience of green or natural places in childhood may inhibit the desire to visit green places as an adult (Ward Thompson *et al.* 2008). Making the link between childhood experience and adult behaviour or perceptions, Hansen (1998) has suggested that if children miss out on playful access to the natural environment – their 'earth period' – they may lose their bond with nature as adults. This has important implications, since experience of the outdoors and green or natural spaces offers vital support for young people's physical, mental and social development (Natural England 2010). Indeed, children's contact with the natural environment appears to be crucial to their social and cognitive development, as it provides them with space to play, to interact with each other and to understand the outside world (Hart 1979; Valentine and McKendrick 1997; Faber Taylor *et al.* 1998; Louv 2005). Benefits from play in natural settings appear to be long-term, realized in the form of emotional stability in young adulthood and meaningful engagement with outdoor environments in later life (Travlou 2006). Recent evidence also points to the serious consequences of restrictions on such experiential play for children's cognitive and conceptual development; in Britain, 11- and 12-year-old children have been demonstrated to be between two and three years behind their counterparts 15 years ago, with significant implications for the next generation (Shayer *et al.* 2007). Shayer and colleagues have speculated that it is partly because they do not have free experience of playing with natural and manipulable environments: 'Computer games may have usurped what might have been, for boys [at least], many hours playing outside with friends with things, tools and mechanisms of various kinds rather than virtual reality' (Shayer *et al.* 2007: 37). Urban wildscapes provide exactly the kinds of places where such play can afford young people real-world, multisensory and embodied experiences of enormous educational benefit. They can be a place to learn about the tensile strength of wood by bouncing on a branch until it breaks, or about fluid dynamics by damming a water channel, or about building structures that keep out the cold and rain (or fail to), and where none of this will be immediately condemned as vandalism.

These things have been understood by many throughout history but perhaps given appropriate expression for the modern and post-industrial era by one of the earliest British landscape architects (and much else besides), Patrick Geddes. Geddes' motto, *vivendo discimus* (by living, we learn), emphasized sensory education and the primacy of learning by doing, emotional before intellectual engagement, anticipating phenomenological approaches to understanding through perceptions and lived experience (Ward Thompson 2006). He believed all children should learn through practical and direct experience, including that of growing vegetables and fruit, but should also be led to learning through delight and wonder in the natural world. He attempted to put this into practice in his innovative design (with architect Frank C. Mears) for the Royal Zoological Garden in Edinburgh in the early decades of the twentieth century. His ideal was a naturalistic zoo (quite a radical idea for its time) 'in which not only should the animals be happily free or happily tame, but in which we ourselves should be again in nature, free in greenwood or forest belt or grassy glade, like

Adam watching and naming the creatures' (Geddes 1904: 81). While he was not able to fully realize this in Edinburgh, when he subsequently had the chance to develop a zoo in Lucknow, India, he proposed allowing boy scouts to build 'a veritable anthropological museum of primitive dwellings': a series of shelters that would include huts, cabins, pile-dwellings and dugouts, giving concrete expression to his idea of enjoyment leading to learning and of physical experience of the primitive being a key to understanding the evolution of human dwelling in the environment (Geddes c.1920: 31–32). No doubt the opportunity that he hoped to offer children as part of such an experience – to build freely with locally available materials – is one that children today would enjoy just as much as 100 years ago and which, too often it seems, they are not able to access (Figure 3.7). Research continues to demonstrate that the personal autonomy of children and the range of their access to outdoor environments has been dramatically reduced over the last fifty years or so (Cole-Hamilton *et al.* 2001; Louv 2005; Travlou 2006).

The evidence shows that the appropriate level of wildness, and the degree of involvement and oversight by adults necessary to enable good use of urban wildscapes, varies according to age and experience as well as the individual context and personality of young people. Just as for mature adults, there is no 'one size fits all' in terms of landscape and management that will satisfy every need for all conditions of young person. However, what is clear is that young people see opportunities to derive enjoyment and satisfaction in many different ways from access to wildscapes and other kinds of natural and adventurous space, and there is a growing body of research to support this. Such wildscapes may not be particularly attractive to older adults, or indeed to very young children and their parents, but it would seem that the urban environment is lacking in

Figure 3.7
At Emdrup 'Junk Playground' in Copenhagen, designed by the Danish landscape architect Carl Theodor Sørenson (1893–1979), and opened in 1943, children are still encouraged to build their own houses from recycled and found materials (photograph: Anna Jorgensen, 2008)

important ways if it lacks such places, and that all of society is likely to suffer in the long run if this is the case. Further, if the opportunity for free and playful adventure in natural environments has not been available from early childhood, it seems that it is harder in later life to perceive the potential for such benefits or to take advantage of them.

Roger Hart's seminal work (1979) showed that children need to find and 'make' places for themselves which are quite different from those identified by adults. The kinds of environments often found in abandoned sites or the wilder natural places in urban areas offer unplanned or 'loose-fit' spaces that can be appropriated by young people and allow for a proliferation of activities that may be more culturally inclusive than those afforded by designed spaces (Ward Thompson 2002). These spaces can offer a place for the marginalized – in this case young people – whose presence in conventional well-designed and managed spaces in the urban environment is often challenged. For younger age groups, the opportunity to make dens and 'secret places' is enhanced by wild and natural environments, while for older teenagers such places may simply offer a space that can be temporarily considered their own: part of the local environment and at the same time out with the adult gaze (Bell *et al.* 2003). For planners, designers and managers of the urban landscape, however, understanding unstructured use of local wild space is a real challenge, precisely because it lacks organization, formality, and is not under an official umbrella. Shifting spaces and temporary sites around the urban environment, changing over time, offer one kind of possibility, and involving young people in looking at what is available may be a valuable approach. Yet there will always be the need for more permanent but unregulated spaces, urban wildscapes that welcome changing uses and users and offer rich, edgy, exciting opportunities for so many young people who otherwise endure such poverty of environmental experience.

REFERENCES

Alston, G. (1847) Letter to *The Times of London*, September 7, 1847. Online: www.victorianlondon.org/entertainment/victoriapark.htm (accessed 23 August 2010).

Bailie, M. H. (2005) '...*and by comparison*'. Adventure Activities Licensing Authority. Online: www.aala.org/guidance_details.php/pArticleHeadingID=144 (accessed 10 December 2007).

Baines, C. (1999) 'Background on urban open space', in *Scottish Urban Open Space Conference Proceedings*, Dundee: Scottish Natural Heritage/Dundee City Council.

Barrett, J. and Greenaway, R. (1995) *Why Adventure? The Role and Value of Outdoor Adventure in Young People's Personal and Social Development. A Review of Research*, The Foundation for Outdoor Adventure.

Bartlett, D. W. (1852) 'London by day and night, Chapter 2 – The Parks', in L. Jackson, (ed.) *The Victorian Dictionary: Exploring Victorian London*. Online: www.victorianlondon.org/publications/dayandnight.htm (accessed 13 August 2010).

Bell, S., Ward Thompson, C. and Travlou, P. (2003) 'Contested views of freedom and control: children, teenagers and urban fringe woodlands in Central Scotland', *Urban Forestry and Urban Greening*, 2: 87–100.

Bingley, A. and Milligan, C. (2004) *'Climbing Trees and Building Dens': Mental Health and Well-being in Young Adults and the Long-term Effects of Childhood Play Experience*, Research Report, Lancaster: Institute of Health Research, Lancaster University.

Burke, E. (1757 [2008]) *A Philosophical Enquiry into the Origin of Our Ideas of the Sublime and Beautiful*, Routledge Classics edition, J. T. Boulton (ed.), London: Routledge.

CABE Space (2004) *Is the Grass Greener? Learning from International Innovations in Urban Green Space Management*, London: CABE Space.

—— (2005) *Decent Parks? Decent Behaviour? The Link Between the Quality of Parks and User Behaviour*, London: CABE Space. Online: www.cabe.org.uk/publications (accessed 13 August 2010).

Cahill, S. (1990) 'Childhood in public space: reaffirming biographical divisions', *Social Problems*, 37(3): 390–402.

Coke, D. (2005) *Vauxhall Gardens 1661–1859*. Online: www.vauxhallgardens.com/index. html (accessed 13 August 2010).

Cole-Hamilton, I., Harrop, A. and Street, C. (2001) *The Value of Children's Play and Play Provision: A Systematic Review of Literature*, London: New Policy Institute.

Cooper, G. (2005) 'Disconnected children', *ECOS*, 26: 26–31.

Cramer, M. (1993) 'Urban renewal: restoring the vision of Olmsted and Vaux in Central Park's woodlands', *Restoration and Management Notes* 11(2) Madison: University of Wisconsin Arboretum.

Faber Taylor, A., Wiley, A., Kuo, F. and Sullivan, W. C. (1998) 'Growing up in the inner city: green spaces as spaces to grow', *Environment and Behavior*, 30(1): 3–27.

Geddes, P. (1904) *City Development: A Study of Parks, Gardens and Culture-Institutes, a Report to the Carnegie Dunfermline Trust*, Geddes and Company, Outlook Tower, Edinburgh; Bournville, Birmingham: the Saint George Press.

—— (c.1920) *Report on Planning for the Lucknow Zoological Garden*, Lucknow: NK Press.

Gill, T. (2006) *Growing Adventure: Final Report to the Forestry Commission*, England: Forestry Commission.

—— (2007) *No Fear: Growing Up in a Risk Averse Society*, London: Calouste Gulbenkian Foundation.

Halseth, G. and Doddridge, J. (2000) 'Children's cognitive mapping: a potential tool for neighbourhood planning', *Environment and Planning B: Planning and Design*, 27: 565–582.

Hansen, L. A. (1998) *Where We Play and Who We Are*. The Illinois Parks & Recreation Website. Online: www.illinois-parks.com (accessed 1 January 2007).

Hart, R. (1979) *Children's Experience of Place*, Irvington Publishers: New York.

Henley Centre HeadlightVision (2005) *Paper 2: Demand for Outdoor Recreation. A Report for Natural England's Outdoor Recreation Strategy*, London: Henley Centre HeadlightVision.

Louv, R. (2005) *Last Child in the Woods: Saving our Children from Nature-Deficit Disorder*, North Carolina, Chapel Hill: Algonquin Books of Chapel Hill.

Natural England (2010) *Wild Adventure Space: Its Role in Teenagers' Lives*. Natural England Commissioned Report NECR025, First published 20 May 2010. Online: http://naturalengland.etraderstores.com/NaturalEnglandShop/NECR025 (accessed 5 September 2010).

Pope, A. (1731) *Of false taste; an epistle to the Right Honourable Richard Earl of Burlington. Occasion'd by his publishing Palladio's designs of the baths, arches, theatres, &c. of ancient Rome*, London: L. Gilliver.

Rosenzweig, R. and Blackmar, E. (1994) *The Park and the People*, New York: Henry Holt.

Schuyler, D. (1986) *The New Urban Landscape: The Redefinition of City Form in Nineteenth-Century America*, Baltimore: Johns Hopkins University Press.

Shayer, M., Ginsburg, D. and Coe, R. (2007) 'Thirty years on – a large anti-Flynn effect? The

Piagetian test volume and heaviness norms 1975–2003', *British Journal of Educational Psychology*, 77: 25–41.

Travlou, P. (2006) *Wild Adventure Space for Young People: WASYP 1, Literature Review – survey of findings*, Edinburgh: OPENspace. Online: www.openspace.eca.ac.uk/pdf/WASYP1LitRevSurvey220906.pdf (accessed 23 August 2010).

Tucker, F. and Matthews, H. (2001) '"They don't like girls hanging around there": conflicts over recreational space in rural Northamptonshire', *Area* 33(2): 161–168.

Valentine, G. and McKendrick, J. (1997) 'Children's outdoor play: exploring parental concerns about children's safety and the changing nature of childhood', *Geoforum* 28(2): 219–235.

Ward Thompson, C. (1998) 'Historic American parks and contemporary needs', *Landscape Journal*, 17(1): 1–25.

—— (2002) 'Urban open space in the 21st century', *Landscape and Urban Planning*, 60(2): 59–72.

—— (2006) 'Patrick Geddes and the Edinburgh Zoological Garden: expressing universal processes through local place', *Landscape Journal*, 25(1): 80–93.

—— (2007) Playful nature: what makes the difference between some people going outside and others not? In C. Ward Thompson and P. Travlou (eds) *Open Space: People Space*, London: Taylor & Francis.

—— (2011) 'Linking landscape and health: the recurring theme', *Landscape and Urban Planning*, 99 (3–4): 187–195.

Ward Thompson, C., Aspinall, P., Bell, S., Findlay, C., Wherrett, J. and Travlou, P. (2004) *Open Space and Social Inclusion: Local Woodland Use in Central Scotland*, Edinburgh: Forestry Commission.

Ward Thompson, C., Aspinall, P. and Montarzino, A. (2008) 'The childhood factor: adult visits to green places and the significance of childhood experience', *Environment and Behavior*, 40(1): 111–143.

Worpole, Ken (2007) '"The health of the people is the highest law": public health, public policy and green space', in C. Ward Thompson and P. Travlou (eds) *Open Space: People Space*, London: Taylor & Francis.

Chapter 4: Playing in industrial ruins

Interrogating teleological understandings of play in spaces of material alterity and low surveillance

Tim Edensor, Bethan Evans, Julian Holloway, Steve Millington and Jon Binnie

INTRODUCTION

Industrial ruins, along with other kinds of wasteland, unkempt parks, alleyways, culverts, edgelands and ramshackle spaces on the urban fringe, comprise informal, marginal spaces that continue to be found in most cities. Old mills, factories and workshops in various stages of decay, and originating in diverse eras testify to Britain's industrial past and the vicious cycles of capitalist expansion and contraction that characterize the volatile composition of cities throughout the twentieth century and beyond. Thatcherite economic policies throughout the 1980s rendered whole areas of industrial production suddenly obsolete. Subsequent processes of regeneration have swept away many of these derelict sites, erasing them entirely, or converting buildings into homes, offices and retail outlets as part of the promotion of a new industrial aesthetics (Muller and Carr 2009). However, in areas that have been less successful in attracting inward investment, such ruins continue to linger. Moreover, a new phase of ruination has been heralded by the severe economic downturn.

In this chapter, we explore the specific uses of these ruins as sites for play, first assessing the material and less tangible qualities that promote the numerous playful practices that are subsequently identified. Following this, we critically examine theories about play and discuss the shared characteristics which allow identification of analogies between play and ruins. Finally, we critically analyse how and why ruins are exemplary realms through which we might adopt a critical perspective that highlights both the limitations and potentialities for play in other kinds of urban space.

Despite their negative associations, industrial ruins are the location for a wide range of social practices, including a host of leisure activities. While the pace of urban regeneration and increasingly rigorous zoning policies make such sites less prevalent than they were in the 1980s, they remain spaces in which unauthorized and improvisational activities may occur, providing a space for bodies and activities that are excluded from regenerated, gentrified urban space.

Recently academics have adopted various accounts about such sites, focusing on myths of political and social progress (Trigg 2006), exposing 'the dark genealogies and destructive operations of the contemporary world' (Gonzalez-Ruibal 2008: 262), interrogating dominant notions of curation and remembering (DeSilvey 2006), critiquing current constructions of heritage (Edensor 2005a; 2005b; High and Lewis 2007), investigating material vitalism (Edensor 2005c), assessing the potential for urban exploration (Romany 2010; Ninjalicious 2005), exemplifying human ambivalence towards 'nature' (Jorgensen and Tylecote 2007; Qviström 2007), and identifying the potential for numerous activities to take place (Shoard 2003; Doron 2000).

In the following section we explore the interconnections between play and industrial ruins and consider the extent to which industrial ruins may offer spaces within which the potentialities and becoming of play can be realized.

PLAYING IN THE RUINS

Before identifying the playful activities that take place in industrial ruins, it is vital to recognize that they are sites for a host of other, ostensibly more utilitarian practices. These include the use of derelict space for sex work, living in a temporary home, growing vegetables, fly-tipping, car-parking and walking the dog; as a resource for building materials, firewood and home furnishings; not to mention the ecological potential that such sites offer as they decay over time and are colonized by flora and fauna that augment urban experience. These activities sit problematically in any division between play and work, and between those activities deemed 'productive' and 'unproductive' or 'illicit' and 'legitimate', for they may be playful or associated with leisure and pleasure, whilst also having 'work'-like qualities, as we discuss later. Such practices also rely on the absence of direct regulation, though they may have their own informal modes of regulation.

A lack of overt regulation is a key attribute of ruins, important in relation to play since this provides a space outside the strictures of 'health and safety', systematic surveillance and material maintenance. Commonly conceived by planners, business people, local politicians and residents, as the derelict vestiges of former industry, when industrial sites are closed down and abandoned they are unmoored from 'stabilizing networks which ensured an epistemological and practical security' (Edensor 2005a: 313). Though high fences often deter would-be visitors to ruins, along with signs warning about security measures and the likelihood of prosecution, in most cases, these measures are toothless. Usually, somebody will already have found a way past the defensive barriers, and security personnel are rarely employed to protect spaces that are in various states of ruination and abandonment. The ordinary control of the human and the non-human is missing, and plants and animals rapidly move in and colonize the space from which they were formerly expelled. There is an instant alterity to normative urban experience, so that ruined space blurs distinctions between the wild and the tame, and the urban and the rural. This lack of ordering and surveillance thus allows wide scope for activities prohibited or frowned upon in other urban public spaces, and admits those who are intensively surveilled and excluded elsewhere.

A second crucial quality of ruins is their material affordance, to be found within the unfamiliar, unkempt environments that foster a multitude of opportunities for playful interaction with space and matter. The ruin *feels* very different to most other forms of urban space, is full of multiple tactilities, smells, sounds and sights (Edensor 2007). Such spaces may be sought precisely because they confound familiar forms of comfort and mundane sensual experience. The transformed materiality of industrial space, its decay and the distribution of objects and less distinguishable matter, provide a realm in which sensual experience and performance is cajoled into unfamiliar enactions that coerce encounters with unfamiliar things, and encourage playful and expressive performances. The ruin is not characterized by velvety textures and polished surfaces, ceaselessly swept flooring or plush carpeting. Instead, it contains the rough, splintery texture of rotting wood, crunchy shards of glass, the mulch of mouldering paper, moss and saplings, decomposing clothes, corroding steel and the oily residues of industry. These material conditions mean that derelict factories and warehouses invite expressive physical investigation through the material forms that pre-exist ruination and those that belong to it. Industrial ruins offer empty corridors to run along; stairs to ascend; windows to climb through; trap doors to be avoided, entered or to throw objects down; rubble to clamber over; materials of multiple textures and smells; walls and floors that provide blank canvases for art works; spaces of different sizes and materialities that provide opportunities to explore soundscapes; extensive abandoned and cleared shop floors that enable the enactment of expressive and unfamiliar physical performances. This engagement with materiality, whether artistic, experimental, hedonistic or creative, occurs in a context in which the usual conventions about the inviolability of physical matter as property, commodity or other value-laden substance do not pertain, since the site and its contents have already been officially ascribed as worthless and obsolete. There are few consequences for engaging with matter or space in ways that transgress these norms, and the absence of surveillance provides an opportunity to do so with little chance for such engagements to be apprehended. These circumstances thus provide opportunities for an array of playful activities which we now identify.

Destructive play: joyriding, burning and smashing

A particularly obvious range of activities carried out in spaces of dereliction, given the general lack of surveillance and lack of value attributed to these places, are those practices we term 'destructive' play. A common feature of many ruins and derelict landscapes are the vestiges of cars and motorbikes that have been stolen, driven around the challenging slopes, tracks and open spaces without following the norms of careful and 'responsible' motoring, and then burnt or otherwise destroyed (Figure 4.1).

These endeavours, along with other 'destructive' practices, would usually be termed 'vandalism'. However, unlike the destruction of vehicles owned by other people, and the damage caused to public and private property elsewhere, the smashing up of the buildings and fixtures within ruins carries little sanction. Ruins are valuable repositories of potentially found items and loose materialities, which promote playful abandon and development skills, including the qualities of balance, inventiveness and improvisation recognized in accounts about the relationship between playfulness and space (Ward 1978). In most ruins windows have been shattered, and porcelain sinks assaulted and fractured with implements such as heavy boulders or iron poles. Wooden boxes are dropped from upper floors, or down lift shafts, and spectacularly splinter. Even brick walls may be annihilated by experimenting with improvized techniques of demolition, and lighter partitions made of plasterboard and wood can be ripped asunder with gratifying ease. Watching the spectacle as things clatter downstairs, deliriously tumble from assigned positions into a chaotic heap as shelving is tipped over and thick oil spills out from pierced tanks and oozes across floors is a pleasurable experience. There is a transgressive, playful delight in contravening what in other spaces would be restricted interaction with things and space, and letting go of the conventions of public bodily control. These more radical playful engagements with matter offer opportunities for expressive physical performance and a relatively unhindered engagement with the material world. As such, these destructive encounters challenge notions of 'acceptable' play, blurring the distinction between that which appears to be productive and improving and that which seems to be destructive, wilful, undisciplined and 'mindless' (Figure 4.2).

Hedonistic play: drinking, drug-taking, partying and sex

Other playful engagements within industrial ruins can be broadly thought of as hedonistic pursuits. During the emergence of early acid house and rave culture, abandoned industrial premises such as warehouses and factories providing expanses of floor space were popular venues for illegal raves and parties. Moreover, outside of such mass-events, ruins continue to be sites for drinking and

Figure 4.1
Upended car, industrial ruin in Leicester (photograph: Tim Edensor, 2003)

Figure 4.2
Smashed partition, derelict Oldham cotton mill (photograph: Tim Edensor, 2007)

drug-taking, with most derelict sites revealing cans, needles and other drug-related paraphernalia. These activities blur the lines between pleasure and necessity since, for some, ruins provide a safe space in which alcoholics and addicts may carry out their practices with little chance of being disturbed or of disturbing passers-by; while the same spaces provide opportunities for those less dependent on drugs and alcohol to hold parties in which drinking and drug consumption can be undertaken for fun. Similarly, the prevalence of condoms reveals that ruins are also settings for sex. While they may serve as sites for sex-workers to take their clients for business, ruins also provide spaces for other sexual practices. David Bell (2006) and Gavin Brown (2008) have discussed the role of new media in reproducing spaces as cruising areas, or spaces for public sex; and there are websites which provide information on cruising areas including ruined buildings, and how to find and access them. Thus, the sexual adventures that take place in ruins may be spontaneous but can also be organized. Accordingly, this also renders such activities liable to state intervention, with the monitoring and policing of these websites (Chanen and Brown 2007) in the context of attempts by the state to eradicate same-sex play from cruising areas (Walby 2009), and public toilets (Johnson 2007), revealing that whilst ruins may be less directly regulated than other urban spaces, they are not necessarily the unregulated counterpart to more ordered urban spaces.

Artistic play: graffiti and other interventions

A third form of play might be labelled artistic or creative. In ruins there are often numerous objects and forms of matter that cannot be identified or classified, partly because of their transformation under conditions of decay and partly because of the visitor's unfamiliarity with industrial processes. Objects made out of unfamiliar material, off-cuts and residues from production processes, parts never assembled with other bits and other equally enigmatic, unclassifiable artifacts litter ruined scenes. This has the effect of contravening the usual visual order and attuning the eye to an emergent aesthetics, one that cannot be fixed through endless maintenance but is constantly becoming different. Thus, shards of metal, things twisted into peculiar shapes, dead animals, matter and fixtures released from their usual confinement collect and mingle. Scenes are framed by collapsing structures and the decorations of yesteryear mock the ongoing production of the visually modish in commercial space. Such unfamiliar scenes involve the random mixing of artifacts, so that things which were previously separated merge in new juxtapositions, striking chords through their unfamiliar accompaniments. Besides these unusual assemblages, large machines, structural entities and other objects appear as pieces of sculpture, allowing their aesthetic, shapely and textural qualities to be apprehended. Accordingly, an emergent aesthetic effect contrasts with the aesthetic ordering of much urban space. In this context, the ruin renders itself available for artistic and creative play.

Visitors may move objects around, compose impromptu installations. Artists are drawn to ruins because they provide a realm outside official artspace against which artworks can be composed. More organized attempts to utilize ruins as sites of exhibition have been mobilized in recent years. For instance, in 2003 at an old x-ray works in Smethwick, Birmingham, UK, an artistic collective took over the property temporarily, spending some time restoring the building so that it was in a condition to serve as an exhibition space, subsequently utilizing the rooms and the materials to produce a series of artworks (Webb 2003).

Most obviously, ruins serve as venues for graffiti, ranging from tagging and slogans associated with subcultural groups, to more elaborate designs produced by experienced artists (Figure 4.3). Since there is no sanction for composing designs on neglected, often crumbling walls, certain sites are saturated with the work of such artists.

Adventurous and expressive play: action sports and urban exploration

A fourth kind of playful practice draws upon the particular affordances of many ruins, identified above, which offer potential for a range of playful somatic engagements with space and materiality (Figure 4.4).

To access an industrial ruin it is often necessary to climb under a fence or into a window, or pick a route through mounds of rubble. To walk in a ruin, whether it is cluttered by multiple objects and fragments, or comprises vast, open spaces is therefore to move within a material environment that continuously corporeally engages the visitor, distracting, repulsing or luring the body towards or away from particular routes, chambers or fixtures, offering engagements with unfamiliar textures or peculiar shapes, and testing embodied capacities to manage risk, move in unusual ways, crouch, bend and leap, to make a path around, through, under or over things (Edensor 2008). Particular affordances that inhere in expanses of concrete floor, chutes, kerbs, large boards and ramps provide a playground for the vehicular pursuits of skating, skateboarding, motorcycle scrambling and mountain biking. Such disordered space also provides a location for play that entails risk and danger through encounters with unstable structures and surfaces, requiring balance, agility and bravery beyond that encountered in managed play spaces or activities, such as climbing and abseiling, where health and safety regulations restrict the level of risk. Akin to the developmental approaches to play discussed below, it could be argued that these forms of play help develop useful skills of recognizing and negotiating danger, and knowing one's bodily capabilities. Yet beyond these instrumental approaches, as proponents of parkour, urban exploration or free running may argue, such encounters with risk need also be understood as forms of 'extreme', 'adventure' or 'lifestyle' sport, involving self expression, playfulness and heightened embodied sensation (Wheaton 2004), and the production of particularly valorized landscapes (Cloke and Perkins 1998).

The backdrop of the ruin provides a particular aesthetic for such activities, informed perhaps by some of the fantastic scenes featured in the spectacular action movies that use ruins as stage-sets for dangerous, frequently violent action (Edensor 2005a). The exploits of urban explorers who typically focus their

Figure 4.3
Budgie graffiti by
Faunagraphic in the
works shower at the
derelict Hepworth
Refractories site in the
Loxley Valley, Sheffield
(photograph: Ian Biscoe,
2009)

activities upon ruined and forbidden sites, often at night, involve an engagement with such spaces as evidenced by the websites and blogs that communicate experiences, share photographs and recommend derelict sites. The elements of danger chime with action and lifestyle sports, and climbing and other specialist equipment is utilized to access and explore derelict space. The illegality of many of these practices adds a further frisson to these playful endeavours. Spectacular vantage points are sought from which to take photographs, and strategies for avoiding security and police contribute to the sense of adventure (Garrett 2010; Romany 2010; High and Lewis 2007; Ninjalicious 2005).

In addition to these physically expressive and sporting pursuits, many derelict and abandoned sites are littered with a plethora of 'felicitous' spaces (Bachelard 1969), the attics, cupboards, offices, cellars and host of micro-spaces in which children and sometimes adults may linger and create dens. Indeed, evidence of the production of these small affective, atmospheric realms recurs throughout ruined space, testifying to urges to claim space away from control. Typically bordered by obstacles, arranged with office and industrial furniture, decorated with small items, pictures and graffiti, these dens again testify to a material looseness that allows creative play and dwelling in less regulated space (Bingley and Milligan 2004) (Figure 4.5).

Figure 4.4
Running boy, derelict Oldham cotton mill (photograph: Tim Edensor, 2007)

Figure 4.5
Den in Newcastle industrial ruin (photograph: Tim Edensor, 2003)

THEORIZING PLAY IN RUINS

We have argued that wild spaces such as industrial ruins are important spaces for play because of their material affordances and the absence of surveillance. We now extend the focus of this chapter to consider the playful activities we have identified in order to critically interrogate academic theories about the meanings and purposes of play.

Dominant notions of play have foregrounded its relationship with childhood. For instance, according to Bateson (1956: 145), when 'people talk about play, they tend to say what it is not – "it is not real" or "it is not serious" – and then the rest of the sentence gets rather vague when the speaker realizes that play is serious'. As this infers, dominant conceptualizations rely on the temporal or spatial separation of play from work, adulthood, production and the 'real stuff' of life, by viewing play as part of childhood development, as a process of learning and 'trying on roles' for future adult life (Katz 2004). The child's right to play is ingrained in international law under Article 31 of the United Nations International Children's Emergency Fund's Convention on the Rights of the Child (UNICEF 2008). Notably, UNICEF includes the right to play under the banner 'survival and development rights', reflecting the broader instrumental and developmental approach to play in childhood, with play valued as 'a means through which children's physical, mental and creative capabilities are developed' (Valentine and McKendrick 1997: 219).

In contrast, in reviewing theories on play in adulthood, Stevens (2007: 32) argues that play is 'fundamentally non-instrumental', 'purposeless', 'illusory', 'non-reflective'; a 'wasting away of time'. He further defines play as hedonistic and gratuitous, 'emotionally pleasurable to all participants' (36), an opportunity for people to 'fully be themselves and ... transcend the roles which have been defined by them for work and domestic life' (46). Like other dominant conceptualizations of play (see Evans 2008), Stevens' definitions are rooted in a

separation of play from production and work, adult everyday life, and are roman-
tically conceived as being outside power relations. Such notions are more broadly
rooted in neo-liberal ideals about the productive, responsible citizen, and the 'teleological march towards reason' (Katz 2004: 98) which informs 'dominant
Western constructions of childhood and adulthood, the former characterized by
play, frivolity, freedom, innocence, dependency and a lack of responsibility, and
the latter by work, seriousness, independence and responsibility' (Evans 2008:
1663).

In this vein, Huizinga (1950: 7) insists that all play is other to work, 'is a vol-
untary activity' and that '(P)lay to order is no longer play: it could at best be a
forcible imitation of it'. However, significant problems with this definition of play
are encountered when applying this to the numerous forms of play which characterize adult and child everyday life. For instance, commercial children's play
spaces, computer gaming and hen and stag parties reveal a blurring of leisure
and work time that instantiate new, idealized work–play rhythms characterized
by the bonding exercises that involve white-water rafting, paint-balling and role-
playing and which seem to have become integral to work practice and culture.
Defining play as 'other' to work thus becomes problematic.

Assertions that play is the antithesis of production, order and responsibility
are analogous to the ways in which disordered spaces such as industrial ruins are
similarly conceived as marginal, lacking purpose and wasteful; and they are
further typified as excessive, dangerous, and 'out of place' (Edensor 2005a). Official accounts of ruined and derelict sites in planning and local government discourses typically identify them as unproductive spaces, blanks that await more
productive use; as 'blots on the landscape', unsightly spaces that signify economic depression and a lack of vitality; or at worst, spaces of danger, criminality
and deviance; assignations that are not ameliorated by media representations of
such spaces as venues for criminal activity, spectacular police chases, fights and
as the lair of the abject and the malevolent. In the examples of ruined space and
play discussed above, the simplistic reasoning inherent in such assignations of
play and ruin is all too apparent. For ruins are often well-used places, sites of
pleasure and leisure as well as spaces for productive and generative practices. We
have identified a wide range of diverse playful practices that blur distinctions
between productivity and pointlessness, creativity and destruction, legality and
illegality, and respectability and abjection, confounding the simple distinctions
between play and work discussed above. We have also shown that these derelict
spaces, like other species of wasteland and interstitiality, are utilized by both
adults and children for play, highlighting that 'playing is not (just) kids stuff'
(Harker 2005: 59).

As Cloke and Jones (2005: 312) argue, because of the shared associations
with disorder, irresponsibility and freedom, play and childhood have become
'associated with places and spaces which are seen to be outside of adult control
and ordering, where the fabric of the adult world has become scrambled or torn,
and the flows of adult order are disrupted or even abated'. Ruins and urban

wildscapes have become situated within a broader debate regarding children's lack of access to diverse and challenging play environments (Jenkins 2006). Implicit in such discourses is an assumption that the denial of access to wild-scapes has a detrimental impact on children's long-term development. Ruins perhaps provide an ideal environment for this kind of outdoor, unsupervized and risky play; but this is an environment which is commonly perceived as being off-limits to children and young people. As such, ruins and wildscapes are entangled in the paradoxical geography of play space that simultaneously constructs them as both risky and ideally-suited to children's play. Thus, associations between childhood playfulness and innocence and vulnerability produce contradictory understandings of playing in wild spaces. For while 'there is an assumption that in losing themselves in disordered spaces, children actually find their selves – become "true" children – without the ordered surveillance of adulthood with its restrictions and imposition of overarching codes of how children should be' (Cloke and Jones 2005: 312), the disordered, unregulated qualities of wild spaces make them seem particularly fearful and dangerous as spaces of play, and thus children's access may be restricted. This is despite the recent identification of wild spaces as particularly important spaces for children's development through play, with the Royal Society for the Prevention of Accidents (RoSPA 2007) arguing that 'children need wilder places to play where ... children can learn valuable life-long lessons, particularly about risks and how to deal with them, from playing in the natural environment'. Furthermore, such assessments contrast with teleological notions that distinguish absolutely between childhood and adulthood, denying the possibility for the child's acquisition of the adult skills of judgement and responsibility, and similarly, refuting the childish qualities of adult play.

These positive assertions about the value of children's unstructured play in wild spaces have involved moves to increase such play in recent years. However, the converse has been true for young people and adults, for whom play is not seen as an important part of everyday life or development – a product, in part, of the 'teleological closure' (Aitken *et al.* 2007: 5) in dominant conceptions of 'growing up', with adulthood the end point of development, not an ongoing process. Moreover, rather than risk being seen as integral to the value of play (as it may be with regard to childhood), playful activities for adults and young people are commonly seen as dangerous infringements on other, responsible, productive uses of public space, further undergirding the splitting of urban space into 'wild' and 'regulated' realms. Thus, activities which may be considered as 'play' for young people and adults, such as hanging out, drinking, skateboarding and par-ticipating in public sex, have faced increased restrictions in public space in recent years, particularly in the highly regulated spaces of many contemporary Western cities (see, for example, work on restrictions placed on young people hanging out in public space by Collins and Kearns 2001; Skelton 2000; Thomas 2005; and on the regulation of drinking by Jayne *et al.* 2006). As we have seen, ruins provide venues for such pursuits, with the particular material and unregulated qualities of industrial dereliction allowing a range of playful activities.

However, we are aware that there is a danger of romanticizing ruins and neglecting issues of danger and power that influence who plays in such spaces. Ruins may be spaces of exclusion, for they are often protected by barriers and fences that prohibit access for those without particular levels of physical agility. Accordingly, differently abled bodies, the young and the old and those who are fearful of such spaces, may be effectively barred from playing in ruins. In addition, while some may choose to visit industrial ruins to explore multiple, playful, heightened forms of embodied experience, other users may do so because they have no other place to go. Homeless people, sex workers and drug addicts use ruins as spaces of low-level surveillance in which they can carry out that which is forbidden in other urban locations. It is thus essential to attend to the ways in which the activities and bodies encountered within ruins remain implicated in broader power relations. For instance, without the protective gaze of surveillance and supervision, child's play can often become a zone of affective disorder, whereby playful punches and kicks spillover into unacceptable and transgressive acts of bullying and beyond. In this context, industrial ruins reveal the necessity of avoiding any conceptualization of play as purely hedonistic and devoid of power relations, for we subsequently miss the multiple forms of tension, competition, friction and hurt which often accompany different forms of play. As Harker (2005: 52) argues with reference to Gagen's (2000) work on gender, performativity and power in play, 'playing can more often than not be used to reinforce existing spatio-temporal relations and sediment existing power relations'.

Tendencies to over-emphasize the playful virtues of industrial ruins also have implications for the way in which we view wild spaces in dualistic terms, as 'other' to those spaces described as 'smooth', regulated urban spaces. Here, it is imperative not to celebrate certain forms of play within industrial ruins as 'authentic' or heroic, or as essentially 'transgressive' and 'resistant' in contradistinction to more 'inauthentic' and 'mainstream' play within more regulated commercial spaces. More importantly than this though, notwithstanding the restrictive elements of play in ruins that we have mentioned, we argue that the more evident lack of regulation and the particular materialities of industrial ruins throw light on the potential for play in other, apparently more controlled spaces to disorder and disrupt their regulation. For while we do not wish to undermine our depiction of the range of expressive, adventurous, unsupervised and sensual qualities of the playful practices carried out in ruins, nor back-track from the suggestion that the potentialities of play in most other more tightly regulated, materially consistent and controlled environments might be suppressed, such conditions cannot wholly exclude the potential for play.

CONCLUSION

Accordingly, we conclude by reflecting upon how thinking about industrial ruins in relation to play challenges the dominant distinctions that position play as other to work, adulthood, smooth urban space, power and regulation. Rather than maintain these divisions, we contend that the proliferation of playful activities in industrial ruins can divert us to a recognition of the potential wildness and playfulness within managed urban areas, reveal possibilities for challenging structures of governance and regulation, and dispute strict distinctions between 'wild' and 'smooth' urban spaces, work and play, and childhood and adulthood. The sheer effort to maintain the material order and regulatory conditions in even the most highly regulated spaces means that there are always opportunities to capitalize on moments of inattention or failures of maintenance. As Cloke and Jones contend, play can be a means to *make* wild those spaces that otherwise may be seen as 'smooth', revealing their rough edges and the potential these hold to refigure and challenge systems of order and governance:

> However ordered, or unordered those street spaces may be, children [and adults
> engaged in playful activity] are able to disorder the street as adult space when they
> transgress spatial and/or temporal boundaries and thereby enter a more liminal, hybrid,
> inbetween world.

(2005: 312)

It is further worth noting that the inclusion of multiple textures, materials and a certain 'wildness' in planning practices is currently influential, and this provides opportunities for a more playful, experimental, expressive and sensual engagement with urban space. But even where this is not the case the unruly effects of sensual stimuli are always liable to break through the carefully guarded city. Since the distinction between wild spaces and more regulated urban spaces is not as clear cut as it may seem, this opens the potential for more varied forms of playful engagement to occur away from derelict sites. Spatially deterministic assumptions are liable to miss the ways in which ordered spaces are continuously subverted by play. This is especially apparent when we consider the similarities between particular kinds of play in ruins and other forms of urban exploration such as free running, parkour and skateboarding, along with graffiti-writing, public drinking and hanging out, along with some of the other playful activities mentioned above that are often tightly regulated but still extend across urban space.

It remains important to recognize that relative freedom from direct retribution is essential to the playfulness afforded in the industrial ruin, since this foregrounds the affective, embodied and sensual qualities of play. For instance, the untying of objects from obvious position and function within ruins allows them to be interpreted and played with in ways that allow scope for imaginative improvisation and exploration. Hence ruins are spaces in which playing may conjure up and enact the different potentialities that have previously only existed as unactualized possibilities, generating heightened sensual, affective and embodied experiences that open the potential spatial, social, political and material orderings to be confounded and threatened by the immanent, sensual, improvisational qualities of play. If we recognize that play is connected to and integrated within work, production, everyday life and power relations, we can see its potential to not only reinforce existing power relations but also transform them. Like the children's play that Katz maintains is not simply learning or copying adult roles, but playing with them, negotiating and transforming their relations to dominant power structures in the process, play is always potentially transformative or subversive of power. Indeed, Katz contends that rather than being 'banished in the teleological march towards reason', play and 'childishness' may be thought of as positive forces in adulthood, 'ready to be sprung as revolutionary consciousness', figured as 'both a form of coming to consciousness and a way of becoming other' (2004: 98).

Harker (2005) suggests that play may best be conceptualized as always potentially emergent, with the potential to shift the actuality of the moment in unforeseen ways, generating encounters which could always have been otherwise. This infers that it is less important to analytically separate apparently opposing spaces and times of work and play. Accordingly, this provides a means to think non-teleologically about industrial ruins, not as 'dead' or waste spaces but as spaces constantly re-formed by both transgressive and playful activities, capitalist modes of production, broader power relations and contemporary forms of urban governance. Moreover, the kinds of play we have identified in ruins allow us to think non-teleologically about play in other spaces in which powerful forces of exclusion, domination and governance are more readily apparent and come with more immediate reprisals – and in which forms of play occur nonetheless. As such, we have argued that an attentiveness to playfulness in industrial ruins offers an opportunity to think about the role of 'wild' spaces within the contemporary city, and the potential 'wildness' present in more managed urban spaces which might offer possibilities for playful transformation.

REFERENCES

Aitken, S., Lund, R. and Kjørholt, A. (2007) 'Why children? Why now?' *Children's Geographies*, 5(1): 3–14.

Bachelard, G. (1969) *The Poetics of Space*, Boston: Beacon Press.

Bateson, G. (1956) 'The message "this is play" ', in B. Schaffer (ed.) *Processes: Transactions of the Second Conference*, New York: Josiah Macy Jr Foundation.

Bell, D. (2006) 'Bodies, technologies, spaces: on "dogging" ', *Sexualities*, 9: 387–407.

Bingley, A. and Milligan, C. (2004) *Climbing Trees and Building Dens: A Report on Mental Health and Well-Being of Young Adults and the Long-Term Effects of Childhood Play Experience*, Lancaster: Institute for Health Research, Lancaster University, Forestry Commission.

Brown, G. (2008) 'Ceramics, clothing and other bodies: affective geographies of homoerotic cruising encounters', *Social and Cultural Geography*, 9: 915–932.

Chanen, D. and Brown, C. (2007) 'Public-sex crackdown takes place to Internet', *Star Tribune*, Minneapolis-St. Paul, MN. Online: www.startribune.com/local/11593986. html (accessed 22 June 2010).

Cloke, P. and Perkins, H. (1998) ' "Cracking the canyon with the awesome foursome": representations of adventure tourism in New Zealand', *Environment and Planning D: Society and Space*, 16(2): 185–218.

Cloke, P. and Jones, O. (2005) ' "Unclaimed territory": childhood and disordered spaces(s)', *Social and Cultural Geography*, 6(3): 311–323.

Collins, D. and Kearns, R. (2001) 'Under curfew and under siege? Legal geographies of young people', *Geoforum*, 32: 389–403.

DeSilvey, C. (2006) 'Observed decay: telling stories with mutable things', *Journal of Material Culture*, 11(3): 318–338.

Doron, G. (2000) 'The dead zone and the architecture of transgression', *CITY: Analysis of Urban Trends, Culture, Theory, Policy, Action*, 4: 247–263.

Edensor, T. (2005a) *Industrial Ruins: Space, Aesthetics and Materiality*, Oxford: Berg.

—— (2005b) 'The ghosts of industrial ruins: ordering and disordering memory in excessive space', *Environment and Planning D: Society and Space*, 23(6): 829–849.

—— (2005c) 'Waste matter – the debris of industrial ruins and the disordering of the material world: the materialities of industrial ruins', *Journal of Material Culture*, 10(3): 311–332.

—— (2007) 'Sensing the ruin', *The Senses and Society*, 2(2): 217–232.

—— (2008) 'Walking through ruins' in T. Ingold and J. Vergunst (eds) *Ways of Walking: Ethnography and Practice on Foot*, Aldershot: Ashgate.

Evans, B. (2008) 'Geographies of youth/young people', *Geography Compass*, 2(5): 1659–1680.

Gagen, E. (2000) 'An example to us all: child development and identity construction in early 20th-century playgrounds', *Environment and Planning A*, 32(4): 599–616.

Garrett, B. (2010) 'Urban explorers: quests of myth, mystery and meaning', *Geography Compass*, 5 (video article, forthcoming).

Gonzalez-Ruibal, A. (2008) 'Time to destroy: an anthropology of supermodernity', *Current Anthropology*, 49(2): 247–263.

Harker, C. (2005) 'Playing and affective time-spaces', *Children's Geographies*, 3(1): 47–62.

High, S. and Lewis, D. (2007) *Corporate Wasteland: Version 2: The Landscape and Memory of Deindustrialization*, Ithaca: Cornell University Press.

Huizinga, J. (1950) *Homo Ludens: A Study of the Play Element in Culture*, Boston: The Beacon Press.

Jayne, M., Holloway, S. and Valentine, G. (2006) 'Drunk and disorderly: alcohol, urban life and public space', *Progress in Human Geography*, 30(4): 451–468.

Jenkins, N. E. (2006) '"You can't wrap them up in cotton wool!" Constructing risk in young people's access to outdoor play', *Health, Risk and Society*, 8 (4): 379–393.

Johnson, P. (2007) 'Ordinary folk and cottaging: law, morality, and public sex', *Journal of Law and Society*, 34(4): 520–543.

Jorgensen, A. and Tylecote, M. (2007) 'Ambivalent landscapes: wilderness in the urban interstices', *Landscape Research*, 32(4): 443–462.

Katz, C. (2004). *Growing up Global: Economic Restructuring and Children's Everyday Lives*, Minneapolis, MN: University of Minnesota Press.

Muller, S. and Carr, C. (2009) 'Image politics and stagnation in the Ruhr Valley', in L. Porter and K. Shaw (eds) *Whose Urban Renaissance? An International Comparison of Urban Regeneration Strategies*, London: Routledge, 84–92.

Ninjalicious (2005) *Access all Areas: A User's Guide to the Art of Urban Exploration*, Toronto: Infilpress.

Qviström, M. (2007) 'Landscapes out of order: studying the inner urban fringe beyond the rural–urban divide', *Geografiska Annaler, Series B, Human Geography*, 89(3): 269–282.

Romany, W. (2010) *Beauty in Decay: The Art of Urban Exploration*, Berkeley: Ginkgo Press.

RoSPA (2007) 'Children must play in the wild says RoSPA', Press release, 11/6/2007. Online: www.rospa.com/news/releases/detail/default.aspx?id=595 (accessed 12 July 2010).

Shoard, M. (2003) 'The edgelands', *Town and Country Planning*, 4(72).

Skelton, T. (2000) '"Nothing to do, nowhere to go?": teenage girls and "public space" in the Rhondda Valleys, South Wales', in S. Holloway, and G. Valentine (eds) *Children's Geographies: Playing, Living, Learning*, London: Routledge, 80–99.

Stevens, Q. (2007) *The Ludic City: Exploring the Potential of Public Spaces*, London: Routledge.

Thomas, M. (2005) 'Girls, consumption space and the contradictions of hanging out in the city', *Social and Cultural Geography*, 6(4): 587–605.

Trigg, D. (2006) *The Aesthetics of Decay: Nothingness, Nostalgia, and the Absence of Reason*, London: Peter Lang.

UNICEF (2008) *The Convention on the Rights of the Child: Survival and Development Rights*. Online: www.unicef.org/crc/files/Survival_Development.pdf (accessed 15 June 2010).

Valentine, G. and McKendrick, J. (1997) 'Children's outdoor play: exploring parental concerns about children's safety and the changing nature of childhood', *Geoforum*, 28(2): 219–235.

Walby, K. (2009) ' "He asked me if I was looking for fags": Ottawa's National Capital Commission conservation officers and the policing of public park sex', *Surveillance and Society*, 6(4): 367–379. Online: www.surveillance-and-society.org/ojs/index.php/journal/index (accessed 26 July 2010).

Ward, C. (1978) *The Child in the City*, Princeton: Pantheon.

Webb, S. (2003) 'Review: Re:location', *Interface*. Online: www.a-n.co.uk/interface/reviews/single/124147 (accessed 18 August 2011).

Wheaton, B. (2004) (ed.) *Understanding Lifestyle Sports: Consumption, Identity and Difference*, London: Routledge.

Chapter 5: Nature, nurture; danger, adventure; junkyard, paradise

The role of wildscapes in children's literature

Katy Mugford

Note to parents: Why, when the landscapes of children's literature support the principles of adventure, experiment and development, are children given limited capacity for adventure play in the real world?

The intention of this chapter is to study how the authors of a selection of books for children and young people find ways of overcoming the barriers children face in accessing urban wildscapes and other challenging and adventurous environments within their narratives, to find common themes, and to consider whether any aspect of their fictional worlds may provide a means to engage with some of these real-world issues; as well as exploring the possibilities and limitations of adventure space for children. Is there a dialogue in these books that could illuminate the future consideration of barriers to access, such as risk avoidance, perceived danger in woods and water, a perceived lack of judgement in children and growing reliance on surveillance as 'protection' for children and young people?

This chapter will explore a range of books currently in print, which use landscape to develop characters, covering recommended reading ages from seven to sixteen. In reviewing current publications, as part of the process of selecting the shortlist of books for this chapter, it seemed that many current children's books are republications from a generation or more ago, suggesting that the barriers children experience in accessing urban wildscapes today can be more ably circumnavigated by a previous generation of authors.

THE WILDSCAPES OF CHILDREN'S LITERATURE

The books explored in this chapter contain stories that unfold in what could be described as wildscapes. The settings range from readily identifiable urban wildscapes, such as rubbish dumps, abandoned churchyards and woods, to places with some wildscape characteristics, which include streets, rooftops, ex-urban wilderness settings and fantasy landscapes. What they all have in common is an ability to offer the protagonists an environment that challenges them to act independently. In each narrative, a development of the protagonist's character goes hand in hand with their growing understanding of their place within their landscape.

Figure 5.1
(photograph: James Sebright, 2011)

Clive King's (1963) *Stig of the Dump* illustrates the importance and lost recreational value of unsupervized spaces. Left alone for the summer, Barney, a young boy, plays in the local chalk pit, the dump, where he meets an extraordinary companion and learns about his environment. Barney takes ownership of an overlooked space: 'there was nothing to do, nothing to play, and nowhere to go. Except the chalk-pit. The dump.'

Danny, the Champion of the World, by Roald Dahl (1975) explores the world of Danny (aged nine), who learns of his father's secret habit of poaching in Hazell's Woods, and the characters in the village. The woods are the setting for the action: illegal activities in which both Danny and his father are complicit.

His Dark Materials, the trilogy by Philip Pullman (1995–2000) is an epic tale of religion, science, spirituality and human nature, which has at its epicentre a twelve-year-old girl named Lyra, joined in the second and third books by a boy of the same age named Will. The landscape setting changes throughout Lyra and Will's journey, which takes them to the end of the earth and beyond. The universe shifts around these two characters as they struggle through the end of childhood to adolescence, and only settles and rests as they find their adult selves. Crucial to this narrative is Lyra's free will: 'she must fulfil this destiny in ignorance of what she is doing … What it means is that she must be free to make mistakes'.

Little Foxes by Michael Morpurgo (1984) is a story about a ten-year-old boy called Billy Bunch, who is abandoned at birth, failed by the system and passed through a series of foster homes. Stuttering and lonely, by making friends with a fox cub in an abandoned churchyard, he sets out on a journey to find the countryside (referred to throughout as his 'Wilderness'), which eventually leads to his new home.

Skulduggery Pleasant by Derek Landy (2007) tells the story of Stephanie, a remarkable twelve-year-old girl, who inherits both her Uncle's house and the mystery of his death. Her uncle is an author of fiction, full of remarkable characters that Stephanie discovers are real, with magical powers, and far more dangerous than anyone in the sleepy town where she grew up. Stephanie's wildscape is the underworld of magic, lying hidden and unseen within the city. Her search to understand the death of her uncle leads her through this world. She is bored by 'Main Street. Normality. Kids playing football, riding bikes and laughing … and the world being as she'd always thought it was.' She is excited by the unknown: 'the lights of the city looming ahead'.

Frozen in Time by Ali Sparkes (2009) (categorized as suitable for readers aged nine and above) tells the story of Ben and Rachel on their school holidays. Bad weather has left them alone with only the TV for company, until it blows up. They discover two children from the 1950s in cryonic suspension in a submerged shelter at the bottom of their garden, release them, and together start to unravel the mystery of their father's disappearance. Their journey takes them through an exploration of their garden, town and surroundings, seeing these once familiar surroundings through different eyes.

Bella, a sixteen-year-old girl, is the protagonist of the *Twilight* saga by Stephanie Meyer (2005–2008), popular with teenage and young adult readers. Bella is moving from Phoenix to Forkes, a place of never-ending mist and rain, to live with her father. She falls in love with a vampire, who with his vampire family, deny themselves human blood, feeding only on animals. The vampire, Edward, loves Bella, but also desires to drink her blood. As the story unfolds, it takes Bella further into the forest and into her emotional landscape. This saga is the journey that Bella takes through adolescence to adulthood, exploring facets of love and responsibility.

A consideration of how access to, and exploration of, challenging and adventurous environments is being presented in children's literature, may present clearly the challenges that are faced in enabling children's adventurous play in the real world. Can common themes be identified and translated into the discussion of urban wildscapes?

I SPY UNSUPERVIZED PLAY

Lack of supervision is key to the development of physical and mental strength, character and resourcefulness in the protagonists of all the books. It works in tandem with a lack of restriction in developmental play.

In the first book of the *His Dark Materials* trilogy, *Northern Lights*, Lyra is a child playing in the marginal and forgotten spaces of Oxford: 'the catacombs under the Oratory kept Lyra and Roger busy for days'. She plays in the unseen places: 'What she liked best was clambering over the College roofs ... or racing through the narrow streets, or stealing apples from the market'.

In the second book of the trilogy, *The Subtle Knife*, we catch a glimpse of the ruins of a beautiful city, deserted by adults, where

> there was a group of boys fighting, and a red-haired girl urging them on, and a little boy throwing stones to smash all the windows of a nearby building. It was like a playground the size of a city, with not a teacher in sight.

In *Frozen in Time* a 'normal summer' is described: 'the garden was perfect for playing in ... most of the time it was left to do its own thing – as was the tangled wood beyond the stream'. It is a perfect wildscape, where 'foxes would flit' and 'Jays would clack'. The absence of Ben and Rachel's parents leaves them free to explore this landscape, which is the setting for the underground vault in which they find Freddy and Polly frozen in time from the 1950s, who join them to explore the twenty-first century. This time slip allows the author to explore many of the generational differences between childhoods in these two eras. In place of absent parental authority Ben and Rachel are left with their absentminded uncle, a scientific genius, who is however, also physically absent for most of the time.

The implication is that children should be left alone to acquire the necessary life skills to deal with unforeseen circumstances, rather than being protected from exposure to risk and challenge through constant supervision.

MISSING PARENTS

Conspicuous by their absence, parents in children's literature are removed. They are presented as ignorant or incapable as parent figures, as child-like themselves, or are killed off before the story even starts. Their absence enables the child protagonists of these stories to make their own choices and to enter new realms that are normally unavailable to them, often with adventurous consequences.

In *Little Foxes,* Billy's parents are removed from the story, having abandoned their son on the doorstep of a police station: 'Billy Bunch came in a box one wintry night ten years ago. It was a large box with these words stencilled across it: "Handle with care" '. Billy's development has been impaired through lack of nurture: 'He did not walk when it was expected of him, for he saw no need to [and a] stutter made him all the more reluctant to communicate'. Billy was passed from home to home, which 'confirmed that he was indeed alone and unwanted in this world'. However, Billy 'had his Wilderness down by the canal'. His Wilderness (always spelt with a capital 'W') is where he learns involuntarily, and feels the responsibility of care that has been missing in his own life: 'He was lord of his Wilderness, its guardian and its keeper'. Of a rescued swan he states 'Not a bit like an ugly duckling, you aren't ... Course you're not as beautiful now as you're going to be, but I 'spect you know that', mirroring his own developmental path. 'Billy at last found peace' in this wildscape.

Stephanie's mother, in *Skulduggery Pleasant*, is a two-dimensional token figure who is portrayed as caring, but unsophisticated. Her father is depicted as a loving, yet foolish man: 'I have a big meeting this afternoon but I left the house without something important ... I forgot my underwear'. With this simple statement his authority as a father figure is dissolved. Tempted by risk in his youth, but then finding security as a father and husband, he becomes risk averse:

> When I was younger, I believed. I believed even more than Gordon did. But I stopped. I made a decision to live in the real world, to stop indulging this, this *curse* [magic]. Gordon introduced me to your mother and I fell in love. I put it all behind me.

Five pages of dialogue help to explain the plot and plant the parental figures firmly in the 'real' world, and then they are gone.

In the *Twilight* saga, the role reversal that we see between parent and child in *Skulduggery Pleasant* is exaggerated even further. Bella's parents are consigned to the role of children; incapable, irresponsible and afraid, needing to be fed, cared for and protected, reduced to bit parts in the plot, in stark contrast to the protagonist's role as independent, resourceful, decisive and brave. Her mother is 'loving, erratic [and] harebrained' with 'wide, childlike eyes'. Her father, Charlie, is a bachelor with childish needs: 'Charlie couldn't cook much besides fried eggs and bacon'. In *New Moon* Bella states that 'I shuddered at the thought of dragging my lethal shadows into my mother's safe, sunny world. I would never endanger her that way.'

In *Danny, the Champion of the World*, Danny's father William is a rare example in children's literature of an adult who engages in adventure with his

Figure 5.2
(photograph: James Sebright, 2011)

son. He is an adult of 'otherness', with an alternative perspective, affiliated with travellers living in a gypsy caravan that Danny 'loved living in'. Danny describes his father as 'the most marvellous and exciting father any boy ever had', who smiled with his eyes: 'my father was an eye-smiler. It meant he never gave me a fake smile'. Perhaps significantly in this context, he was also 'a marvellous story-teller'. Whereas Stephanie's father dismisses magic as a curse, Danny's father embraces it. He is not afraid to blend the boundaries that would seem to restrict the adult (to non-play), and the child (to not being an equal, responsible figure). In *Danny, the Champion of the World* these roles are shared.

Danny does everything that the young protagonists in the other narratives can only do away from parental supervision. Danny's father, though not perfect, 'no father is perfect', embraces the risk involved in a young boy growing up. In this book the role of parent is not synonymous with restriction.

SURROGATE PARENTS AND TRAVELLING COMPANIONS

In place of parents the children are provided with fantastical uncles, surrogates, guardians and travelling companions, sometimes good and sometimes bad. The children are listened to, considered and have a mutual reliance on the adopted companions of their journeys, who are often given animalistic qualities, or represent the exceptional adult engaged with 'otherness', rather than the normative orderings of everyday life. They do not fit within the child's recognized conception of adulthood.

In *Little Foxes*, running away from 'Aunt May' leads Billy to the countryside, both liberating and harsh, and to the river where he is rescued by a kindly man on a barge named Joe, who, with his wife, adopts Billy into a life engaged with the natural environment, and in balance with his own nature, treating him with kindness, acceptance, respect and friendship. Joe also teaches Billy about letting go, and of respecting 'wildness'. Of Billy's companion fox cub he explains:

> He loves you like a mother, Billy. But foxes leave their mothers, old son. If he comes to rely on you he won't be a real fox any more … and that would be a terrible thing, almost like taking his soul away from him.

The emotional difficulty of letting the fox become independent certainly has resonances with the child/parent relationship: 'The younger he goes, the more chance he has of surviving out there'. Billy's friends are the swan and fox, both rescued and rescuers. There is a mutual respect between the boy and these animals that he has not experienced before. This makes him courageous and he learns from the fox about friendship and trust.

Stephanie's companion is Skulduggery Pleasant, an adult of the underworld that she becomes a part of. There is a mutual respect between them. They support each other as a partnership but Skulduggery does not dissuade her from making her own choices:

> You should be realising by now that looks are, more often than not, deceiving. A neighbourhood like this, with its graffiti and litter and squalor, is the safest neighbourhood you could possibly visit. Open the door to any one of these houses around us and you walk into a veritable palace. Surface is nothing, Stephanie.

Skulduggery's description evokes 'otherness' existing alongside the everyday. As with all urban wildscapes, unpredictability brings possibilities.

For Stephanie it provides the freedom to choose risk over endured safety. This is the urban landscape made available by travelling beyond the safe idyll. 'Stephanie sensed an opportunity … it occurred to her that she had never spent a whole night without her parents nearby. A small taste of freedom and it almost tingled on her tongue.' Stephanie is demonstrably a child but develops aspects of adult behaviour. This is a key theme throughout the books. Each protagonist takes on responsibility that is recognized as an adult trait, but within the adventure. The authors blend the boundaries between adulthood and childhood within these landscapes, providing the possibility of a balance of skills and capacities. Partnerships make the exploration of wildscape and the success of the narrative journeys possible. The adults/guardians in these narratives have the playfulness and creativity of perceived childishness and the protagonists have responsibilities often reserved for the 'adult' role.

In the *Twilight* saga Bella has her vampire and werewolf friends, and in the *His Dark Materials* trilogy, Lyra has many companions, including the Gyptians (leading the 'alternative' lifestyle of river people) and an armoured bear. The calm strength of John Faa, Lord of Lyra's Gyptians, bears a striking resemblance to Billy's Joe in *Little Foxes*. She also has the constant companionship of Pan, her 'dæmon' (an animalistic extension of her spirit) which means she is never alone. Although her parents figure in the trilogy, it is not in the traditional role of 'parents', as they leave her in the care of Jordan College as a young child, so that they can court power, only reappearing sporadically during the story.

In *Stig of the Dump* the companion figure, Stig, is a caveman and is thus distanced from contemporary 'sensible' figures of authority. Barney would be bored by himself. He needs some help and guidance to find the love of the dump, to learn the new skills, to learn to think beyond normal situations. He also needs some protection, a buffer so that he can make friends without fear and call on someone in times of trouble.

These surrogate figures support the protagonists in their wildscape adventures, allowing them to use their judgement and exercise freedom of choice in ways that are not permitted in the normal adult world of these narratives.

FRIEND OR FOE?

The authors of these narratives address the issue of adult threat that children may face when unsupervised in a wildscape. The vulnerable child protagonists are confronted by the dangerous 'stranger'. The protagonist in each case identifies the danger and evaluates it. The child is always shown as resourceful. The predator is exposed time and time again. The unnamed threat is therefore challenged and given an identity, which varies from narrative to narrative: a librarian, the government, the church, thieves, kidnappers, poachers and keepers and vampires. A positive reflection on the theme of danger is repeatedly presented.

Lyra is confronted with a predator on many occasions throughout the *His Dark Materials* trilogy. One predator figure is a charming man 'wearing a beautifully tailored linen suit', whose handkerchief 'was scented with some heavy cologne like those hot-house plants so rich you can smell the decay at their roots'. This man preys on Lyra: 'On the one hand he was kind and friendly, [on the other] she sensed, not a smell, but the idea of a smell, and it was the smell of dung, of putrefaction'. She is groomed by him and lured into his car thinking that she is safe. The man steals from Lyra, but she reclaims what is hers. Lyra has to make character judgements throughout her journey and when she is wrong is not afraid to address the mistake. Over time she learns to trust her instincts.

Billy and his fox are pursued by poachers, 'each of them carrying a gun': 'They could hear behind them that the hunters were in the woods too'. As the drama unfolds it is reflected in the landscape: 'It was a different forest now, with great tall oaks clinging dangerously to the hillside. Many had fallen, their roots ripped out, leaving vast craters where young saplings were sprouting again'. In contrast to this Danny and his father are poachers themselves, hunted by keepers with guns.

Bella takes a considered risk by choosing to have a relationship with Edward. As a vampire he explains, 'It's not only your company I crave!... Never forget I am more dangerous to you than I am to anyone else'. Her ability to understand the perspective of others turns threatening strangers into friends and lovers.

Judgement is a learnt skill, not one that can be presented as a package to a child. It encompasses misjudgement and development through choice and experience. It is natural for children to make mistakes, choose companions and identify foes. These choices cannot always be forestalled by adult intervention. Children need to exercise choice and judgement.

SINK OR SWIM

As well as introducing children to an adult world of judgement and responsibility, wildscapes are also shown to be an arena for managing risk through the acquisition of bodily strength and physical dexterity. Game playing, unfamiliar environments and unusual circumstances in each of these narratives permit the development of these skills.

Learning about the materiality of the world is explored in all the books. Lyra learns about alternative dimensions; Bella fixes up motorbikes to increase her experience of risk, joyriding along tracks. Barney climbs a tree: 'As he climbed higher he could feel something about the swaying of this tree. It did not have the

Figure 5.3
(photograph: James Sebright, 2011)

springy exciting sway of a sound tree'. Learning about the environment through exploring wildscapes teaches an inbuilt risk management. In *Stig of the Dump* 'Barney had a feeling ... that it was probably true about the ground giving way. But still, there was a difference between being told and seeing it happen'.

Lyra has similarly learned from experiences of battling with other children, raiding 'the Claybeds, pelting the brick-burners' children with lumps of heavy clay ... before rolling them over and over in the clinging substance they lived by'. It is visceral, filthy and aggressive play. This learnt experience is put to good use in self-defence in the frozen wastes of the North:

> She remembered hurling a handful of clay in the broad face of a brick-burner boy ...
> She'd been standing in the mud. She was standing in the snow. Just as she'd done that afternoon, but in deadly earnest now, she scooped a handful together and hurled it at the nearest soldier.

These are not just learnt traits of aggression, but of judgement, aim, balance and risk assessment.

In *Frozen in Time*, the time slip device allows a comparison between the management of childhood risk now and in the 1950s. The two boys have a discussion about the river:

BEN: 'Swim the river? ... Are you mad? We can't swim it!'
FREDDY: 'Why ever not? We used to swim it all the time in 1956.'
>   People did paddle at the edges sometimes, but the kids were always being warned not to bathe in it. There were big signs forbidding it. He [Ben] didn't know why. Probably so the local council didn't have to worry about being sued if somebody stood on a broken bottle.
FREDDY: 'Don't you do that here any more?'
BEN: 'Council doesn't allow it'.
FREDDY: 'Sounds like your council members are a bunch of lily-livered old codgers to me! Where on earth did you get them from?'
BEN: 'Well ... er ... most of them probably used to swim the River Am with you.'
FREDDY: 'Oh. Well, pretty poor show then, the lot of them!'

Sparkes takes the time to make this point in the middle of the action, namely that risk aversion has been foisted on today's children by those who experienced freedom only a generation before. She also illustrates the immense pride and satisfaction such risk taking can bring: 'Freddy helped him out of the water at the other side and for a moment Ben just stood, shivering with excitement and delight'.

Instead of being a potential threat, the versatility and unpredictability of the natural environment is seen as a vital component of children's life experience. Rivers are also used as metaphors for the children's personal journeys, linking Lyra and the Gyptians through the riverways to the Fens and beyond in the *His Dark Materials* trilogy. The water represents freedom and a growing sense of self, as with Billy, who finds words to express himself through his river journey, and Danny who we see at the end of his story leaving to poach trout.

Conditional and pre-determined risk-assessed play does not figure in these stories. The heightened sense of adventure is evoked through risk, unknown outcomes and physical exertion.

JUNKYARD OR PARADISE?

Spaces that are good to play in are not always the ones designated for that role. 'Adult' and 'child' spaces are often the same, just perceived from differing perspectives.

Frozen in Time also has a rather contrived discussion of playground play equipment: 'It's all very colourful now'. Today's play equipment is contrasted with that from the 1950s:

> FREDDY: 'The pirate ship was the best … One time it cracked Gus Blaine in the back of the head and knocked him out cold! It was hilarious!… I wonder why they took it away. It was heaps better than this. This is all little kids' stuff!'
> BEN: 'Um…' 'I think with this stuff people tend not to get knocked out so much.'
> FREDDY: 'Safe … But jolly dull.'

Stig teaches Barney to use found objects as play: 'Stig seemed very pleased with all of the things he could do with his bits of umbrella'. This engages with the child's ability to invent. Danny's toys 'were the greasy cogs and springs and pistons that lay around all over the place, and these, I can promise you, were far more fun to play with than most of the plastic stuff children are given these days.'

Danny's father breaks the rules by not sending Danny to school aged five, teaching him the art of mechanics instead. Lyra was not taught a regular curriculum, picking up odd lessons from the Scholars at the Oxford college where she lived. Danny's world 'consisted only of the filling-station, the workshop, the caravan, the school, and of course the woods and fields and streams in the countryside around'. His wildscape is a blend of nature and junkyard. Danny and his father play with fire together, build tree-houses, make bows and arrows, all the things that Barney does with Stig.

Found objects and spaces can often initiate unexpected imaginative play. Children use interpretative skills to translate found objects and places into tools for play.

MUD, MUD, GLORIOUS MUD?

The issue of washing versus adventure came up in some of the books. Instead of being seen as an extra washing chore for parents, dirt is presented as the by-product of play, adventure, survival and life.

Mud is frowned upon by Aunty May (Billy's foster mother) in *Little Foxes*: 'can't be for ever spending on extra washing [and] can't think why you don't go and play in the adventure playground with the other children. It's all concrete there, and much better for you'.

Ben and Rachel in *Frozen in Time* 'were getting filthy, but did not worry. Uncle Jerome wouldn't notice ... there was nobody to give a sharp exhalation and fold their arms in annoyance when they traipsed back to the house later.'

Danny in *Danny, the Champion of the World* is covered in dirt. It is a matter of fact, distinguishing him from other characters with more authoritarian parents. 'I was now a scruffy little boy as you can see, with grease and oil all over me'; it is the sign of labour, an adult preoccupation 'because I spent all day in the work-shop helping my father with the cars.' With no bath, his father washes Danny by standing him up and scrubbing him down: 'This, I think, got me just as clean as if I were washed in a bath – probably cleaner because I didn't finish up sitting in my own dirty water.' Here, inventiveness works alongside cleanliness, where dirt is a fact rather than a sin. 'My sneakers were the wrong colour too. They were white. But they were also dirty and that took a lot of the whiteness away.'

Throughout the *His Dark Materials* trilogy Lyra is safe in her coating of dirt: 'Lyra's furs looked ragged and they stank, but they kept the warmth in'.

This theme raises the question of how many of the barriers to children's adventurous play are not for the protection of children and based around genuine health and safety concerns, but are purely for adult convenience.

CONCLUSION

Although these stories are fiction, they ably illustrate the opportunities that wild-scapes provide for children's development and there are key themes that help illuminate the debate around danger/adventure.

In these books, wildscapes are a vehicle for having adventures and learning through experience. In the security of the fictional realm children often visit unsu-pervised and risky spaces, and recognition is given to the special qualities of urban wildscapes. In these stories the barriers to accessing these places and experiences that are increasingly present in modern childhood are addressed head on. Water is used to represent journey and independence, and independent choice is key to strength. Dirt is liberating, predators are exposed, darkness embraced and unsupervised play with found objects enhances the skills and development of each character. These protagonists appear to grow within their wildscapes. The real-world fears propagated by the media, of child as vulnerable victim, are countered from childish perspectives of curiosity, learnt judgement

Figure 5.4
(photograph: James
Sebright, 2011)

and understanding of the world. Engagement with the wildscape surroundings is synonymous with personal growth. In the quieter moments of these plots, the protagonists use their solitude and 'otherness' to reflect on both themselves and their situation. This demonstration of independent consideration is a valuable lesson in self-reflectiveness. Landscape in these books represents engagement with self and with the world.

A common theme is the complete separation between the protagonist's development through landscape and any parental engagement. Most commonly the parents are removed from the story line, in order to give the protagonist the opportunity to engage in adventure, in 'growing up'. It is clear that in this literature, the role of 'parent' constitutes a barrier to children's access to challenging places and experiences. The clear line between the 'normal' 'adult-ordered striated space' and the 'otherness' encountered through the child gaze is absolute (Cloke and Jones 2005). Cross-over of the parenting role into the imaginative space is avoided. These books raise the question of whether an understanding and enjoyment of challenging places and experiences has been counteracted by the developed moral code of 'good parenting'. Cloke and Jones (2005) suggest that the rigid demarcation between the worlds of adulthood and childhood creates 'conditions for spaces both of [inappropriate] childhood mischief and of potentially inappropriate adult intervention'. Are parents, and adults more generally, also losing the ability to experience childish mischief themselves?

It could be suggested from the evidence identified in children's literature and from the popularity of these texts that a more balanced approach to children's protection and development is needed. The popularity of the film versions of the *His Dark Materials* trilogy and the *Twilight* saga with both adults and children suggest that this elusive freedom to enjoy challenging places and experiences is a quality treasured in both adult and children's cultures. Adults often supply these books to children and it is adults who have written them. It seems that the current generation of parents may be using their own real-life experiences of freedom to engage their children with the now fictional concept of adventure.

Roald Dahl is one of the few authors to really engage with the possibility of naughty parents. His irreverence towards conventional parental role models is refreshing, which may help explain his popularity. In his books parents face consequences. They lose their children if they are dull and/or bad parents. In *Matilda* (Dahl 1988) the parents are forced by their daughter to sign her away for adoption. Most importantly, mischievous behaviour is celebrated and rewarded. The perceived roles of 'adult' and 'child' are consciously blended in such narratives.

Children can develop skills of self-sufficiency if they are given the space to learn how and why. They create opportunities for play, learn through risk taking and develop a sense of responsibility that is not always the preserve of the 'adult'. Adult figures can engage with creative and playful enterprises. Climbing on rooftops and throwing mud is not the preserve of fiction. Creative learning can engage more than a school curriculum. Adventures are possible within the real world. Children should learn to be resourceful, to use found objects as tools for play and experiment. What is frequently perceived as anti-social behaviour is often constructive and is not a precursor to development into a 'bad' adult. It is healthy play.

It could also be suggested that the distinction between reality and fiction has become too absolute and that this is one of the main barriers to young people's access to urban wildscapes. The line is not so clear in the literature reviewed in this chapter and the blurring is believable to its readers, desired and engrossing. The clear difference between these books and the 'real' world is that the threat of danger is not avoided and danger is not lessened by pre-emptive action. Danger has to be understood and negotiated. As Danny says: 'Most of the really exciting things we do in our lives scare us to death. They wouldn't be exciting if they didn't.'

REFERENCES

Cloke, P. and Jones, O. (2005) 'Unclaimed territory: childhood and disordered space(s)', *Social and Cultural Geography*, 6(3): 311–333.

Dahl, R. (1975 [2010]) *Danny, the Champion of the World*, London: Penguin Books Ltd.

Dahl, R. (1988 [2010]) *Matilda*, London: Penguin Books Ltd.

King, C. (1963) *Stig of the Dump*, London: Puffin Books.

Landy, D. (2007) *Skulduggery Pleasant*, London: HarperCollins Children's Books.

Meyer, S. (2005 [2007]) *Twilight*, London: Atom.

Meyer, S. (2006 [2007]) *New Moon*, London: Atom.

Meyer, S. (2007 [2008]) *Eclipse*, London: Atom.

Meyer, S. (2008) *Breaking Dawn*, London: Atom.

Morpurgo, M. (1984 [2008]) *Little Foxes*, London: Egmont UK Ltd.

Pullman, P. (1995 [1998]) *Northern Lights*, London: Scholastic Ltd.

Pullman, P. (1997 [1998]) *The Subtle Knife*, London: Scholastic Ltd.

Pullman, P. (2000 [2001]) *The Amber Spyglass*, London: Scholastic Ltd.

Sparkes, A. (2009) *Frozen in Time*, Oxford: Oxford University Press.

PART 2

WILDSCAPE CASE STUDIES

Chapter 6: Brown coal, blue paradise

The restoration of opencast coal mines in Lusatia, Germany

Renée de Waal and Arjen de Wit

If you choose to leave the regional train from Berlin to Senftenberg at the little town of Großräschen, you will find yourself on a desolate platform. The presence of five other railroad tracks indicates that it must have been busy in the past, but now birches and pine trees shoot up between the rusty steel. The newly asphalted road to the town centre will invite you to continue on your way. If you follow this road to the very end, the view will explain the – somewhat provocative – choice for the name 'Seestraße', or 'Lake Street' in English. What you see is a former opencast brown coal mine, which is being flooded to become part of the Lusatian Lakeland, the biggest artificial chain of lakes in Europe.

The previous account aptly summarizes what is going on in a region that is recovering from decades of exhaustive coal mining activities. Lusatia, the region in which Großräschen is situated, is not singular in this regard. Abandoned mining regions can be found all over Europe, for example, Cornwall in the United Kingdom, Nord-Pas de Calais in France, the region around Ostrava in the Czech Republic and the Portuguese pyrite belt. After heavy industrial activities, these areas are left behind with poor economies, high unemployment and destroyed landscapes. They are all in need of fundamental economic, social and environmental change, yet they have very different ways of dealing with the mining legacy (IBA 2010a).

Former mining regions are wildscapes by definition, that is, post-mining wildscapes. Buildings, mining machines and infrastructure are either dismantled or left behind in a deserted landscape of extensive brownfield (Figure 6.1). Appreciated by many as fascinating post-industrial wilderness, the deserted landscape painfully reminds locals of more prosperous times. How can a region deal with this contradiction? Is it possible to preserve the wildscape character of these wastelands without blocking new economic development, or even to use it as a basis for a new future for the region? In this chapter, the role of wildscape is analyzed in the process of structural change which is taking place in Lusatia after the collapse of the mining industry.

Figure 6.1
Derelict conveyer bridge
in Lusatian post-mining
wildscape (photograph:
Henning Seidler, 2004)

ENERGY CENTRE LUSATIA

Lusatia is situated in the east of Germany. Before the region became established as a mining area, it was rather isolated, and agriculture was the main land use. The mining started with accidental findings of brown coal (lignite) around the town of Lauchhammer in 1789. But soon the brown coal at the surface ran out, which caused a change to shaft mining first, and then to opencast mining at the end of the nineteenth century (Großer 1998). Brown coal was used in the emerging glass, brick and iron industry in Lusatia, where it replaced fuels such as peat, charcoal and wood (Steinhuber 2005). Later the brown coal was converted into electricity in power plants, which is its main use nowadays.

After World War II, the communist regime in the German Democratic Republic (GDR) strived to make the country self-sufficient in its energy supply, since it could not trade with capitalist states and it was expensive to import oil from the Soviet Union. Because brown coal was the GDR's only fossil fuel, everything was done to increase production, which increased steadily to its peak in the late 1980s (Wittig 1998). At that time, seventeen opencast coal mines were operating simultaneously (Pflug 1998), producing almost 200 million tonnes of brown coal per year (Wittig 1998). Lusatia had become the energy centre of the country (Steinhuber 2005; Wittig 1998). The environmental impact of the large-scale opencast mining only became an issue later, when it became apparent that the restoration of these sites was lagging far behind the excavation activities (Pflug 1998; Steinhuber 2005).

The brown coal occurs under most of Lusatia. The excavations ate up large agricultural, forestry and nature areas (Drebenstedt 1998; Steinhuber 2005). But as the mining expanded, housing areas were also sacrificed.

Großräschen, being one of the Lusatian towns that quickly developed as a mining town, offers a paradoxical example of this. In 1888, the Ilse mining stock corporation was founded in the nearby village of Bückgen. The company built its head office, several works and dwellings for workers and employees south of Großräschen, where the Meuro opencast mine was opened. One hundred years later however, in 1989, the mining company started to excavate this new part of the town as well, because brown coal was also found here. About 4,000 people had to be resettled, and an entire part of the town was demolished (IBA 2010b). Only three characteristic buildings remained along the Seestraße. Not surprisingly, a common Lusatian saying is 'Die Kohle hat's gegeben, die Kohle hat's genommen', which means 'the coal gave it and the coal took it' (IBA 2010c).

The German reunification in 1990 caused the collapse of the Lusatian industries (Hunger *et al.* 2005). Energy from plentiful and cheaper sources, like natural gas or oil, could now be imported from other countries. This led to a sharp decline in brown coal production. On top of that, companies in western Germany took over many of the mining-related industries in Lusatia, only to close them down to avoid competition. This caused high unemployment and population shrinkage, since many people moved to the West in search of better opportunities. The city of Hoyerswerda for example, also a mining town, which had expanded from 7,000 to 70,000 inhabitants since the 1950s (Baxmann 2004), shrank back to its current population of 38,000 after the reunification (Stadt Hoyerswerda 2010).

The Lusatian former mining districts are among the economically and socially weakest in Germany (IW Consult 2009). Whether the shift to a capitalist economy was really for the better is still doubted by people who miss the (apparent) securities of the communist time.

Nowadays, brown coal accounts for 24–26 per cent of total power generation in Germany (Schiffer and Maaßen 2009; OECD/IEA 2009), despite landscape destruction by the opencast mining process and the problem of high carbon dioxide emissions, which have to be solved by the new Carbon Dioxide Capture and Storage (CCS) technique (OECD/IEA 2010; Vattenfall Europe AG 2010). At present, there are three large opencast mines being operated in Lusatia, producing almost 60 million tonnes of brown coal per year (Schiffer and Maaßen 2009).

POST-MINING WILDSCAPE

In Lusatia, the brown coal occurs at a depth of 40–120 metres (Pflug 1998). In the opencast mining process, a large conveyer bridge excavates and transports overburden deposits back to where the coal has already been removed (Figure 6.2). In the meantime, smaller machines excavate the brown coal at the bottom of the pit, after which conveyer belts transport it to the power plant nearby. This mechanical structure slowly moves through the landscape, totally reshaping the land and affecting its ecology, water table and soil.

The newly dumped soils are very unstable, because they have had no time to stabilize through natural processes, resulting in a serious risk of landslide (Steinhuber 2005). The soil deposits that come to the surface cause acidification of the top soil and the ground water. Large drainage systems, necessary to keep the deep pits free from ground water during the excavation, cause severe aridification in large parts of Lusatia (Drebenstedt and Möckel 1998). The combination of aridification, acidification and a bad soil structure with little to no soil activity makes the dumped soils very infertile. Without human intervention, they could stay bare for decades (Katzur and Haubold-Rosar 1996). The mining machines leave ridges of soil behind at the dump area, waiting to be levelled. Beside the dump, a wide pit remains, having the same volume as the brown coal that was excavated.

Figure 6.2
Active opencast brown coal mine in Lusatia with power plant in the background
(photograph: Rianne Knoot, 2008)

As previously indicated, mine restoration did not keep pace with mining activity during the GDR, which magnified the effects of opencast mining on their surroundings. After the industrial collapse due to reunification, former power plants, coke ovens and briquette factories became desolated ruins. Leftover machinery and old industrial buildings are direct references to the high days of mining and industry.

The Lusatian post-mining landscapes of the 1990s are sometimes compared to lunar landscapes, or the planet Mars. If, eventually, young pine trees start to grow, the landscape looks like a prairie. These bizarre manifestations contrast highly with the original flat, humid, half-open rural landscape which used to characterize Lusatia (Baxmann 2004).

People from outside the area are attracted to this unfamiliar landscape. They see qualities in the rough, desolate, silent and ominous atmosphere. They experience a visit to a former mine pit as adventurous, exciting and out of the ordinary. People are fascinated by the dynamics of a region that was an important industrial centre once, then in serious decline and now at the brink of redevelopment.

However, if no-one interfered, a landscape like this would need hundreds of years to recover by itself, morphologically, hydrologically and ecologically. Until then, it can hardly be used for agricultural or other economic activities. Although such areas might be exciting to outsiders, many local people consider them as unwanted wastelands that must be restored.

Notwithstanding the weak economy in Lusatia after the industrial collapse, the mine restoration deficit has to be solved. Since the state owns the decommissioned mines of the former GDR, by law it is also responsible for creating a safe and healthy landscape system with viable land uses (Steinhuber 2005). Despite the infertility of the post-mining soils, agriculture, forestry and nature development are the most common new land uses (Drebenstedt 1998), because many other uses, such as housing or industry, are excluded from a safety point of view. Basically, given the limited financial resources, the aim is to reinstate the land uses to the pre-mining situation in a quick and cost-effective way.

NEW WAYS OF DEALING WITH POST-MINING WILDSCAPE

After the fall of the GDR, a growing number of landscape professionals acknowledged that mining has influenced Lusatia so profoundly, that returning to the pre-mining situation is not a desirable strategy. In 1994, the Lusatian architect, Wolfgang Joswig, and others managed to convince the District Administrator of their ideas concerning the region's future (IBA 2010c). In their opinion, the economy in Lusatia needed to diversify to overcome the industrial collapse. After decades of landscape destruction, the people deserved a landscape providing a high quality of life; at the same time, erasing the mining history by quick and efficient landscape restoration felt too rigorous, and also needless. On the contrary, the presence of the unique post-mining wildscape should be seen as an opportunity. As a result, a way of landscape restoration that makes use of the opportunities of the post-mining wildscape became a new strategy for regional development.

To implement this strategy, five regional authorities, supported by the federal state of Brandenburg, established the Internationale Bauausstellung Fürst-Pückler-Land (IBA). Since 2000, the IBA initiated a new dialogue concerning the post-mining landscape. The actors in Lusatia were inspired by the IBA Emscher Park in the West German Ruhr area (1989–1999), which successfully guided the restructuring of a post-industrial region by making use of the relics of industry, instead of erasing them.

The IBA Fürst-Pückler-Land considers Lusatia as 'the biggest landscape construction site in Europe'. In its visions, planning concepts and thirty concrete projects, IBA addresses environmental, social and economic aspects of regional transition in an integrated way. The starting point is always the post-mining wildscape, yet the approach to this wildscape differs from place to place. Below, this is exemplified by three cases.

The Lusatian Lakeland

As early as the 1960s the German landscape architect Otto Rindt envisioned transforming mine pits into lakes, and connecting them by navigable canals (Reitsam 1999): a 'blue paradise' for locals and tourists would be developed to succeed the once inhospitable and inaccessible mining areas. Financed by the federal and state government, the Lusatian and Central German Mining Administration Company (LMBV) is currently flooding ten lakes, interconnected by thirteen canals.

Along their shores, an infrastructure for tourism is being developed from scratch. An extensive network of cycle paths is under construction. Beaches and parks provide possibilities to lie down and relax, to swim or play sports. Investors are attracted to open up cafés, restaurants, hotels, camping sites, holiday parks, boat rental and diving schools. Some areas in the Lakeland will remain restricted, partly because of the risk of landslides, but mainly because the areas are predestined for nature conservation. Within ten years, this otherwise dry area will be the largest artificial Lakeland in Europe (Von Bismarck 2010). The IBA aimed to set this region apart from other lake areas with integrated planning concepts, innovative architecture and spectacular landscape design. As well as arguing for the connection of ten lakes by navigable canals, it planned several remarkable buildings along and on the lakes and initiated land art projects, striving to enhance the spatial and architectural quality of the necessary reconstruction activities.

Turning the former mines into lakes is an efficient way of mine restoration, since it saves extensive ground work to fill in the pit. Topographic changes caused by the mining are the basis for the development of a new land use, in which the new lakes are a distinct reference to the mining past. The creation of lakes near Hoyerswerda and Senftenberg in the 1960s, following Otto Rindt's ideas, have shown that flooding opencast final voids can result in geotechnically safe and attractive leisure landscapes (Figure 6.3). The obligation to re-establish a safe, stable and self-preserving soil and water system can thus be used as a steppingstone for the development of tourism as a new economic driving force (Müller 1998), and a way to diversify the Lusatian economy.

Sielmann's Nature Landscape Wanninchen

Another approach to development was chosen for a pit and dump area of 3,000 hectares near the town of Luckau. This former mine was bought by the Heinz Sielmann Stiftung, a private foundation for nature conservation. In Sielmann's nature landscape, Wanninchen, named after one of the villages destroyed by mining, LMBV takes only minimal measures to restore geotechnical safety.

Figure 6.3
Development of tourism
in the Lusatian Lakeland:
beach at Lake
Senftenberg
(photograph: Renée de
Waal, 2007)

In contrast to other former pits, this one is not artificially flooded. Whilst several small islands and slopes have been created, no effort is made to prevent erosion and landslides as the groundwater slowly rises (Figure 6.4).

As a consequence part of the area is not open to the public. This is a disadvantage for the visitor, but allows nature to conquer the place undisturbed. In this way, a dynamic landscape of forest, water, marshland and sand dunes is developing. It turns out that the acid water and the bare, dry, infertile soil offer a habitat for pioneer species, which are followed by birds and amphibians.

Figure 6.4
Sielmann's Nature
Landscape Wanninchen
(photograph: Frank
Döring, 2010)

With the support of the IBA, educational and tourist programmes were developed in conjunction with an information centre to make the process visible and to show an alternative way of dealing with the post-mining landscape (IBA 2010c; Heinz Sielmann Stiftung 2010).

Landscape Project Welzow

IBA's most controversial idea was a project originally named Desert/Oasis Welzow. As part of the mining process in the mine Welzow-Süd, the machinery would shape the dump for its future purpose. Over many years, the desert-like features of the dump were not to be erased as in the traditional approach, but to be emphasized, to become a desert with high, bare sand dunes and a green 'oasis' in the middle (Figure 6.5). It would have been a land art project of a unique kind, which was supposed to serve as a leisure landscape, drawing international attention and economic benefits to the region.

Desert/Oasis Welzow turned out to be a bridge too far. Although the mining operator was interested in the project, it soon acknowledged the technical difficulties in the realization. Even more problematic however was the resistance from a large part of the population of the city of Welzow and the surrounding villages. There was little faith in the economic benefits of the project as a tourist attraction. People feared sand storms over their houses. Above all, after decades of mining on their doorsteps, people longed for the green, rural landscape of pre-mining times. To them, it did not make sense to create a landscape they perceived as useless. Six years after the first sketches were drawn, the project was cancelled.

However, the idea of using the operated mine for tourism purposes was not completely lost. An association supported by the city of Welzow and the mining operator successfully organizes guided tours through the mine, showing their visitors both the impressive process of mining and the bizarre landscape aftermath (IBA 2010c).

IS THE POST-MINING WILDSCAPE A PARADISE AT ALL?

In the Lusatian Lakeland, the physical characteristics of the post-mining wildscape are used to create an artificial lakeland for leisure and tourism. The adventurous character of wildscape slowly vanishes in the name of economic and environmental progress. In this case, the post-mining wildscape is a 'landscape-in-between', an ephemeral landscape, which will gradually give way to another, more structured, lake landscape: a 'blue paradise'.

In Wanninchen, the specific natural conditions of the post-mining wildscape are purposely used for nature development from the first stages of succession. Funding by a private foundation was a key condition, which indicates that this landscape is valued by a number of people, but that it would not be feasible for all post-mining areas in Lusatia. In this case, the post-mining wildscape is a landscape-in-between as well, but the natural process of succession will take

Figure 6.5
Impression of the Desert
Oasis design for the
Landscape Project
Welzow. View from an
imagined hotel window
(image: Archiscape/bgmr,
2002)

much longer than the development of the Lusatian Lakeland. There is a growing interest in visiting this area to watch the process of succession in this bizarre, clear-felled landscape.

In the last project mentioned above, Desert/Oasis Welzow, the features of the post-mining wildscape as described earlier inspired the design of a safe and controlled wildscape for leisure purposes: refined wildscape. In fact, it is questionable whether this is wildscape at all, since it is not the by-product of former land use, but a deliberately produced landscape.

The three different cases indicate how planning and design concepts dealt with the opportunities that the post-mining wildscape has to offer for development. The question of whether it is possible to preserve the wildscape character of these wastelands without blocking economic development, or even to use it as a basis for a new future for the region, is still difficult to answer unambiguously; but the cases certainly provoke some interesting alternative thoughts.

The first two cases show that the unique features of post-mining wild-scapes can be a good physical basis for leisure, tourism and nature development. However, an adventurous or risky atmosphere, typical of a wildscape, is hard to retain because post-mining wildscape is a real threat to people's safety. This makes retaining wildscape on a large scale unfeasible. Besides, wildscape is most valuable when it is a contrast to neater, safer and more structured surroundings. Urban wildscapes are a relief in the dense network of civilization, which makes them – on a small scale – acceptable and exciting. On a regional scale however, the case of Lusatia demonstrates that it is unacceptable for a regional landscape to be unsafe and without use or economic value.

The third case particularly, shows that it is hard to make use of the adven-turous atmosphere of the post-mining wildscape as a basis for landscape design. There seems to be a difference between local people and outsiders in their per-ception and valuation of post-mining wildscape. Whereas tourists from afar are interested in the extraordinary landscape and history of Lusatia, local people long for a new and prosperous view of their region. To refine the wildscape in a con-trolled and safe, but artificial and inauthentic way, like in the Welzow case, appears to be an illusion, since refined wildscape is a *contradictio in terminis* (contradiction in terms).

It may be that the only way to make use of the adventurous and exciting character of post-mining wildscape is by cherishing and making accessible real remnants of it. For example, in the form of nature landscapes like Wanninchen, or by using active mines as a location for guided tours, which is now the case in Welzow. As small remnants, pieces of post-mining wildscape could become ephemeral pearls in the otherwise healthy, rationally used, economically valuable and progressing landscape. The transience of these places is inevitable, and even contributes to their extraordinary qualities. It is this ephemerality that makes the post-mining wildscape paradisiacal.

REFERENCES

Baxmann, M. (2004) *Zeitmaschine Lausitz, Vom 'Pfützenland' zum Energiebezirk, Die Geschichte der Industrialisierung in der Lausitz*, Dresden: Verlag der Kunst.

Drebenstedt, C. (1998) 'Planungsgrundlagen der Wiedernutzbarmachung', in W. Pflug (ed.) *Braunkohlentagebau und Rekultivierung*, Berlin: Springer.

Drebenstedt, C. and Möckel, R. (1998) 'Gewässer in der Bergbaufolgelandschaft', in W. Pflug (ed.) *Braunkohlentagebau und Rekultivierung*, Berlin: Springer.

Großer, K. (1998) 'Der Naturraum und seine Umgestaltung', in W. Pflug (ed.) *Braunkohlentagebau und Rekultivierung*, Berlin: Springer.

Heinz Sielmann Stiftung (2010). Online: www.sielmann-stiftung.de (accessed 5 August 2010).

Hunger, B., Weidemüller, D. and Westermann, S. (eds) (2005) *Transforming Landscapes: Recommendations Based on Three Industrially Disturbed Landscapes in Europe*, Großräschen: International Building Exhibition (IBA) Fürst-Pückler-Land.

IBA Fürst-Pückler-Land (ed.) (2010a) *Bergbau Folge Landschaft/Post-mining Landscape*, Berlin: Jovis-Verlag.

—— (2010b) *Project 1: IBA-Start Site at Grossräschen-Süd* (updated 29 April 2010). Online: www.iba-see2010.de/en/projekte/projekt1.html (accessed 21 April 2010).

—— (2010c) Neue Landschaft Lausitz/New Landscape Lusatia, Berlin: Jovis-Verlag.

IW Consult (2009) *Regionalranking 2009, Untersuchung von 409 Kreisen und kreisfreie Städten*, Köln: Institut der deutschen Wirtschaft Köln Consult GmbH.

Katzur, J. and Haubold-Rosar, M. (1996) 'Amelioration and reforestation of sulfurous mine soils in Lusatia (Eastern Germany)', *Water, Air, and Soil Pollution*, 91: 1–2. Online: www.springerlink.com/content/p7164132783pk08l (accessed 30 April 2010).

Müller, L. (1998) 'Freizeit und Erholung', in W. Pflug (ed.) *Braunkohlentagebau und Rekultivierung*, Berlin: Springer.

OECD/IEA (2009) Share of total primary energy supply in 2007. Online: www.iea.org/stats/pdf_graphs/DETPESPI.pdf (accessed 30 April 2010).

—— (2010) *Carbon Dioxide (CO2) Capture and Storage (CCS)*. Online: www.iea.org/subjectqueries/cdcs.asp (accessed 30 April 2010).

Pflug, W. (ed.) (1998) *Braunkohlentagebau und Rekultivierung*, Berlin: Springer.

Reitsam, C. (1999) 'Otto Rindt', *Garten + Landschaft*, 5: 37–40.

Schiffer, H. W. and Maaßen, U. (2009) *Braunkohle in Deutschland 2009*: *Profil eines Industriezweiges*, Köln: DEBRIV Bundesverband Braunkohle.

Stadt Hoyerswerda (2010) *Stadtporträt.* Online: www.hoyerswerda.de/index.php?language =de&m=1&z=236.65#content (accessed 10 April 2010).

Steinhuber, U. (2005) 'Einhundert Jahre bergbauliche Rekultivierung in der Lausitz: Ein historischer Abriss der Rekultivierung, Wiederurbarmachung und Sanierung im Lausitzer Braunkohlenrevier', unpublished doctoral thesis, Olomouc: Palacký Universität.

Vattenfall Europe AG (2010) *CCS: eine Technologie für den Klimaschutz.* Online: www.vattenfall.de/de/das-ccs-projekt-von-vattenfall.htm (accessed 9 January 2011).

Von Bismarck, F. (2010) 'Land in motion: opencast restoration and recultivation in Lusatia', in IBA Fürst-Pückler-Land (ed.) *Bergbau Folge Landschaft/Post-mining Landscape*, Berlin: Jovis-Verlag.

Wittig, H. (1998) 'Braunkohlen- und Sanierungsplanung im Land Brandenburg' in W. Pflug (ed.) *Braunkohlentagebau und Rekultivierung*, Berlin: Springer.

Chapter 7: Wildscape in Shanghai

A case study of the Houtan Wetland Park – Expo 2010 Shanghai

Yichen Li

INTRODUCTION

Shanghai is the biggest industrial city in China. It covers an area of about 6,340 km², of which about 1,100 km² is industrial. The industrial sector consists of industrial development areas of 920 km² (mostly ex-urban), and traditional manufacturing areas covering 180 km² (mostly located in the city centre) (He 2005). In 2000, in order to create a sustainable urban environment, the local government started to relocate highly polluting industries – most of which are traditional manufacturing such as steel manufacture and shipbuilding – from the city centre to rural areas. By the end of 2006, around 90 per cent of the highly polluting industries had been moved from the city centre (Office of Shanghai Government 2009). Redevelopment of these post-industrial sites started immediately. Amongst these regeneration projects, Expo 2010 Shanghai is the biggest and most important to Shanghai as well as China.

The World Expo is an important stage for people from all over the world to present their cultures and histories, exchange information, enhance co-operation and look forward to future development. In 2010, the 150-year-old world exposition was held in China.

The aim for Expo 2010 was to attract 200 countries and international organizations, 70 million visitors, 25 partners and sponsors as well as the general public as participants. In order to fulfill this aim, therefore, the Expo site was developed not only for the exposition uses, but also as a multi-functional and highly efficient space.

Shanghai hosted Expo 2010 on a site located between the Nanpu and Lupu Bridges in the city centre. It was positioned there due to the site's good transport links with the metro, bridges, tunnels, expressways and traffic hubs. The Expo site covers 5.28 km², comprising 3.93 km² in the Pudong district (south-east of the Huangpu River) and 1.35 km² in the Puxi district (north west of the Huangpu River). The enclosed area (admission by ticket only) was 3.28 km² and the surrounding service area was a further 2 km². The Bailianjin Canal joins the Huangpu River in the Pudong (south-east) section of the site, creating a pleasant waterfront area (Figure 7.1).

THE EXPO 2010 SITE

Historically, the site was first developed in the nineteenth century after the First Opium War with Great Britain, which ended in 1842 when the Treaty of Nanjing was signed, and saw Shanghai's treaty port, amongst others, opening for international trade. The intersection of the Huangpu River and the Bailianjin Canal made this site the most ideal location for industry and shipping trade. Later, the first heavy industry, 'Jiangnan dock yard', was established in 1865 by a Chinese merchant in Puxi district. After a few years, the great success of Jiangnan dock yard made it the foundation of China's modern industry. Shipbuilders, merchants and chemical refiners soon copied Jiangnan and their businesses developed rapidly in the subsequent decades (Figure 7.2). With the development of local industry, several settlements were established by factory and dock labourers in the locality.

The second development phase happened after the Communist Party of China took control of Shanghai in 1949. A clear development strategy for Shanghai was formulated immediately by central government. The shipping trades and heavy industries' markets were standardized and reinforced by new regulations.

Figure 7.1
Masterplan for the World Expo 2010, Shanghai (image: Shanghai Urban Planning and Design Institute)

Figure 7.2
The site for the World
Expo 2010 in its industrial
heyday (photograph:
photographer unknown,
thought to date from the
1940s)

This stable economic environment led to new logistics centres and industrial plants being built in the Puxi district of the site. At the same time, new residential blocks were constructed by the government among the former settlements to improve local residents' standard of living. However, at this time, the Pudong district was still dominated by a mixture of agriculture and derelict sites dating from the Second World War.

The third phase of development started in 1991 after a process of economic reform. At this stage, the new developments took place mainly in the Pudong part of the site. Light and high-tech industries and dockyards started to appear and replaced the former agriculture and wasteland. New neighbourhoods grew up around these industries.

Subsequently, the site started to empty as most of the heavy industries moved out of Shanghai, and in 2002 it was decided to hold the Shanghai Expo at this location.

FORMER, EXISTING AND AFTER USES

There was about 1.1 km² and 3.5 km² post-industrial land in the Puxi and Pudong districts respectively. The rest of the site was covered by dwellings, most of which were constructed between 1970 and 1980. The pre-existing natural environment in the site was worse than expected: after 100 years of industry, the ground was severely contaminated by heavy metals, affecting vegetation, and limiting human activities. However, a natural wetland covering 2.25 hectares, named 'Houtan', remained within the brownfield area, located in the west of the Pudong district along the Huangpu River. The tidal mudflat was formed by the deposition of sandy sediments along the banks of the Huangpu River over hundreds of years. The Expo, which adopted the slogan 'Better City, Better Life', aimed to adopt an exemplary and sustainable approach by preserving the Houtan wetland and extending it to create an urban wetland park. A detailed description of the Houtan Wetland Park will be given in the following section.

The planning for Expo 2010 took into account factors such as appropriate walking distances and visitor perceptions. The strategic planning divided the Expo site into one main area with multiple auxiliary parts, two of which are located in Pudong, and one in Puxi. The main area is located beside the riverside green corridor running along both sides of the Huangpu River (see Figure 7.1). The Expo site is partitioned into five zones. Within each zone, there are groups of pavilions which contain public amenities such as small canteens, shops, telecommunications, toilets, and medical services, amongst other facilities.

The dominant uses of the site changed from the previous industrial functions to exhibition, conference and cultural uses for the Expo. Quite a few of the industrial buildings remained and were renovated for exhibition and conference use, or public facilities, depending on their condition, location and historical value. Some of them were protected as city culture relics. The rest were demolished and replaced by civic squares, urban parks and green spaces.

Now the Expo has ended, the site is being converted into a multi-functional area providing different functions (exhibition, activity centre, convention, recreation, education and interpretation of Shanghai's industrial past) (Wu 2010a).

APPROACH TO THE POST-INDUSTRIAL LANDSCAPE: HOUTAN WETLAND IN THE EXPO SITE

Houtan Wetland Park is an ecological park located in the western corner of the Expo site. It was developed from an existing natural wetland along the Huangpu River and stretches out over 1.7 kilometres. The whole park covers an area of about 13.43 hectares, including 2.25 hectares of natural wetland (Figure 7.3). Generally, the site is relatively flat, ranging only from 4 to 7 metres above sea level. There is a 100-metre-long beach lying on the south-west side of the site gently sloping down to the Huangpu River (Yu et al. 2007).

Spontaneously occurring vegetation and the buildings and structures from former heavy industry coexist on site. An iron and steel works (known as Shanghai's 'Third Steelworks') was vacated in 2004, leaving behind several heavy industrial facilities, such as gantry cranes, pontoon dock, tracks, overhead pipes and storage tanks, which all reflect the defunct industrial characteristics.

The natural wetland has a tidal range of 3 metres and is located at the river bank and outside the flood defence wall. For this reason, there have been almost no human activities within this area, mitigating pollution from heavy industries. After construction of the flood defence wall the river bank became vegetated thus preserving Houtan's wetland. The undisturbed situation provides a habitat for diverse plant and animal species, including 50 Gramineae and Asteraceae, 12 woody species, 45 Phytoplankton, 25 Protozoa and Tardigrada and 18 Zoobenthos (Zhang 2007).

There were two main challenges facing the project from its inception:

1 Should the existing wetland be influenced directly by human intervention during the preservation process? If not, how would this wetland be restored and maintained?
2 How would the heritage and culture of the site be conserved and developed?

Figure 7.3
Masterplan for the
Houtan Wetland Park
(image: Turenscape
Design Institute)

According to the site survey and analysis, the existing natural wetland faced two main threats. One was from the former iron and steel works. The cumulative industrial waste from the steel plant had deposited heavy metals (iron, copper and zinc) over a long period of time. These elements had permeated and inter-fused into the ground, as a result of the action of the tidal river, causing serious contamination to the local wildlife and damaging the wetland ecosystem. The other threat was from the Huangpu River, which was classified as 'seriously pol-luted', with dangerous substances at levels over ten times greater than the levels specified in environmental quality standards (EQS), with fauna absent or seriously restricted (Shanghaiwater 1998; Office of Scottish Environment Protection Agency 1974). Nevertheless, due to the purifying function of the natural wetland, the water quality within the wetland was rated 'fair', was compliant with EQS, and supported a sustainable coarse fish population with the possibility of Salmo-nids, although the ecosystem was judged to be 'impacted'.

Natural wetland plays a very important role in absorbing carbon dioxide and, especially in this case, relieving the city's heat island. Therefore, Houtan's natural wetland is quite precious to the ecosystem of Shanghai. In order to deal with the contamination and restore the natural wetland, it was necessary for human intervention to take place. However, this raised another question regard-ing the extent of the intervention necessary for the function of an urban wetland park, as well as finding the fine ecological balance within the local wetland eco-system. After a long period of discussion among the relevant experts, and com-parison between different plans, the final plan was resolved. An artificial wetland was constructed on the south side of the natural wetland, running through the whole site from west to east and connecting with the Huangpu River (Figure 7.3 and 7.4). A water channel flows through the middle with an average width of 10 metres. An accompanying riverside walk was designed between the natural

Figure 7.4
Houtan Wetland Park: (From top left) The park was developed from an existing natural wetland along the Huangpu River and stretches out over 1.7 km (photograph: Yichen Li, 2010); a riverside walk has been designed between the natural and artificial wetlands, creating the opportunity for the visitor to experience a wetland with wilderness-like characteristics within a highly urban setting (photograph: Yichen Li, 2010); spontaneously occurring vegetation and the buildings and structures from former heavy industry coexist on site (photograph: Yichen Li, 2010); a water channel flows through the middle of the artificial wetland with an average width of 10 metres (photograph: Yichen Li, 2010)

wetland and the new one, creating the opportunity for the visitor to be completely immersed in a wetland with wilderness-like characteristics within a highly urban setting. As well as enhancing and complementing the local ecosystem the artificial wetland has a water purification function and is a visitor attraction in its own right. New water treatment technology combined with the introduction and enhancement of natural wetland flora and fauna will establish and maintain a healthy wetland system. Although the hydrology of the two wetlands is not connected (to minimize the impact from the artificial wetland), some interaction takes place through tidal fluctuation, and as a result the outer wetland environment will be improved.

In addition to rebuilding the overall wetland ecosystem, the artificial wetland plays another important role in the Expo site: purifying water for irrigation of the green spaces throughout the whole Pudong site. It is believed that the combination of the ecological water treatment technology and the power of the wetland will create a highly efficient purification system (Wu 2010b). The water is guided from the Huangpu River into the water channel at the western end of the artificial wetland. Then the water will run through the purification system and finally, at the end of this process, the water quality should reach the same standard as within the natural wetland, suitable for irrigation.

THE SITE AS CULTURAL RELIC

In order to express the cultural background of the site, the Houtan Wetland Park is designed according to its timeline. The site has experienced three different periods of evolution, the pre-existing nature, cultivation, and industrial eras (Yu *et al.* 2007). Consequently, this cultural background is displayed in three different landscapes.

Prior to the Tang Dynasty (AD 618–917), the land lay undisturbed. At that time, Shanghai was just a small fishing village and wetland covered the whole site: an undisturbed biodiverse ecosystem rich in plants and animals. Farming started in the Tang Dynasty and continued for over 1,000 years. With the development of modern manufacturing in the nineteenth century, heavy industries soon began to replace the farmland, whose outputs changed from crops to industrial production. The rapid change marked the foundation of Shanghai and China's modern industry. However, at the same time, it brought great damage to the local environment.

The combination of existing wetland, artificial wetland and riverside landscape is intended to evoke the original landscape elements for visitors. The character of the farming era is re-established through the idea of urban production. Different kinds of crops, such as paddy rice, wheat, sunflowers and corn have been planted in a terraced landscape, located to the south of the site. It is hoped that this productive landscape will enrich the diversity of green space, as well as functioning as an experimental urban production base open to college students and researchers. Finally, there are a number of selected relics, which have been restored as symbols of the modern industrial era, including gantry cranes, the pontoon dock, tracks, overhead pipes and industrial buildings. According to the site planning, these relics will be renovated in order to serve as part of the site's tourist attractions, which are placed in a new context through the opening up of the public open space, so that they can be enjoyed as part of the new landscape. For example, the floating garden is located in the southern part of the site, close to one of the main entrances of the Houtan Wetland Park. The focus of the garden is a former industrial building, stripped down to its steel infrastructure (Figure 7.5). The garden itself provides multi-functional facilities including a tourism centre, a cultural education centre and several public facilities, such as a café and toilets. The environment around the building has been transformed into a connection with the artificial wetland, turning this 'dead land' into a vital and attractive place.

APPROACH TO POST-INDUSTRIAL LAND IN SHANGHAI

Whilst most Western countries finished the accumulation of original capital from the secondary sector and started to develop their tertiary sectors as a major part of their national economies at the end of the twentieth century, agriculture is still the predominant economic activity for most of the population of China. According to the census in 1990, roughly 79 per cent of the population were peasant farmers (He 2005). At that time, the industrial part of the secondary sector in big coastal cities in the east of China was the main support to the Chinese economy. In order to grow its economy, China has to bridge the development gap with developed countries. However, if China follows the traditional economic model, evolving from primary to tertiary sectors step by step, problems faced by industrial cities in developed countries recently such as shrinking and depopulation will occur in China. Therefore, as well as updating the primary and secondary sector, the new concept of 'urban industry', based on the principle of creative industries, was put forward in the 'Eleventh Five-year Plan' (the first Five-year Plan – a strategic plan covering development objectives for the next five years – began in 1953) by central government in 2003 (Office of Shanghai Government 2009). Shanghai follows this policy closely.

According to the 'Eleventh Five-year Plan', the redevelopment approach to post-industrial land in Shanghai is clear. Most post-industrial sites have been

Figure 7.5
The focus of the garden is a former industrial building, stripped down to its steel infrastructure (photograph: Shanghai Urban Planning and Design Institute, 2009)

regenerated to house creative industries over the last decade. The first creative industry was housed in a 2,000 m² former industrial building in 1998 (Office of Shanghai Government 2009). The building was renovated and turned into a design studio. By the end of 2008, the number of areas given over to creative industry in Shanghai was around 100. Over 6,000 creative enterprises in different fields including art, design, advertising and music were located in these areas. These industries also produce considerable revenue (China News 2010). In 2008, creative industries generated over GBP£341 billion, over 7 per cent of Shanghai's overall GDP. By the end of that year, there were at least 300,000 people working in creative industries. It has become the new economic growth area in Shanghai (Office of Shanghai Government 2009).

At the present, the judgment as to whether a city is suitable for living in no longer depends on how fast the city's economy is growing, and how many job opportunities the city can provide. As the biggest industrial city in China, Shanghai has got abundant potential post-industrial land in the city centre. Creative industries are a good way of regenerating these areas. However, this approach may benefit the city government more than its residents. Therefore, new ways of dealing with these sites should be discovered that not only help to develop the city economy for the local government, but also improves the living standard for the city's inhabitants. The regeneration of the Shanghai Expo site into a multifunctional area is a good attempt to maximize the benefits of rehabilitating a post-industrial site.

REFERENCES

China News (2010) *The Initiation of Shanghai's Largest Creative Industrial Project*. Online: www.chinanews.com.cn/cj/cj-cyzh/news/2010/04–01/2204159.shtml (accessed 1 April 2010).

He, Z. (2005) *Creative City and Creative Industry: The Exploration and Practice of Shanghai Creative Industry*. Online: www.soufun.com/news/2009–05–26/2596427.htm (accessed 16 November 2010).

Office of Scottish Environment Protection Agency (1974) *River Classifications Scheme, Annex 1*. Online: www.sepa.org.uk/science_and_research/classification_schemes/river_classifications_scheme.aspx (accessed 16 November 2010).

Office of Shanghai Government (2009) *The Connection between Creative and Industry*. Online: www.shanghai.gov.cn/shanghai/node2314/node2315/node4411/userobject21ai366940.html) (accessed 14 October 2009).

Shanghaiwater (1998) *The Water Source Bulletin*. Online: www.shanghaiwater.gov.cn/web/sw/98_5.jsp (accessed 16 November 2010).

Wu, Z. (2010a) *2010 Shanghai EXPO Construction Series: Landscape Section*, Beijing: China Building Industry Press.

—— (2010b) *Sustainable Planning and Design for the World Expo 2010 Shanghai China*, Beijing: China Building Industry Press.

Yu, K., Ling, S., and Jin Y. (2007) 'Back to riparian wetland: the Houtan park of Shanghai 2010 Expo', *Urban Environment Design*, 5: 54–59.

Zhang, Y. (2007) 'Characteristics of macrobenthic communities and environment analysis of Houtan wetland in Shanghai', *Wetland Science*, 5(4): 326–332.

Chapter 8: Christiania Copenhagen

A common out of the ordinary[1]

Maria Hellström Reimer

INTRODUCTION

Years of development boom on both sides of the Øresund, the strait separating Sweden and Denmark, has resulted in an urban landscape of great wonder. On the Swedish side, in Malmö, the new talisman, the twisted high-rise of Santiago Calatrava, towers behind old wharfs and docks. Erected by a labour movement housing association,[2] it signals a new era and a new way of manifesting the spatial relationship between individual and group. With promises of both comfort and participation, the spiralling edifice has not only settled in with the surroundings, but also developed into a symbol for a welfare society keeping abreast of the times.

Concurrently, on the Danish side, metropolitan Copenhagen expands. Its latest ramification, Ørestad, provides a new arena for the social manifestations of the new, entrepreneurial class. In the enchanting gleam from Jean Nouvel's Concert Hall cube, Henning Larsen's new IT University building markets its tantalizing choices, and further down along the driver-less infrastructural artery,[3] BIG's terraced mountain capriciously challenges the Danish flatlands. Daniel Libeskind has similarly responded to the call, in a posh marketing video presenting a series of welcoming public spaces for the new Ørestad Down Town. 'For me,' Libeskind says while finishing his Espresso, 'architecture is all about people – architecture without human beings to enjoy it is meaningless.'[4]

As difficult as it is to disagree with such a vision, it is hard to recognize it in current urban development. To what extent are the urban landscapes unfolding around us at present really developed for 'people'? What kind of 'enjoyment' do they provide? And what kind of 'meaning'?

'The urban landscape' appears in many different guises and with many different connotations. As a modern notion, it unfolds as an inclusive and continuous rationality, an ordering, airy and visual backdrop, that, as Le Corbusier (1927/2008: 210) put it, would help 'eliminate from our hearts and minds all dead concepts' as regards housing and living.[5] Today, the urban landscape has developed into an even more vitalizing expanse of opportunities and expectations, of leisure and wonder. If it was once associated with social botheration and distress, it now appears as a coffee-scented and colourful environment for cordial encounters. Or as the message has been framed by the Copenhagen developers: 'Follow your heart to Ørestad (or simply take the metro)' (Figure 8.1).

Marketing the urban landscape as a hotbed not only for technological innovation and economic development but also for the development of new life-styles, today's developers whole-heartedly adopt what may be interpreted as a radical urban rhetoric of the transformative and alternative. Nevertheless, just off the new and abundant urban landscape, you still find alternative aberrations, suckers shooting off from the recognized multiplicity.

One such offshoot is the Free Town of Christiania. In the beaming light of the new and semi-transparent developments, this threadbare, self-governed settlement in central Copenhagen, now in its forties, may seem more wicked than ever. Yet, at the same time, its special anthem *Christiania – You Have My Heart*, still hovers in the air (see Figure 8.1). For if Copenhagen has a heart, it is likely to be found somewhere close to the appropriated military barracks in Bådsmans-stræde, Christianshavn (Figure 8.2). And the localizing of this heartfelt site was always easy: 'You simply take Bus no 8 to Princess Street. Cost: One token' (Ludvigsen 2003: 22; Hellström 2006: 34).

Figure 8.1
(From top) 'Follow your heart to Ørestad (or simply take the metro)'. Header from the homepage for Udviklingsselskabet By og Havn (The City and Port Development Association) as it appeared on their 2008 homepage. Still from the film *Christiania – Du Har Mit Hjerte (Christiania – You Have My Heart)*, Nils Vest, 1991

Figure 8.2
Courtyard in Christiania: the lower photograph is a close-up of the historical image to the left of the notice board depicting the same courtyard at the time of the military garrison (photograph: Anna Jorgensen, 2010)

OUTSIDE THE WALLS

Christiania – this urban hybrid brought forth in 1971 – has so far survived. Situated within the historic centre of the Danish capital, the Free Town covers an area of 49 hectares and comprises half of what is still left of the historical ramparts, Christianshavns Vold, one of Denmark's major historical landmarks and heritage landscapes (Figure 8.3).[6] The southern parts of the military garrison had already been abandoned in 1916 and turned into a public park. From 1967 to 1971, the military also phased out its activities in the remaining parts, in spite of the fact that there were no explicit plans for the area. These historical circumstances, combined with an acute housing shortage and a youth movement in full bloom, thus opened the area for new and informal usages. During the summer of 1971, people from the neighbouring, overpopulated slums came to enjoy the green and open spaces, even starting to use some of the abandoned buildings as summer houses. At the same time, a burgeoning squatter movement saw the opportunities, initiating a 'conquest expedition' to the prohibited territory. The happening, which took place on 26 September 1971, is often referred to as the 'official' founding of the Free Town. In the political climate of the time, the program for the take-over was clear: 'It is the biggest chance yet to build a society from scratch – but one still to a certain extent based on the remains of what was there before' (Ludvigsen 2003: 28). The possibilities were many, and by November, the new urban formation counted several hundreds of inhabitants.

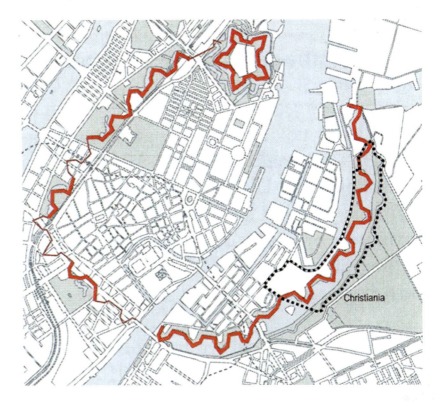

Figure 8.3
Plan showing Christiania in relation to the historical ramparts of Copenhagen in 2004

Although formally illegal, the settlement thus already initially enjoyed a public legitimacy, eventually leading to its political acknowledgement in 1972 as a 'social experiment'.[7]

Located not more than a stone's throw from the capital's political epicentre, the Free Town's physical presence is still more than evident. Moreover, as an un-intentional community, representing a cross section rather than a segment of the city's population, its social entanglement has been difficult to disregard. Explicitly relational, one of the most current slogans for the alternative community has also been '[y]ou cannot eradicate us – we are a part of you'.[8] As a watchword, the phrase was directed not only towards politicians and developers, but perhaps pri-marily towards architects and planners; or in other words towards those, whose responsibility it is – or should be – to develop alternatives.

Yet, neither market forces nor master plans have so far been capable of eliminating the Free Town, which today has a population of around 900, many of whom have hung on since the start.[9] And even if its pulse over the last decade has diminished in strength, some fervent or aesthetic move; be it a TV documen-tary, a street theatre event, a collaborative planning workshop, or an art exhibi-tion, has sufficed for it to resume its off-beat.

One of the reasons why Christiania has managed to avoid eradication is its developing of a spatially conscious and aesthetically informed urban tactics. Paying attention not only to the physical appropriation of space, but also to its discursive reproduction, the inhabitants of Christiania have delivered a swift stream of aesthetically conscious, yet playful urban ruses, thus contributing to the diversifying of the urban imaginary. Recent political happenings may, however, have enforced a more juridically-conscious approach. If Christiania was at times possible to dismiss as an aesthetically expressive, yet extreme 'loony bin' (Løvehjerte 1980: 27; Hellström 2006: 230), it has now taken on the more serious role of urban advocate, particularly as the defence counsel for the collect-ive right to use/appropriate urban space.

Since the historic elections in 2001, when a single right-wing party in Denmark received more votes than the social democrats for the first time since 1920, the legal battle around Christiania has intensified; especially since 2004, when the Danish State unilaterally cancelled its special agreement with the com-munity, giving it eighteen months' notice to dissolve itself. Yet, this was not the first time the relationship between the Free Town and the state had been articu-lated in legal terms. When defending their rights, the Christiania dwellers usually refer to the governmental ratification of the community as a 'social experiment'. Yet this ratification has been questioned and disallowed repeatedly, not least in a verdict by the Supreme Court in 1978, when the 'social experiment' claim was dismissed, albeit with the proviso that the verdict was strictly legal and did not take any political, social and human aspects into consideration. Eventually, this led to the passing of the special 'Christiania Law' in 1989, which regulated the relationship between the owner of the site, the Ministry of Defence, and the Free Town.[10] Based upon the idea of a collective right of use to land and buildings, this agreement was then extended several times before its final cancellation in 2004 through the implementation of the new Christiania Law, or 'the law on the change of the law on the use of the Christiania area' (Hellström 2006: 81). With reference to *the normal*, i.e. standard planning legislation and urban forms of organization, the claim for a collective right of use accumulated over time was dismissed. When, in 2008, Christiania chose to put the validity of this law to the test, the District Court again ruled against the community and in favour of the authorities' demand for *normalization*: a submission of the Free Town to regular planning and building legislation.

But what – or where – is the normal? In an ambiguous urban landscape characterized by recurrent exceptions; by intimate subjectivities and systems of surveillance; by pulsating street life and driver-less trains; by limitless commodity supplies and selective spending power; the standard or ordinary is as ambiguous as it is imperative. If normality on the one hand constitutes an indispensible conditioning force in a distributed power structure, it is on the other hand no more than an ideal abstraction, independent from any spatial materializations. And what does normality signify in relation to a cityscape that does its best to promote itself as a stimulating and transformative experience?

In Scandinavian, the notion of 'Free Town' has a double meaning, with connotations of both the unregulated and the safe.[11] By referring to itself as 'refuge', Christiania has thus deliberately manifested itself as a space allowing for deviations from the norm; at the same time providing protection for those who deviate. In early appeals for Christiania, the Danish architect Steen Eiler Rasmussen referred to a pre-modern, medieval urbanity, in relation to which the refuge figured as a significant, yet indispensible, exception (Rasmussen 1976). According to Rasmussen, Christiania's function was that of 'the commons' – an urban border phenomenon or a secondary product of regulated urbanity – akin to the unclaimed territories south of the Thames, at Southwark in medieval London. These areas, situated outside of both royal control and burghers' decency, functioned as vital gathering grounds bringing together all those who had left their close-knit villages; all those without land of their own; those who had given up their belonging without replacing it with something else; those who had been thrown out of the city or who did not fit into its day-trading system. In this medieval geography the commons emerged first and foremost as a social aberration; a temporary and diffuse form of commonality, whose only necessary characteristic was its *spaciousness*; its inclusion of all that which had been excluded from urban normality.

INSIDE THE COMMONS

In the contemporary urban debate, the idea of commons has once again gained attention. The commons has come to represent a non-proprietary, collective form of spatial organization based on a localized relationship to land, resources and ideas (Holder and Flessas 2008). In this sense, 'the commons' expresses a situated relationship, which develops through social interaction and responsible usage over time. As in the seminal studies of Elinor Ostrom (1990), it is a concept which refers to an informal yet regulated situation, often a collective use of natural resources such as pastures or fishing grounds. The idea of the commons can in this respect be compared with what in Roman law was designated as *res nullius*; that which belongs to nobody but may be acquired by any one, i.e. the fish in the sea; and *res communis*; that which may be used by all but belongs to no one, like the sea as such (Holder and Flessas 2008: 301–302). Indistinct and shifting, it has also been referred to in terms of 'tragedy': over the commons hovers the threat of impoverishment caused by unrestrained individual exploitation of common resources; an exploitation that certainly provides maximized returns but at the same time rapidly exhausts the commons and therefore also hits back at the collective as such (Hardin 1968).

Explored or contested, the commons has nevertheless become an increasingly important geo-political notion. As an alternative form for negotiating not only accessibility but also *enjoyment of rights*, the commons actualizes the dilemmas of resource distribution and spatial justice. At the same time, it generates new and unpredictable convergences, and thus also new societal patterns, not because of its internal logic but because of its emergence; its continuous embodiment of the fact that 'we are part of you'.

This emergent quality is perhaps all the more conspicuous when it comes to urban commons. Within the framework of urban real estate logic, non-proprietary conditions of commonality constitute an apparent disturbance. An urban commons does in this sense open up a wider, yet also agonizing, spatial imaginary; an imaginary explicitly addressing the political function of a shared space, where the enabling source code of relational agency remains accessible, from the point of view of the individual facilitating continuous change.

In Christiania, this relational definition of the commons has repeatedly been on probation: the legal case of Christiania's status as a commons is still pending. In the summer of 2008, the community decided to reject the proposal from the government for a negotiated solution. Even if the Christiania community had given up the idea of acquiring undisputed collective tenancy rights, it could not accept the proprietary structure of the agreement. The most problematic part of this was the authorities' reluctance to distinguish between proprietary commonality and action-based sociability. Instead of acknowledging the societal qualities and dynamics of usages generated through collective ownership, the government (now represented by The Palaces and Properties Agency),[12] insisted upon propriety-based multiplicity, instrumentalized through the normalizing procedure of the detailed development plan, assigning for the Christiania aberration a special or proper place.

Yet what makes the commons so politically charged is not its idiosyncrasy but its paradoxes. On the one hand, the commons is a result of a situated claiming of place or a local instigation of community. On the other hand, the commons relates to a larger, normative and ordinary placeboundedness, from which it deviates. As such, it represents as much a departure or a vagabonding escape away from territorial normativity. The connectedness offered by the commons is thus impregnated with a socially conditioned desire for vagrancy, for the exploration of 'escape routes' (Papadopoulos *et al.* 2008), intensifying both spatial experience and social life.

BEYOND IDEALS

In relation to the spatial ordinary, Christiania has accordingly offered not only refuge, but escape routes and loopholes, thus also actualizing deep-seated urban regimes and mechanisms of control. As a relationally performed amplification, the alternative community has employed both political and aesthetic means to break through all the 'little hypnoses' (Vaneigem 1967) of the propriety-based urban identity policy, which today characterizes the urban customary.

The lingering question is what this chipped haunt for a motley crew of tramps and renegades, of stray children and marginalized migrants, could possibly add to contemporary urban landscape discourse (Figure 8.4). As a free zone, is it not already hijacked by an urban experience economy? As a social experiment, has it not already lost its innovative capacity long ago? As an asylum for

Figure 8.4
Christiania, Melkevejen
(The Milky Way)
(photograph: Maria
Hellström Reimer, 2008)

mavericks, has it not petrified into an exclusive reserve for a shrinking circle of airy-fairy utopians? In relation to the new creative commons that we now see emerging, these are not unimportant questions. As opposed to Christiania, the new commons are often less geographically bound and more interlaced with the system from which they deviate. They are informal networks within the network, virtual machines of change, flashmobs,[13] spontaneous social platforms, temporary squatter initiatives – non-finalized and fragmented commons, managing nevertheless to modify the urban operating system.

Ubiquitous and easily modifiable, these new commons may render superfluous a more inert formation such as Christiania. At the same time, they complement and sustain a socially motivated locality production, further actualizing the spatial principle at work. While the normative ordering of space conventionally is seen as a primary condition for viable social life, the commons operate in the other direction. Intensifying social and material interaction, the commons produce, if not solid establishment dependent on the normal, so at least a local engagement strong enough to allow for deviations.

In this sense, the Free Town of Christiania is not an ideal, but an important relational agent in an urban field of forces. Agitated and atypical, it can help us understand not only the working principles of urban commonality, but also the urban implications of the new, emerging commons, which, rooted in a strong, social engagement, produces new urban spaces, new housing communities and new public spheres; spaces which are not grounded in private ownership but dependent on localized common interests.

While the governing or planning of such off-hiving spatial formations may seem an anomaly, they also address the very motive and meaning of spatial knowledge. Based upon a logic of relational agency, the commons force us to develop a spatial thinking capable of dealing not only with territorial definitions, partitions and borders, but also with the workings of an open situation of resourcefulness. This requires new forms of spatial learning and knowing; new forms of communication and new stages for negotiation. If the imaginary of 'the market' once made it possible to acquire a coherent understanding of a modern and transient commercial urbanity, it is today the idea of 'the common' that will enable us to understand the world as a paradoxical and shifting, yet shared concern.[14]

In the recent negotiations about the legal status of Christiania, the District Court, fortunately enough, took pains to unravel some of the 'loose ends' of the Free Town (Dahlin 2008). One of these savage threads concerned the future managing of the community and the possibility of pronouncing alternatives to the private ownership structure. Maybe there are possibilities that come closer to the ambition expressed back in the Christiania manifesto of 1971 – possibilities of developing formations and languages for a common, dynamic urbanity, including a more itinerant relationship between individual and collective. As a common out of the ordinary, the Free Town of Christiania therefore still offers an underestimated reservoir of socially innovative and politically provocative expressions.

'Christiania provides both a feeling of freedom and a feeling of community', it was said during the court proceedings (Dahlin 2008). One can only hope that it was also entered in the minutes.

NOTES

1 A Swedish version of this article entitled 'Den avvikande allmänningen' ('The Aberrant Common') has previously appeared in Pløger, J. and Juul, H. (eds) (2009) *Byens Rum* 1.5. Juul and Frost Arkitekter in collaboration with Roskilde Universitetscenter.

2 The Turning Torso is owned and managed by the HSB Swedish Tenant-Owner Cooperative Housing Association (HSB National Association), an NGO with 350,000 member households. Founded in 1923, HSB has been one of the major actors in the development of modern Sweden.

3 The metro system connecting Ørestad with its surroundings is serviced by driverless trains.

4 Online: www.orestaddowntown.dk (accessed 26 April 2010).

5 Le Corbusier's *Vers un architecture*, published in 1923, may in this sense be understood as a deliberate movement towards an idea of architecture as a landscape machine; an apparatus productive of a unitary and visually coherent environment (Le Corbusier 1927/2008: 210).

6 Christianshavns Vold, fortification ramparts and moat, can be traced back to the twelfth century, with its present design of linked bastions forming a combined sea and land fortification dating back to the latter part of the seventeenth century (Hellström 2006: 33).

7 The notion of 'the social experiment' appeared for the first time in the minutes from a meeting between the Ministry of Culture and Christiania's negotiation group in the spring of 1972, and in a report of the same meeting by the Minister of Defence a year later (Hellström 2006: 44).

8 'I kan ikke slå os ihjel' ('You cannot eradicate us') was the title of a song composed by Tom Lundén and recorded by the group *Bifrost* for 'Christianiapladen', ('The Christiania record') a compilation album released in 1976 in support of the at that time severely threatened Free Town. Ever since, this song has served as the 'national anthem' of the Free Town.

9 More information on the current situation in Christiania can be obtained through the Free Town's official website. Online: www.christiania.org.

10 *Lov om anvendelse af Christianiaområdet (Law concerning use of the Christiania area)*, law number 399, 7 June 1989. The objective of the law was to put an end to the untenable situation of insecurity that had marked the first two decades of the Free Town's existence, thus enabling a continuous use according to the planning directives yet to be developed. Furthermore, the purpose was to invest the Ministry of Defence with sole responsibilty for the negotiations with and supervision of the Free Town (Hellström 2006: 70–71).

11 Fristad; primarily signifying sanctuary; yet with the words separated (fri stad) denoting a free city or town.

12 Shortly after the passing of the new Christiania Law, the ownership of the area was transferred from the Ministry of Defence to the Ministry of Justice, to be administered by Slots- og Ejendomsstyrelsen (The Palaces and Properties Agency), which is the authority responsible for historical landmarks.

13 Flashmob (or flash mob); a quite recent socio-spatial phenomenon relying on the use of communication technology or social media for the rapid assembly of a large group of people in a public space, often with the purpose of 'aesthetically' performing an odd or aberrant act.

14 Jonathan Rowe (2001) reminds us of how Adam Smith introduced the concept of 'the market' 200 years ago, and thereby succeeded in creating a wider understanding of how a diverse number of different, more or less sprawling and deviating phenomena related to each other. The idea of 'the common' can in a similar way, according to Rowe, help us understand and handle a situation, in which our future existence depends on our ability to imagine a world of limited common resources.

REFERENCES

Dahlin, U. (2008) 'Landsdommere så lysbilder fra Christiania' ('Judges watched slides from Christiania'), *Information*, 11 November 2008.

Hardin, G. (1968) 'The tragedy of the commons', *Science*, 162 (3859): 1243–1248.

Hellström, M. (2006) 'Steal this place: the aesthetics of tactical formlessness and the free town of Christiania', unpublished thesis, Alnarp: Acta Universitatis Agriculturae.

Holder, J. B., and Flessas, T. (2008) 'Emerging commons', *Social and Legal Studies*, 17(3): 299–310.

Le Corbusier (1927) *Vers un architecture*, trans. Fredrick Etchells (2008) *Towards a New Architecture*, New York: Dover Publications.

Ludvigsen, J. (2003) *Christiania: Fristad i Fare (Christiania: The Free Town Threatened)*, København: Extrabladets Forlag.

Løvehjerte, R. (1980) 'Christiania … et socialt eksperiment og mere og andet end det' ('Christiania … a social experiment and more and other than that'), in M. Bakke, B. S. Østergaard, and O. Østergaard (eds) *Christiania – Danmarks grimme ælling? Et exempel på et alternativt samfund (Christiania – Denmark's Ugly Duckling? An Example of an Alternative Community)*, København: Munksgaard.

Ostrom, E. (1990) *Governing the Commons: The Evolution of Institutions for Collective Action*, Cambridge: Cambridge University Press.

Papadoupoulos, D., Stephenson, N. and Tsianis, V. (2008) *Escape Routes: Control and Subversion in the 21st Century*, London: Pluto Press.

Rasmussen, S. E. (1976) *Omkring Christiania (Around Christiania)*, København: Gyldendals.

Rowe, J. (2001) 'The hidden commons'. *Yes! Magazine*, Summer 2001. Online: www. yesmagazine.org/article.asp?ID=443 (accessed 9 December 2010).

Vaneigem, R. (1967) *Traité de savoir-vivre à l'usage des jeunes generations (The Revolution of Everyday Life)*, Paris: Gallimard.

Chapter 9: The River Don as a linear urban wildscape

Ian D. Rotherham

INTRODUCTION

South Yorkshire's River Don runs from its Pennine source through Sheffield to the great River Humber, which pours into the North Sea through one of the largest estuaries in Europe, emptying a river basin covering much of the UK's East Midlands. The river arises as a clean acidic stream, gushing from peat bog and heather moorland, to arrive in the urban catchment of Sheffield. Then, it heads eastwards to cut through the Don Gorge, and pours out onto what was once the great wetland of the South Yorkshire Fen (Figure 9.1). During its journey the Don passes through some of the formerly most industrial and degraded landscapes in western Europe (Walton 1948); a complete contrast with its historical origins as a river forming part of a wildlife-rich landscape of meandering channels and floodland (Bownes *et al.* 1991). Two hundred years of urbanization, manufacturing and agri-industry had constrained its flow and gutted its ecological soul, so by the 1970s I witnessed the river and many of its tributaries biologically dead, detergent foam laced with raw sewage blowing across their filthy banks. Once naturally meandering, the urban river was now trapped inside fixed banks of brick and concrete, and the rural watercourse was canalized in levees of clay and rubble. Today, its ecology transformed, the Don has re-emerged as a central feature in the region's urban ecology and even in the new lifestyles of city dwellers (Firth 1997; Gilbert 1992a).

As the region's main river, a newly emergent and vibrant artery for wildlife and people, the Don presents many dilemmas in its relationships with nature and local residents. In 2007, the normally placid river turned into a torrent and swept destructively through the region, causing massive damage for 80 to 90 kilometres or more (Figure 9.2). This abruptly reawakened a greater awareness of the Don, as the river in spate responded to major land-use changes in its catchment over many decades (Rotherham 2008a; 2008b). Now clean, but once badly polluted, how can we celebrate the river and engage the public in planning and nurturing its future? In 2010, the Don Catchment Trust was launched to do exactly this. The river is symbolic of the region's post-industrial renaissance, but suffers both from a vision of a preconceived politically correct ecology that is often at odds

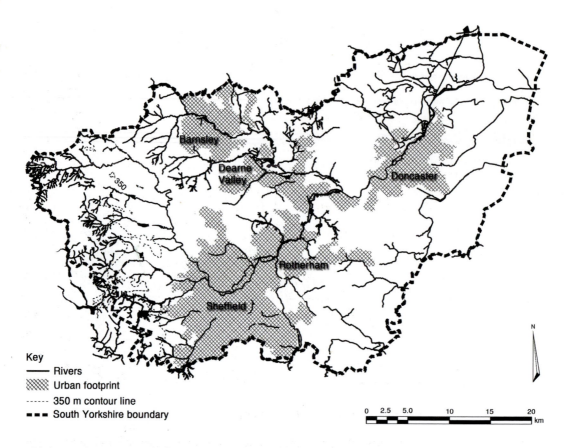

Key
— Rivers
▧ Urban footprint
------ 350 m contour line
■ ■ ■ South Yorkshire boundary

Figure 9.1
Plan of the River Don
catchment in South
Yorkshire (illustration:
Laura Silva Alvarado).
Plan based on OS and
UKBORDERS 2001 Census
boundary data. © Crown
copyright Ordnance
Survey, All rights reserved

with its exotic nature, and of a lasting image as dirty and polluted. For much of the last two centuries the riverside was deliberately closed to the public as factory owners sought to hide their discharges and to protect their premises from thieves. A major catalyst for recovery has been the development of the Five Weirs Walk since the 1980s that again provides open access to the public. This raises awareness of the river and fosters custodianship and conservation (Firth 1997).

A CONTEXT FOR SHEFFIELD, SOUTH YORKSHIRE AND THE RIVER DON

Sheffield is a remarkable city, growing from around 10,000 people in the early 1700s to over 300,000 by 1900 (Walton 1948; Warman 1969). A city of rivers and valleys, it extends from the high western ground down to the lowlands in the east, covering 300 km² of varied landform. These river valleys converge like the spokes of a wheel on the city centre, forming a network of green corridors and semi-natural wildlife habitats (Figure 9.1). It has 80 ancient woodlands, extensive heather moorland and bog, urban relict grasslands, and ecologically-rich post-industrial sites (Bownes et al. 1991).

THE DON: A RIVER WITH A HISTORY

Figure 9.2
Aftermath of the 2007
flood in Sheffield –
uprooted vegetation and
shoal made of brick
rubble from buildings
and structures damaged
by the flood
(photograph: Richard
Keenan, 2007)

In the early 1900s a dugout canoe was found in sediments near what is now Meadowhall Shopping Centre; testimony to the wet prehistoric landscape of extensive wet alder and willow woodland, with meandering river channels, pools and marshes, the long-lost 'Lake Meadowhall'. Place-names such as Holmes Farm at Blackburn Meadows suggest an island settlement in a marsh. The Don is a river with 'attitude', and a tendency to flood, but over time, people colonized the area and farming pushed back the water's edge. By medieval times the river would have been lined by rich, productive waterside meadows and winter flood-lands. These provided valuable summer grazing and hay crops, and marsh resources for basket making, peat fuel, reed thatch, fish and wildfowl. In 1546, the ancient chapel at Attercliffe was still in use, and the curate of Rotherham, the major town and main ecclesiastical centre, would come to his flock when it was too wet for them to come to him:

> to mynistre to the seke people, as when the waters of the Rothere and Downe [Don] are
> so urgent that the curate of Rotherham cannot to them repayre, nor the inhabitants
> unto hym nether on horseback or bote.

(Hunter 1819)

Along the Rivers Don and Rother, until the 1950s, many local people had boats in case the river burst its banks; all part of living near the water.

A lost wetland: the River Don catchment and
the great South Yorkshire fens

Oliver Rackham (1986) suggested that 'about a quarter of the British Isles is, or has been, some kind of wetland'. Like many great rivers, the Don draws its life from a vast catchment and watershed. For the most part, the rivers and streams run from the high western land, down to the lowland plains of Doncaster. Across this vast network of streams and rivers, especially to the east where the waters spilled out over the Doncaster plains, were extensive marshes, bogs and reed-beds, forming around 2,000 km² of the great South Yorkshire Fens. In Yorkshire, south of the confluence of the Ouse and the Trent, 284 km² of Hatfield Chase were constantly inundated before Vermuyden and his fellow Dutch undertakers started to drain it in 1626. At its heart was Thorne Mere, almost a kilometre and a half across. Close by, the 16 km² of wetland at Potterick Carr near Doncaster fell to John Smeaton and his engineers after a private Act of Parliament in 1764 (Rotherham 2010). This was one of the Yorkshire Carrs, famous with local people for its bitterns (*Botarus stellaris*) or 'butter bumps'. By the early 1900s, around 99 per cent of this rich wetland resource had been destroyed (Rotherham 2010). Indeed, as I describe elsewhere (Rotherham 2010), for most Yorkshire people, all memory of these wetlands has gone. Smout (2000) states that 'it is surprising how ... Yorkshire ... fenlands have evaporated from general memory'.

The main rivers were also comprehensively straightened and canalized, and once tortuous sluggish meanders converted to clinical drains for speedy removal

Figure 9.3
Early Morning on the Don, Sheffield by Walter Hayward Young 1868–1920 (pseudonym 'Jotter'). Reproduced with the kind permission of Sheffield City Council

of water. Many smaller streams and even sections of major Sheffield rivers such as the Sheaf and Porter were lost underground to culverts. The straightjacketed river has huge environmental consequences in the urbanized landscape. Culverted and canalized both upstream and downstream of the city, the river and its tributaries become 'flashy', rising and falling quickly and powerfully. Tributary rivers such as the Rother exemplify the impacts, with massive floods in the 1940s and 1950s. In 1991, the *Sheffield Nature Conservation Strategy* (Bownes *et al.*) finally established a baseline for a future vision of the rivers, aiming to re-connect the threads of the Don catchment, and some progress to this end has been made.

Urban expansion, decline of nature, and natural re-colonization

By the early 1900s, Sheffield had grown from a minor medieval settlement centred on a significant river crossing, with a castle and a manor and one of the greatest deer parks in England, to a thriving industrial centre (Walton 1948). One consequence was that the urban core was biologically dead, with gross levels of pollution of air, water and land (Bownes *et al.* 1991). Many who lived and worked there would not expect to live beyond their early twenties. The air was heavy with dust, smoke and grime, and sunshine rarely penetrated except when the factories had their Sunday break (Figure 9.3). The rivers, once vibrant with life and famous for salmon (*Salmo salar*) and eels (*Anguilla anguilla*), were now devoid of anything living. Used for cooling machinery as well as sewage disposal, they ran at temperatures constantly in the region of 20°C (Walton 1948; Gilbert 1989, 1992a).

From the 1970s onwards, action was taken to control these impacts and create opportunities for the river to recover. At the end of a process of thirty years of change, the River Don has re-emerged as a central feature in regional ecology, and increasingly in the lives of local people. However, even the wildest parts of today's river are not 'natural', and its fauna and flora mix native and exotic in equal proportions. It is argued by Gilbert (1992b) and Barker (2000) that this is a new ecology; that of 'recombinant species' of exotic plants and animals intimately mixed with natives. This newly emerging recombinant ecology challenges many precepts of nature conservation; though neither wildlife nor local people generally differentiate between native and exotic as species occupy vacant niches in the post-industrial river. Sheffield people have themselves actively contributed to the recombinant ecology by bringing Himalayan balsam (*Impatiens glandulifera*), Japanese knotweed (*Fallopia japonica*), and Mediterranean fig (*Ficus carica*) to the river.

It was in the 1980s that these wild figs were found growing along the River Don by naturalist and industrialist Richard Doncaster, and local botanist Margaret Shaw. Oliver Gilbert followed these observations with detailed fieldwork and experimentation. Thermal pollution of water used for cooling the steel works and the abundance of raw sewage containing fig seeds combined to establish a major, urban fig forest along the River Don (Gilbert 1989). This exotic plant is recognized and protected as 'Industrial Heritage' by Sheffield City Council, in its *Sheffield Nature Conservation Strategy* (Bownes *et al.* 1991); the only such case of protection of an exotic plant species in Britain.

Otters play under a canopy of knotweed, sycamore (*Acer pseudoplatanus*) and balsam with a ground flora of 'ancient woodland indicator' flowers, including bluebells (*Hyacinthoides non-scripta*), wood anemones (*Anemone nemorosa*) and other woodland flora washed down from upstream. This major green corridor through Sheffield, Rotherham and Doncaster even has red deer (*Cervus elaphus*) and roe deer (*Capreolus capreolus*) in most urban areas. After its recovery from gross pollution the River Don had become a rich haven for species such as water voles (*Arvicola terrestris*), but in recent years, the exotic American mink (*Mustela vison*) and growing populations of urban brown rats (*Rattus norvegicus*) now out-compete the voles. All these mammals are frequently seen by local people walking the waterside footpaths.

The remarkable recovery of this major watercourse is the result of changed regulation, planned action and the decline of polluting industries through economic change. Ecological renewal is all the more impressive when the depth of the original decline is realized.

New life, new living: retail therapy for the River Don in the twenty-first century

After 2,000 years of change and decline the River Don is re-emerging in a process driven since the late 1970s and early 1980s by bodies such as the charity, the Five Weirs Walk Trust, and the public good arm of local business, the Sheffield Junior Chamber of Commerce (Firth 1997). As the river became cleaner there was renewed demand for bank-side access for wildlife watching, fishing, walking, cycling and even water-based sports like canoeing. All these helped fuel the cry for an improved waterside environment, and following the dramatic industrial collapse of the 1970s and improved pollution regulation there has been a swift upturn in the river. Also, as industry declined, the renovation of vacant warehouses and other industrial premises, together with new-build on derelict sites, provide offices, apartments, student villages and more as Sheffield seeks to reinvigorate its urban centre; a remarkable turnaround in less than 50 years (Figure 9.4). Central to the recovery was the transformation of the Lower Don Valley in the 1980s and 1990s into a new landscape of leisure, sport, and retail with the Tinsley Canal and the River Don forming two key 'green' spines. The greening of the valley was a keystone of its rejuvenation, a turning point in its history, and at its core is the massive Meadowhall Shopping Centre with a footprint of about 140,000 m^2. The river has become a catalyst rather than a hindrance and waterfront dwellings and offices are now premium locations.

BUT HOW SHOULD WE CELEBRATE THE NEW RIVER AND ENGAGE THE COMMUNITY?

Figure 9.4
New riverside
developments along the
River Don in the Wicker
area of Sheffield
(photograph: Richard
Keenan, 2007)

Although the River Don, its tributaries and its environs have changed almost beyond recognition, they are still the artery of a region and the lifeblood of its ecology. This new vibrant ecology emerged from industrial wasteland and both native and exotic species jostle for position. Finely balanced, the outcome fluctuates as plants and animals come and go. There is no long-term stability, but a dynamic continuum that ebbs and flows like the river. Urban rivers are mirrors to the wider landscape and ecological stresses like global climate change. New species like *Buddleia* and figs are winners in the re-shuffling of the environmental pack of cards (Figure 9.5). But this need not mean that natives will necessarily lose out; many native plants and animals thrive in this recombinant post-industrial ecology. As Oliver Gilbert (1992a) pointed out so eloquently in the 1980s, these species were in any case entirely removed by the gross pollution and other impacts over 200 years or so of industrialization and urbanization. The new ecosystems are bustling dynamic mixes of old and new; a rich mixture reflecting the dynamic and exciting human populations that now re-colonize the urban heartland. Seen from this perspective, the tale of the River Don, for all its pollution and depression, is one of heartening optimism for the future.

Whilst there are many successes in the story of the Don (Firth 1997) the release of the canalized river back into its dynamic floodplain and its meandering

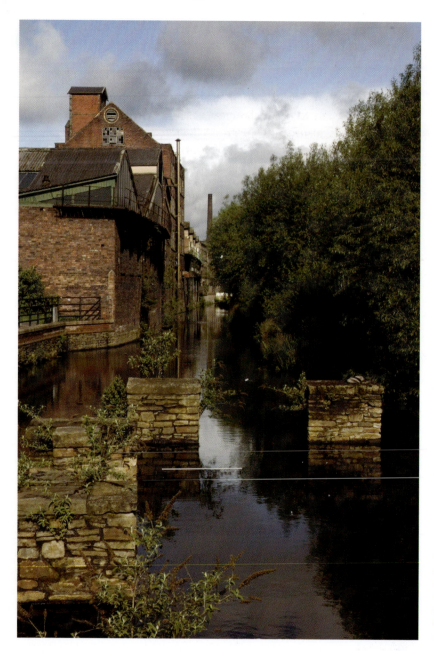

Figure 9.5
Buddleia growing on industrial ruins in the Kelham Island goit (mill race) in Sheffield (photograph: Richard Keenan, 2009)

watercourse is a very long way off. Indeed, recent widespread tree felling along the re-naturalized riverbanks and islands for 'safety' reasons, together with scouring and de-silting of the watercourse, suggests that a long-term view of the river as a wild resource remains out of reach. These were a hasty response to the flood events of 2007, but from my personal research it seems that public debate and effective dialogue on this post-flooding response was very limited and most local people were perplexed by these actions and excluded from the process. Even if the actions were necessary, such drastic works would be better framed by public consensus. Similarly, responses to the spread of invasive alien species remain patchy and uncoordinated; and this is despite long-held views that to be effective, such actions need to be at a catchment level and to be embedded within a realistic strategy (Rotherham 2009). So, in the early twenty-first century it is time to regard this great urban river as an important resource worthy of holistic management plans. With new challenges such as global climate change and the increasing risks of flooding it is sensible to bring together all stakeholders and facets of our great rivers and to address them in coordinated, long-term, publicly accountable ways. It is also clear that current policies and strategies at national and regional levels are uncoordinated and weak. With issues of biodiversity conservation, flood management, access and recreational or sporting use, and riparian ownership, management and development, it is time to take a more robust and visionary approach to the sustainable future of the Don and other rivers. This is why the Don Catchment Trust was launched in 2010.

Above all, it is important to recognize and plan for the bigger role of the rivers. As witnessed in 2007, the way that we manage the landscape and the climate-induced extreme weather conditions mean the river remains central to the region's environment. It is important to learn the lessons of the floods and consider how best to work with the river and its floodplains to make a more sustainable future for all of us. This is a message that is easily overlooked but a newly-resurgent river offers opportunities for living, for recreation, for business and for conservation. A former publicity officer for Sheffield City Council once touted the image of 'Sheffield by the Sea', with candy floss and ice-cream along the Meadowhall waterfront. His plans to dam the River Don to form a lake were flawed, because they neglected the core functions of the river in its landscape, and the impacts on the city's main trunk sewer. He left shortly afterwards. Any new vision needs to take into account the nature and character and environmental significance of this great river. Will twenty-first-century residents need to take to the boats as often as they once did? Only time will tell, but in the meantime the emergence of new community-based networks and charities like the Don Catchment Trust will help to focus interest, awareness and efforts into more effective and strategic custodianship for the future.

REFERENCES

Barker, G. (ed.) (2000) *Ecological Recombination in Urban Areas: Implications for Nature Conservation*, Peterborough: English Nature.

Bownes, J. S., Riley, T. H., Rotherham, I. D. and Vincent, S. M. (1991) *Sheffield Nature Conservation Strategy*, Sheffield: Sheffield City Council.

Firth, C. (1997) *900 Years of the Don Fishery: Domesday to the Dawn of the New Millennium*, Leeds: Environment Agency.

Gilbert, O. L. (1989) *The Ecology of Urban Habitats*, London: Chapman & Hall.

—— (1992a) 'The ecology of an urban river', *British Wildlife*, 3: 129–136.

—— (1992b) *The Flowering of the Cities: The Natural Flora of 'Urban Commons'*, Peterborough: English Nature.

Hunter, J. (1819) *Hallamshire, The History and Topography of the Parish of Sheffield*, London: Lackington, Hughes, Harding, Mavor and Jones.

Rackham, O. (1986) *The History of the Countryside*, London: Dent.

Rotherham, I. D. (2008a) 'Landscape, water and history', *Practical Ecology and Conservation*, 7: 138–152.

—— (2008b) 'Floods and water: a landscape-scale response', *Practical Ecology and Conservation*, 7: 128–137.

—— (2009) 'Exotic and alien species in a changing world', *ECOS*, 30(2): 42–49.

—— (2010) *Yorkshire's Forgotten Fenlands*, Barnsley: Pen & Sword Books Limited.

Smout, T. C. (2000) *Nature Contested: Environmental History in Scotland and Northern England since 1600*, Edinburgh: Edinburgh University Press.

Walton, M. (1948) *Sheffield: Its Story and Its Achievements*, Sheffield: The Sheffield Telegraph and Star Ltd.

Warman, C. R. (1969) *Sheffield Emerging City*, Sheffield: The City Engineer and Surveyor and Town Hall Planning Officer.

Chapter 10: Enhancing ruderal perennials in Manor Fields Park, Sheffield

A new park on the 'bandit lands' of urban green space dereliction

Marian Tylecote and Nigel Dunnett

INTRODUCTION

> The vegetation, and therefore the character of the park, has come about mainly by accident: through successional growth, neglect, abandoned allotments and local community use and misuse … Development has largely worked around this, with this or used it as inspiration.
>
> (Brian Hemingway, Project Manager at Manor Fields Park)

At the new Manor Fields Park (formerly known as 'Deep Pits'), located in the Manor and Castle district of Sheffield, UK, the aesthetic and experiential qualities of the site have been determined by a transformation of the site and its vegetation over time, through historical changes from medieval deer park to public allotments and eventual abandonment as a purposeful/working space. Remnants of hedges, a large pond and a brook running the entire length of the park, have provided a framework filled in by spontaneous vegetation (Figure 10.1). Recently, since the site became a designated District Park, it has been the focus of a long-term regeneration project that seeks to work sensitively within the existing landscape fabric and social context. The goal has been to transform what was a dumping ground for burnt-out vehicles and other depredations, known locally as 'bandit lands' – symbolic of the problems of the district – into a place with a positive interface for the local people, via the vision of a social enterprise company, Green Estate Ltd.[1] At Manor Fields, we challenge the view that the characteristic plants spontaneously arising in urban areas are of no value. We are undertaking experimental work at the park within one plant community, namely 'tall herb' (ruderal herbaceous perennials/forbs; originating from different parts of the world), and adding compatible non-native tall perennials. Our work seeks to promote the use of these tough, dependable and beautiful perennials, with their adaptability to urban conditions and potential for spectacular effects.

It seems clear that many people regard the unmanaged vegetation associated with abandoned, vacant or untended places as weedy and disorderly (Hands and Brown 2002; Breuste 2004); whilst the image of such places bespeaks failure 'made tangible in an anthropomorphized landscape' (Corbin 2003: 15). The little

Figure 10.1
A small pond created along the brook that runs the entire length of the park, surrounded by spontaneous tall herb vegetation (photograph: Nigel Dunnett)

empirical research that has been done into attitudes towards previously used spaces (Bauer 2005) seems to show that people value urban 'nature', despite its diverse meanings (Ozguner and Kendle 2006). However, they appear to like this spontaneous, feral nature least (Rink 2005). Following on from earlier 'habitat creation' schemes in cities in the 1970s and 1980s (using strictly native species), there is now new evidence of the ecological significance of urban habitats (Thompson *et al.* 2003; McKinney 2008) and of the novel plant communities that may arise there.

For at least a century in north-west Europe 'the practice of ecological planting has been important in defining the concept of nature' (Woudstra 2004: 53). 'Naturalistic' planting, making use of non-natives for the enhancement of visual effect (loosely based upon the structure of natural habitats), was an idea first explored by William Robinson in 1870 (Bisgrove 2008). The concept of using 'weeds' may have started with the work of Louis Le Roy, a visionary Dutch environmental activist working in urban landscapes from the 1970s, espousing 'co-operation between natural and creative processes' (Woudstra 2008: 200). Le Roy believed that because spontaneous nature will always produce varied, pleasing scenes, elaborate planting plans may be dispensed with. We agree that such planting plans are superfluous but we believe that aesthetic enhancement and evidence of maintenance (Nassauer 1995) of feral vegetation is needed in public parks.

Ruderal vegetation has been retained in post-industrial parks like Landscape Park Duisburg-Nord, Germany, with the object of respecting nature's regenerative capacity, whilst contrasting this with design: tree planting in grids, clipped vegetation and 'garden' areas in the park. The use of spontaneous urban vegetation has also been investigated by Norbert Kuhn on test plots in Berlin (2006). Our aim is similar but in a different context – a public park – and in different climatic conditions, i.e., mild and maritime; where vigorous grasses such as false oat (*Arrhenatherum elatius*) grow all year round, producing highly competitive effects on other plants.

The interventions being undertaken in the area of tall herb vegetation will not normalize or formalize the existing nature of the site but will engage with the type and ecology of the vegetation as it functions in-situ, to produce, using extensive management techniques, minimally disturbed, relatively stable plantings. Simultaneously, ways are being devised to enhance the aesthetic appeal for people who may have a conventional image of what a park should be, providing a long flowering season and colourful plantings, strongly linked to the site's cultural and natural history.

This case study describes the background to the park development, and then outlines the experimental planting research, which is an important part of the park regeneration. It is based on documentary evidence, semi-structured interviews with individuals working for Green Estate, and a diary of comments and conversations with park visitors kept whilst working on site for the duration of the planting work.

THE PARK'S HISTORY AND CONTEXT

Sheffield, famous for its metal trades and steel making, was badly hit by de-industrialization in the late twentieth century: 60,000 people were employed in the steel industries in 1971, falling to 10,000 by the 1990s (O'Connell 2006). The Manor housing estate, built after the First World War for the city's steel workers, reflects this industrial decline: following the collapse of the steel industry, 68 per cent of the residents of Manor and Castle ward were said to be 'hard pressed', against a Sheffield average of 31 per cent (LASOS 2010).

The 25-hectare Manor Fields Park site (located three kilometres south-east of Sheffield city centre) was originally part of 'Sheffield Park', one of the largest deer parks in England, belonging to the Lords of the Manor of Sheffield and existing until the 1600s (Jones 2007). Later, the deer park was divided up into smaller units for agriculture, and during the 1800s, three mine shafts were sunk on the Deep Pits site. Archaeological work undertaken in 2005 by ARCUS (Archaeological Research and Consultancy at the University of Sheffield) (Bell 2006), revealed numerous coke ovens, probably constructed in the early nineteenth century. By the 1853 Ordnance Survey, the ovens were marked as 'disused'. Between 1921 and 1939 the Manor housing estate (with 3,600 dwellings) was laid out on Garden City principles (Jones 2007) over a large area of the former deer park; Deep Pits was designated an important allotment site, and was opened by the Queen Mother in 1936. Gradually the allotments declined in popularity and they were eventually cleared by the City Council in the 1980s. Since then, the site has been going through several stages of natural development/succession. It is roughly at the later stages of 'tall herb' succession (Gilbert 1989), with shrubs like blackberry (*Rubus fruticosa*) and dog rose (*Rosa canina*) coming in strongly amongst the forbs. Blackberry, the most competitive, is gradually establishing a foothold, and has to be dealt with if the perennial vegetation is to continue to provide its present colour and diversity. According to Brian Hemingway:

> Our challenge is to retain these existing assets and to integrate ... a complete set of facilities expected of an urban park ... an apparently natural landscape can be full of colour and beauty while at the same time offering a full set of recreational facilities ... To achieve this we identify suitable, naturally occurring plant systems, create the correct conditions or augment those already existing ... This may mean using plants which do not occur in the wild but which have the same habit and more and longer lasting colour ... Ultimately the effect should be that of a wild landscape with little evidence of intervention where only a trained eye should be able to perceive the levels of manipulation.

These 'naturally occurring plant systems' in the wilder spaces, reflect the site's history (natural and cultural), biogeographical conditions, urban surroundings and social context. Reflecting these conditions, disturbance can be regarded as unproblematic, contributing, as it does, to the dynamism of the site; the lighting of a fire by youths destroyed a patch of bramble, but brought in its wake lupins (*Lupinus polyphyllus*), and tansy (*Tanacetum vulgare*). Other plant communities of interest include damp acid grassland (overlying poorly-drained coal mining spoil) with heather (*Calluna vulgaris*), sheep's fescue (*Festuca ovina)* and a vivid display of early summer lupins (*Lupinus polyphyllus* agg.) (Figure 10.2).

SHAPING THE PARK

In 1998, Roger Knowle, attached to Green Estate but employed by Sheffield City Parks Department as Project Officer to develop Deep Pits as a park, took the lead on site development and inspired its future direction and vision. He said: 'Big cultural change is the vision needed here ... There are multi-issues, multi-communities and multi-territories, so better to take it slowly.' The need for cultural change was also emphasized by Sue France (Chief Executive Officer of Green Estate): 'There was never a park culture in the area. People saw green space as trash and waste land.'

Figure 10.2
A vivid display of early summer lupins (photograph: Nigel Dunnett, 2009)

An incremental approach has meant that changes in the landscape have developed alongside changes in culture. According to Sue France:

> Due to lack of money green space is designed by thrift and poverty. We have learnt how to do things with no money. This is quite unlike the prestige parks which get the money, produce something overnight and then do not follow through with long term management goals. We try little bits at a time in our different green spaces and wait for the ideas to be assimilated by the local people. Our process involves layering over time. We are simultaneously trying things out on a small scale in other places all the time before implementing into final schemes.

The overall strategy for the park's development has been to create recreational pocket parks at the entrances whilst retaining the wild/naturalistic core. A new pocket park containing a children's playground was created at one end of the park, whilst at the other a new 'urban edge' adjacent to the main transport artery to the city centre, with park offices and ornamental planting, is being developed. Constructing solid paths for main routes was among the first works undertaken, as well as new decorative fencing and stone walling. Secondary mown paths through existing vegetation defined and connected spaces of varying sizes to the main paths (Figure 10.3). Adjacent to the playground, a large and imaginative sustainable urban drainage scheme, collecting run-off from surrounding new housing (overlooking the park), was designed by Roger Knowle; introducing large permanent and temporary water bodies (and habitat), where

Figure 10.3
(From top) Secondary mown paths through existing vegetation define and connect spaces of varying sizes to the main paths (photograph: Marian Tylecote, 2009); Part of the sustainable urban drainage system at Manor Fields Park (photograph: Nigel Dunnett, 2010)

many people come to fish and play (Figure 10.3). Hard materials are reused or recycled throughout the park, giving it a strong sense of local identity. Roger has now left the team and Brian Hemingway, who worked with him for a time, is the Operational Manager for the site.

It is becoming apparent that many users empathize with the direction the work has been taking. According to Andrea Marsden (also employed by Green

Estate): 'Some people have told me that they like the park in different ways. They have a choice between the tidy places and the wild places'. Andrea says most of the comments made to her are positive; many people tell her that they are now visiting Manor Fields rather than Norfolk Park (a heritage park) further away. She says that recently she has seen new faces at the park, including ramblers and people using mobility scooters. In her opinion, the most positive sign yet of the success of the new work is that families with children are now having picnics – in a place once feared and shunned.

THE EXPERIMENTAL PLANTING

This planting has been inspired by Nigel Dunnett's work on integrating wild and designed vegetation, and developed collaboratively with Marian Tylecote at Manor Fields Park from 2007. First, additional tall herbs were selected, having the appropriate character to fit in with the existing tall herb vegetation; which were then tested for persistence under the competition from the existing tall herb perennials.

The tall herbaceous vegetation (where the experimental work is taking place) consisting of mainly naturalized non-native species, covers a substantial area in the centre of the site on either side of the brook (Figure 10.4) (Species such as goat's rue (*Galega officinalis*), rosebay willowherb (*Chamerion angustifolium*), golden rod (*Solidago canadensis*), Michaelmas daisy (*Aster spp.*), lupin (*Lupinus polyphyllus*), tansy (*Tanacetum vulgare*), shasta daisy (*Leucanthemum × superbum*), soapwort (*Saponaria officinalis*), tufted vetch (*Vicia cracca*), hedge bindweed (*Calestegia sepium*) and teasel (*Dipsacus fullonum*) are prolific here.

Figure 10.4
Existing tall herbaceous vegetation consisting mainly of naturalized non-native species covers a substantial area on either side of the brook in the centre of the site (photograph: Marian Tylecote, 2009)

Natives (except for grasses) are few. Creeping thistle (*Cirsium arvense)*, growing strongly, mixes in with these. With in-depth awareness of the site, research undertaken has been guided as far as possible by ecological knowledge of the dynamics of the existing plant communities, following Grime (2002) and Dunnett (2004).

Three experimental plots randomly selected during winter (containing as little bramble as possible) were set up in the existing tall herb vegetation, which was supplemented by ten additional non-native herbaceous perennial species. These were: *Achillea grandifolia*, *Campanula lactiflora* 'Loddon Anna', *Helianthus laetiflorus* (hybrid), *Inula magnifica*, *Leucanthemum* 'Becky', *Lysimachia ciliata* 'Firecracker', *Lythrum salicaria* 'Zigeunerblut', *Persicaria amplexicaulus* 'Firetail', *Persicaria polymorpha* and *Veronicastrum virginicum* 'Temptation'.

The larger pond and brook, with species such as great willowherb (*Epilobium hirsutum*), watercress (*Nasturtium officinale*), and flag iris (*Iris psuedocorus*) also adds another layer of interest and potential for designers, where for example, *Lythrum salicaria* 'Feuerkerze' has been added to great effect (Figure 10.5).

This list of potential plants is not exhaustive: many more would be suitable but funding is scarce; further testing of other suitable alternatives will therefore have to wait.

Figure 10.5
Lythrum salicaria 'Feuerkerze' has been added to great effect at the water's edge (photograph: Marian Tylecote, 2010)

The results to date have been very promising, with seven of the selected species thriving amongst the rosebay willowherb and bindweed, etc., with increasing numbers of flowering stems being recorded since work began (Figure 10.6). Management has simply consisted of cutting down vegetation after harvesting (for measurements of dry mass).

The work that will follow will make use of the plants that are shown to be successful in the experiments by planting them in 'borders' along the edges of the tall herb, thereby 'framing' and conserving the tall herb behind the borders. This will serve to enhance the visibility of the tall herb as a distinctive visual element in the park, adding to its appreciation by visitors. Some of the existing vegetation, such as shasta daisy, could also be used in this manner. More paths (added to existing desire lines) and spaces will be carved out amongst the vegetation. This will provide more intimate contact with the plants, whilst serving to control the encroachment of blackberry.

Many users have expressed interest in the planting experiments, stopping and enquiring. Several have commented on the colour that the selected plants have added to the park. A young man, passing by in July 2009 commented: 'I used to play here when I was small. It is fantastic to have some more flowers and colours in the park.' However, an older man responded differently:

Figure 10.6
Achillea grandifolia and *Persicaria polymorpha*, additions to the existing tall herb vegetation flowering in July (photograph: Marian Tylecote, 2010)

'The flowers are nice but I also like the wildness here. I don't want this place to be changed too much – like you know, a garden.'

The experiments have attracted interest in the wider use of these techniques as shown by the enthusiastic response of an environmental maintenance Team Leader from Telford, UK in 2010.

CONCLUSION

The landscape aesthetic embodied at Manor Fields Park employs few of the traditional forms associated with park design. Losing little of the amalgam of past human influences offers the freedom to engage with an urban ecosystem interpreted through the agency of human transformation.

Whilst deliberately controlling succession in the area of the ruderal tall herb vegetation (and in other semi-natural parts of the park that merit sympathetic intervention in order to retain and enhance their character), it may not be desirable to stop all change that may follow at a later stage, such as the succession from scrub to woodland. But some arrest of succession by sympathetic changes, such as those we are currently engaged in with the tall herb planting, adds emphasis and focuses attention on the aesthetics of biodiversity and the meaning of the transformations since the allotments fell from use. Naturalizing suitable non-natives into different types of plant communities and habitats (depending on site conditions and context) could be applicable to many other urban sites.

NOTE

1 Formerly the Green Estate Programme, set up in 1998 as a ground-breaking partnership between Sheffield City Council, Sheffield Wildlife Trust and the Manor and Castle Development Trust. The Green Estate now manages all the green space (500 ha) in the district.

REFERENCES

Bauer, N. (2005) 'Attitudes towards wilderness and public demands on wilderness areas', in I. Kowarik and S. Korner (eds) *Wild Urban Woodlands: New Perspectives for Urban Forestry*, Berlin: Springer.

Bell, S. (2006) *An Archaeological Watching Brief at Deep Pit, City Road, Sheffield*. ARCUS: Sheffield.

Bisgrove, R. (2008) *William Robinson: The Wild Gardener*, London: Frances Lincoln.

Breuste, J. H. (2004) 'Decision making, planning and design for the conservation of indigenous vegetation within urban development', *Landscape and Urban Planning*, 68: 439–452.

Corbin, C. I. (2003) 'Vacancy and the landscape: cultural context and design response', *Landscape Journal*, 22(1): 12–24.

Dunnett, N. (2004) 'The dynamic nature of plant communities', in N. Dunnett and J. Hitchmough (eds) *The Dynamic Landscape*, London: Spon Press.

Gilbert, O. (1989) *The Ecology of Urban Habitats*, London: Chapman & Hall.

Grime, J. P. (2nd Edn. 2002) *Plant Strategies, Vegetation Processes and Ecosystem Properties*, Chichester: Wiley.

Hands, D. E. and Brown, R. D. (2002) 'Enhancing visual preference of ecological rehabilitation sites', *Landscape and Urban Planning*, 58: 57–70.

Jones, M. (2007) 'Deer parks in South Yorkshire: the documentary and landscape evidence', in I. D. Rotherham (ed.) *The History, Ecology and Archaeology of Medieval Parks and Parklands*, Sheffield: Wildtrack.

Local Area Statistics Online Service (LASOS): Manor Neighbourhood Profile. Online: www.lasos.org.uk/PublicProfile.aspx?postcode=S2%201GF (accessed 23 August 2010).

Kuhn, N. (2006) 'Intentions for the unintentional: spontaneous vegetation for innovative planting design in urban areas', *Journal of Landscape Architecture*, Autumn: 46–53.

McKinney, M. L. (2008) 'Effects of urbanization on species richness: a review of plants and animals', *Urban Ecosystems*, 11: 161–176.

Nassauer, J. I. (1995) 'Messy ecosystems, orderly frames', *Landscape Journal*, 14(2): 161–170.

O'Connell, D. (2006) 'Sheffield regains cutting edge', *The Sunday Times*, 17 September.

Ozguner, H. and Kendle, A. D. (2006) 'Public attitudes towards naturalistic versus designed landscapes in the city of Sheffield (UK)', *Landscape and Urban Planning*, 74: 139–157.

Rink, D. (2005) 'Surrogate nature or wilderness?', in I. Kowarik and S. Korner (eds) *Wild Urban Woodlands: New Perspectives for Urban Forestry*, Berlin: Springer.

Thompson K., Austin, K. C., Smith, R. M., Warren, P. H., Angold, P. G. and Gaston, K. J. (2003) 'Urban domestic gardens (1): putting small-scale plant diversity in context', *Journal of Vegetation Science*, 14: 71–78.

Woudstra, J. (2004) 'The changing nature of ecology: a history of ecological planting (1800–1980)', in N. Dunnett and J. Hitchmough (eds) *The Dynamic Landscape*, London: Spon Press.

—— (2008) 'The Eco-cathedral: Louis Le Roy's expression of a free landscape architecture', *Die Gartenkunst*, 20(1): 185–202.

Chapter 11: Pure urban nature

Nature-Park Südgelände, Berlin

Andreas Langer

INTRODUCTION

Around 50 years of natural succession have converted the Südgelände, a derelict shunting station in the heart of Berlin, into a highly diversified piece of natural urban landscape. Originally a hub of activity, then a virtually untouched new wilderness for a stretch of more than four decades, today the site is one of the first official conservation areas in Germany in which urban-industrial nature is both protected and accessible to the public.

Two thirds of Berlin's open spaces are under protection. Protected sites cover about 15 per cent of the city's total area; 2.2 per cent of these are nature protection areas. The remainder are landscape protection sites. If you take a closer look at the location of the protected sites in general you will find most of them on the fringes of the city, thus protecting the remnants of natural or semi-natural habitats like forests, lakes, moors or meadows. In the inner city you will only find a few areas where urban-industrial nature is granted official protection status. One of them is the Nature-Park Südgelände. Officially designating and thus ennobling urban nature has to be seen as a milestone of nature protection, even in a city. It acknowledges the value of nature's wild spontaneous growth, leading to a much broader acceptance and appreciation of what had once been perceived as a symbol of decline and neglect, in other words, wasteland.

Designing wilderness, and making it accessible to the public is a further step in overriding these perceptions. The following paragraphs describe the conceptual and design principles that were applied at Nature-Park Südgelände, demonstrating how different goals have been brought together on the site.

HISTORY: FROM FREIGHT RAILYARD TO NEW WILDERNESS

The Nature-Park Südgelände is situated on part of a formerly much larger freight railway yard that was built between 1880 and 1890. It remained in use until the end of World War II. Train service was discontinued in 1952. From this time on, the Südgelände was mostly, but not entirely, abandoned. Trains continued to be shunted on a few tracks for a few years, and a large hall was still used for their repair. However, on most of the site natural succession began to take hold, a process whose results represented the basis and framework for the masterplan of the nature-park 45 years later (Figure 11.1).

How could we have left such a site in the heart of the city undeveloped for such a long period of time? You can find the answer to this particular question simply by looking at the special political situation Berlin found itself in after World War II. Although the Südgelände was located in the former western part of the city, the administration of the West Berlin senate had no jurisdiction over it. In the divided city of Berlin all railway yards were placed under the East Berlin authorities. However, it was not only the political situation which caused the site to be cut off: the infrastructure of railway tracks and heavily used roads made it practically inaccessible to city dwellers. As a consequence the site was removed from the consciousness of the population.

It should also be mentioned that the site was fenced off and guarded by wardens with dogs, which made sneaking through a hole in the fence an adventure, and a bit dangerous, thus keeping its informal use in check. Nevertheless, in the late 1970s a few wilderness enthusiasts (myself included) used to explore the site. In addition there were some homeless people who made their homes there.

Figure 11.1
(From top) The Südgelände site in 1935 (photograph: Carl Bellingrodt); the site in *circa* 1999, after natural succession took over

There were some beaten tracks running through the then much more open vegetation – only a third of the area was wooded – and a fireplace, surrounded by planks serving as benches, that marked the centre of activity within a beautiful clearing under a Swedish whitebeam tree (*Sorbus intermedia*). Today the clearing is still used for resting, and people enjoy using the swing there right beside the whitebeam tree.

At the end of the 1970s, nearly 30 years after the discontinuation of the train services, the site returned to present attention, when the re-establishment of a new shunting station was proposed by the local authorities. In response to this development a local citizens' group put forward the idea of having a nature-park on the site. Rather than clearing the site the citizens' group put pressure on the city government to do an ecological survey. As a result of the survey the Südgelände was shown to be one of the most valuable ecological areas in the city because of the immense diversity of flora and fauna. At the end of an intensive discussion process the government scrapped its plan for the new station, and the concept of a nature-park was adopted.

The establishment of the nature-park was again dependent on history: the reunification of Germany and the rapid development of the city of Berlin that followed required ecological compensation. The idea behind ecological compensation as conceived by German legislation on nature protection is to keep an ecological balance. It is applied as a means of compensating for any negative effects of development on ecosystem services such as climate regulation, hydrological function or habitat for flora and fauna. First, negative ecological effects are to be avoided. Second, any unavoidable impairment, such as sealing soils or destroying biotopes are to be offset by measures of nature conservation and landscape management.

In this case the compensation was the transfer of the property rights of the Südgelände site from the German railway company to the state of Berlin. This happened in 1996. The transfer was a pre-condition for retaining the characteristic qualities of the site in the long term, whilst implementing the nature-park idea, and recognizing the site officially as a nature protection area in 1999. The central part of about 3.6 hectares is protected as a nature conservation site, while the surrounding area of 12.8 hectares is not so strictly protected as a landscape protection site (Senatsverwaltung für Stadtentwicklung, Landesbeauftragter für Naturschutz und Stadtentwicklung 2007) (Figure 11.2). The park was finally opened in May 2000, almost 50 years after the railway yard was shut down, and 20 years after the introduction of the nature-park idea.

Figure 11.2
Plan of the Nature-Park Südgelände (red = nature conservation site, blue = landscape protection site) (image: planland Planungsgruppe Landschaftsentwicklung)

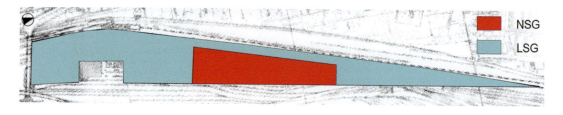

NSG

LSG

FROM NEW WILDERNESS TO NATURE-PARK: CHALLENGES AND APPROACHES OF THE MASTER PLAN

The concept for the nature-park had to address two challenges from its inception: how to open the site to the public without endangering the rich flora and fauna present, and how to address the question of whether the natural vegetation dynamic should be influenced or not.

The diversity of species at the site has, generally speaking, developed without human intervention. The result has been a mosaic of habitat types colonizing the plains, cuttings and embankments, viaducts and ramps (Figure 11.3). Besides the long-term undisturbed development, the different aspects and conditions provided by the varied topography are causal for the rich diversity of flora and fauna including more than 200 species of wild bees and wasps, and 366 different ferns and herbs (Prasse and Ristow 1995, Saure 2001).

The results of two vegetation surveys, undertaken in 1981 and 1992, showed a remarkable increase in woody vegetation in one decade. Within ten years the percentage of woody stands doubled. In 1981, only 37 per cent of the Südgelände was wooded, ten years later this figure had increased to 70 per cent (Kowarik and Langer 1994). The results also showed that ongoing succession would have led to complete reforestation of the Südgelände in a short period of time. The consequence would have been a decline in the characteristic species and plant communities of the open landscapes, and a loss of spatial diversity as well.

We were not willing to accept these harsh consequences, therefore we made the decision to combine both natural dynamics and controlled processes. What did we do? Three principles were adopted, which are essential to the concept.

1 Definition of space typology

We defined three types of spaces, which are constitutive of the site: clearings, groves and woody stands. In order to create different spatial characteristics, clearings were opened and partly enlarged, stands that were light and open were to be maintained as groves, while in the wild woods the natural dynamics would be allowed to proceed fully unfettered.

The spatial determination of the three types of spaces considers both nature conservation and landscape aesthetic criteria. The aim has been to

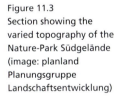

Figure 11.3
Section showing the varied topography of the Nature-Park Südgelände (image: planland Planungsgruppe Landschaftsentwicklung)

demonstrate the transformation from railway yard to wilderness over time and to make the site more attractive both for the rare species, which are bound to the open sites, and for the visitors, who can experience a more diverse landscape.

2 Access concept

To make the site accessible to the public, a path system was developed that was based fundamentally on the linear structure of the earlier railway yard. Train tracks were turned into paths. The ramps and underpasses that were once used for crossing tracks were now being used to establish the path system on different levels. In addition, a few new connections make circular routes possible. The nature conservation area in the middle of the Südgelände is traversed by a metal walkway raised 50 cm above the vegetation while for the most part following the old tracks. The metal walkway represents a linking element between the requirements of conservation and the aspirations of the visitors. It fulfils two criteria: first, it makes the nature conservation area accessible, and second, it simultaneously avoids any direct impact on the vegetation. By combining these functions in a single setting (metal walkway with a connected observation post and a platform to rest on), large areas are protected from disturbance, which in turn allows space for undisturbed succession to take place (Figure 11.4).

Figure 11.4
The raised metal walkway with its associated lookout posts and platforms, designed by the Odious Group, protects the vegetation in the most biodiverse areas of the nature-park, whilst enabling users to access and overlook these areas (photograph: Laura Silva Alvarado, 2010)

3 Preservation of natural and cultural elements

There are a number of selected relics which have been restored, including railway signals, watercranes and the old turntable. The old water tower was also preserved as a landmark (Figure 11.5). These old cultural layers have been enhanced by the contribution of the Odious Group, a group of artists working at the site who have been using their creative talents to the benefit of the developing wilderness. One of their major contributions to the project has been the development of

Figure 11.5
The water tower, one of the remants from the former railway era that references the former use of the site (photograph: Laura Silva Alvarado, 2010)

the previously mentioned metal walkway. You could even add the work of unknown artists in the form of graffiti to the cultural enrichment.

MANAGEMENT

Since the official opening of the park in May 2000, a new factor at the site has been the management of vegetation growth. This has replaced the previous natural vegetation dynamic. Today, management is the key factor in the further development of the park. It has to be seen as part of the design concept. It creates and keeps the different succession stages juxtaposed while maintaining the special character of the site.

The management measures implemented concern the wild woods, the groves and above all the clearings. From the very outset we decided to leave the wild woods unfettered. The light and open character of the groves is kept by cutting down trees and shrubs from time to time.

As to the clearings, reforestation by highly invasive woody species such as black locust (*Robinia pseudoacacia*) and aspen (*Populus tremula*) has to be prevented. The highly diverse dry meadows are to be kept. Every clearing is grazed by a herd of about 50 sheep, which are brought to the site for a few days, normally at the end of June. The sheep serve two purposes: first, they eat up the grass, and second, they eat the suckers of woody species. The sheep's selective grazing habits help perpetuate a diverse and wilderness-like vegetation structure.

Due to the flexible nature of the management approach, a monitoring concept was designed. The vegetation development is recorded with reference to the management measures. This provides a basis for adjusting the purpose and outcome of the upkeep. The management measures have to be continually reviewed and adapted to changing circumstances.

CONCLUSION

The project shows that designing wilderness and making it accessible to the public is a worthwhile endeavour, which can be achieved, making it both visible and valuable for city dwellers. Contrasting nature with fabricated or artistic elements, such as the metal walkway, highlights both nature and culture. The spatially differentiated concept works, and has been very well-received by the general public with an ever-increasing acceptance of the nature-park. Compared to other parks which foster the alleged contradiction between city and nature, the Nature-Park Südgelände is closely connected to the city. Culture has become nature; nature is pure urban.

REFERENCES

Kowarik, I. and Langer, A. (1994) 'Vegetation einer Berliner Eisenbahnfläche (Schöneberger Südgelände) im vierten Jahrzehnt der Sukzession' ('Vegetation on a Berlin railway yard (Schöneberger Südgelände) in the fourth decade of its succession'), *Verhandlungen des Botanischen Vereins von Berlin und Brandenburg (Proceedings of the Botanical Association of Berlin and Brandenburg)*, 127: 5–43.

Prasse, R. and Ristow, M. (1995) 'Die Gefäßpflanzenflora einer Berliner Güterbahnhofsfläche (Schöneberger Südgelände) im vierten Jahrzehnt der Sukzession' ('The vascular plant flora of a Berlin railway yard (Schöneberger Südgelände) in the fourth decade of its succession'), *Verhandlungen des Botanischen Vereins von Berlin und Brandenburg (Proceedings of the Botanical Association of Berlin and Brandenburg)*, 128: 165–192.

Saure, C. (2001) 'Das Schöneberger Südgelände: Ein herausragender Ruderalstandort und seine Bedeutung für die Bienenfauna (Hymenoptera, Apoidea)' ('The Schöneberger Südgelände: an outstanding ruderal site and its importance to bee fauna (Hymenoptera, Apoidea)'), *Berliner Naturschutzblätter (Berlin Nature Protection Newsletter)*, 35: 17–29.

Senatsverwaltung für Stadtentwicklung, Landesbeauftragter für Naturschutz und Stadtentwicklung (Berlin Senat for Urban Development, Commissioner for Nature Protection and Urban Developement) (eds) (2007) *Natürlich Berlin! Naturschutz-und NATURA 2000 Gebiete in Berlin* ('Berlin naturally! Nature protection and NATURA 2,000 sites in Berlin'), Rangsdorf: Natur und Text.

Chapter 12: Upstaging nature

Art in Sydenham Hill Wood

Helen Morse Palmer

Between May 2005 and August 2007, three exhibitions of site-specific contemporary art were held within the urban wildscape of Sydenham Hill Wood, south-east London, UK. These shows were free, curated events featuring local, national and international artists, and were the result of collaboration between arts organization Lookoutpost and the London Wildlife Trust (LWT). This chapter details the exhibitions as a case study for future projects of a similar nature.

AN URBAN WILDSCAPE

Sydenham Hill Wood offers a strange duality. It is a tranquil place of exceptional natural beauty, but it is situated just eight kilometres from the centre of one of the biggest, busiest capitals in Europe. As the largest remaining stretch of the Great North Wood, its history can be traced back to the sixteenth century. The landscape has survived a good deal of transformation, from ancient woodland to wood pasture to luxury Victorian villas with extensive grounds. The ruins of an old folly mark a time when the wood temporarily became private gardens. In 1865, a high-level railway was built from Nunhead to Crystal Palace, cutting a direct route through the trees. A century later the villas were ruins and the railway had been dismantled. In the 1980s, planning proposals were submitted for a council (public) housing estate to be built on the site, but a committee of local residents fought off the developers.

Sydenham Hill Wood is now run as a nature reserve by the LWT. The term 'nature reserve' should be read loosely, however, since the environment is not protected from human access. Joggers continually run through the wood. Cyclists whiz by, in defiance of the 'No Bicycles' signs. Since there are no poop-scoop bins, dog walkers leave little bags of dog poop at the side of the paths or dangling from the trees. Fly tipping is a regular occurrence. Kids from the neighbouring estate ambush pizza delivery boys and hijack their mopeds, which are later found burnt out beneath the trees. Day-trippers, bird-watchers, wildflower collectors and locals of all ages walk in the wood in all seasons for all reasons. Sydenham Hill Wood is a true urban wildscape.

Urban wildscapes attract creative thinkers, including John Deller, who discovered Sydenham Hill Wood in 2003 whilst volunteering for the LWT. John is a contemporary artist and founder of the non-profit arts organization Lookout-post.[1] The chief concern of Lookoutpost is to seek out and reclaim forgotten sites and structures within which artists can develop new work.

Sydenham Hill Wood appealed as an exhibition site for several reasons, particularly the juxtaposition of the permanence of nature with the continual flux of human intervention. The wood's history presents it as a backdrop of constancy against a foreground of social, economic and political change – a rich source of inspiration for creative work. Using an urban wildscape as an exhibition site offers clear advantages to an artist. The environment presents no commercial demands or restraints, instead offering inspiration and space for the nurturing of new work. The challenge of making work that will respond, adapt and survive in such a space encourages different artistic approaches and processes.

Central to the Lookoutpost aim of site reclamation is the encouragement of new audiences for new work. The exhibitions in Sydenham Hill Wood attracted people who might be deterred from visiting a gallery by feelings of intimidation, or by a preconceived idea of contemporary art. Similarly, the wood presented no danger of Lookoutpost patronizing an audience or artificially cultivating interaction with the artwork. The take-it-or-leave-it ambiance of the urban wildscape environment could be transferred to the work, resulting in an atmosphere of discovery rather than pretension.

There were also strategic advantages to this site, which bridges the borough of Southwark and the borough of Deptford, tying the affluent Dulwich to the council estates of Sydenham. The exhibition in Sydenham Hill Wood was intended to encourage partnership on all sides with the potential for positive long-term relationships.

In 2004, John, in collaboration with fellow artist Helen Morse Palmer, and the LWT woodland manager, Ian Holt, began to develop the plan for utilizing the creative potential of the site, which culminated in the exhibitions. The LWT is the only charity dedicated solely to protecting the wildlife and wild spaces of London. It is a politically independent charity that manages over 50 reserves London-wide. It campaigns to save important wildlife habitats and seeks to engage Londoners on conservation and wildlife issues through access to nature reserves, volunteering programs and education work.

Ian saw that by instigating this collaboration with Lookoutpost he could raise the profile of both the LWT and Sydenham Hill Wood. A creative thinker himself, he was open to suggestion, and the realization of many different works of art in unusual locations around the wood (Figure 12.1). If conservation looked to be an obstacle, he was quick to suggest an alternative. This attitude led to the climax of the first exhibition: the opening of the disused railway tunnel to accommodate a high-profile interactive work by Disinformation entitled *The Origin of Painting*. Walking into the cold darkness of the tunnel it was impossible to see anything beyond your own outstretched hand. The air smelled of generator

Figure 12.1
Untitled, Jane Thurley,
2005 (photograph: Helen
Morse Palmer and John
Deller)

fumes, damp and earth. Hard-hats were obligatory. About 25 metres in, you found yourself up against a giant projection screen. As you stood, puzzled, a tremendous flash would dazzle you from behind. Stepping back in confusion it was possible to see your own shadow frozen in time on the screen. It stayed, suspended, for a few moments before fading away. Participants who already understood what was happening would fill the screen, holding all kinds of positions, waiting for the flash to freeze their shadow shapes.

Lookoutpost worked with Ian towards curating and installing the exhibitions, taking responsibility for the artistic and practical considerations. A call for submissions was placed in all major art publications, and artists were selected, based on track record, strength of proposal and relevance of work to the concept of the show. The curatorial vision was balanced with practical possibility, health, safety, risk assessment, impact of the work on the environment and impact of the environment on the work. Protecting the environment was key, and measures were taken on all sides to ensure that work was eco-friendly and as vandal-proof as possible. Lookoutpost designed exhibition fliers, posters and catalogues, occasionally collaborating with students from a local college. The catalogues were subsidized by local businesses placing advertisements and sold on site, although entry to the exhibitions was always free, in accordance with the aims of both Lookoutpost and the LWT. Profit from the catalogues helped to fund the shows, whilst providing a means of evaluating the level of attendance. The LWT provided support in terms of publicity, public liability insurance and input into funding applications. Local steering groups and societies were contacted and helped to publicize, document and steward the events.

THE ART OF PERMANENCE AND CHANGE

Over the course of 2004/5, Lookoutpost and the LWT worked together towards their first exhibition: *The Art of Permanence and Change*. Thematically, this show drew on the history of the woods as a metaphor for permanence and change in a broader context. Eighteen artists were selected through a process of open submission to make new work in response to the environment and the theme of the show.[2]

The show was planned to coincide with the already well-established Dulwich Arts Festival, and ran from 14–22 May 2005 from 10 am to 5 pm. The art form focus was sculpture and installation, and included a weekend of live art and performance. Work spanned the traditional, the fun and mischievous and the conceptual (Figure 12.2).

Amongst the most memorable pieces was a haunting durational perform-ance by Michelle Griffiths entitled *Broken Hearted Promenade*. All day, every day, over the nine-day period of the show, Michelle walked slowly and silently though the wood. Dressed from head to foot in black Victorian period costume, she was accompanied only by a black dog (real) on a lead and a black raven (stuffed) on her shoulder. Attached to her skirts were numerous black helium balloons, which rustled and bobbed as she passed trees and bushes. Attached to the balloons were scraps of paper, on which were written fragments of love quotes. Every now and then she would cut a balloon free, sending the quote floating into the wood, the sky, and away. Describing her work Michelle wrote: 'The capital's parks and woodlands have diminished and changed with time, but shadows from the past remain. In a peaceful spot where, sometimes, one's only companion is a dog, a perpetual Promenade might be glimpsed.' The piece left a lasting legacy as unsuspecting joggers and dog-walkers began to talk about the ghost-lady of the wood...

Another work that caused a major sensation was Roger Nell's *Last Train to Knowhere*. This was an audio piece situated in the centre of the wood under the old railway bridge. It was common for visitors to stop on the bridge and gaze down a leafy path, which once formed the high-level railway line. During the exhibition such visitors were startled to hear the sound of a steam train, far away in the distance. So softly at first that they might question their ears, the noise grew louder and louder until anyone listening felt compelled to look behind for fear the train would come crashing through the trees. It became a favourite pursuit of people familiar with the work to watch the surprise of others encoun-tering it for the first time.

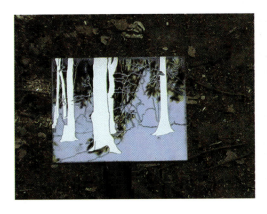

Figure 12.2
You Are Here: In Media Res, John Deller, 2005 (photograph: Helen Morse Palmer and John Deller)

According to exhibition catalogue sales and a tally count kept at a temporary information desk set up for the show, *The Art of Permanence and Change* received approximately 1,500 visitors over nine days. The verbal and written responses were overwhelmingly positive, to the extent that another exhibition was planned for the following year:

Imaginative, thought-provoking and mesmerising – well done.

I loved the casual layout – no determined track to explore.

Loved it! Inspiring, intriguing, evocative, enchanting, unnerving – great stuff. Made you slow down and appreciate and question what's around us.[3]

ECO VANDALISM

During 2005/06, Lookoutpost and the LWT collaborated for a second time to produce an exhibition entitled *Eco Vandalism*. It took place over the weekend of 13–14 May 2006, again coinciding with the Dulwich Festival. The decision to shorten the duration of the exhibition reflected the evaluation of popular viewing times for *The Art of Permanence and Change*.

Two works from the previous show had suffered minor acts of vandalism, so the title of the exhibition was deliberately ironic. It also acknowledged the possibility that artwork placed within the wood might be misinterpreted as vandalism. Once again artists were encouraged to consider the environment and its risks when proposing work for the show. The call for submissions asked for proposals tackling such questions as who should judge eco vandalism, how the context of an object affects these judgments, and whether something that at first glance appears to be eco vandalism might ever turn out to be beneficial. Can eco vandalism have inherent beauty?

Implementing such concerns as guidelines for a curatorial framework, Lookoutpost selected 14 artists from over 50 applicants, to create new work for the show.[4]

Particularly well-received pieces were Verity Gwinnett's multiple bath-time duck sculptures, made from re-formed plastic bags and situated in a muddy swamp. Conceptual artist Paul Lewis attached paintball targets to trees, placing art and eco vandalism under the banner of entertainment. Giles Pritchard's sinister installation of CCTV cameras juxtaposed the necessity for security with the invasion of privacy, whilst simultaneously acting as a deterrent for vandalism during the show. Also popular was Sara Heitlinger's individual audio tour of the wood. Anyone taking the tour was given a CD player with a set of headphones, immediately substituting the tranquility of the environment for pre-recorded surround sound. However, the tour took the form of a gentle, personal narrative, strangely in keeping with the setting. The conclusion of the tour was particularly powerful, leaving participants peering through a protective metal grid used to block the old railway tunnel. Over the headphones Sara's farewell could be heard echoing down the tunnel whilst her footsteps disappeared into the darkness where no one could follow.

UPSTAGING NATURE

> I believe arts events like *Upstaging Nature* play an important role in developing our local civic culture ... The unique setting for the event will allow new and diverse audiences to see excellence in arts in an unusual setting, and foster new use of one of South London's best and oldest wild spaces.
>
> (Extract from letter of recommendation by Councillor Alex Feaks, Forest Hill Ward)

In August 2007, the LWT celebrated its Sylvan (Silver) Jubilee. As part of the celebrations a third exhibition was arranged at Sydenham Hill Wood in collaboration with Lookoutpost. The show took place over the Bank Holiday weekend of 25–27 August. This event, entitled *Upstaging Nature (You Can't See the Art for the Trees)*, was the biggest to date. Thirty-two artists, selected from over 100 submissions, were commissioned to make new work in an attempt to 'upstage' the woodland environment.[5] The title of the show derived from feedback received during the evaluation of the previous exhibitions, where artists reported a sense of trying (and failing) to compete with the natural magnificence of the wood.

The thematic threads running through the exhibition were 'Dominance', 'Commodity' and 'Priority', an exploration of self in relation to, and over and above, the surroundings. Work also addressed 'Mimicry and Manipulation', 'All the Wood's a Stage' and 'Indirect Challenges' that displaced the tranquility of the environment (Figure 12.3).

Figure 12.3
Upstaging Nature, Helen Morse Palmer, 2007 (photograph: Helen Morse Palmer and John Deller)

Artists came from as far afield as Amsterdam and New York to participate in the show. Live art and performance pieces were scheduled back-to-back throughout the weekend. Events included Caroline Kraable's saxophone experiments, Julius Murinde's one-to-one singing, and Weiyee Cheung's participatory piñatas. Humour was added by Etta Ermini's contemporary dance safari and Stuart Silver's art history tour. Joanna Morse Palmer upstaged nature in spectacular fashion with a stunning aerial performance on a rope hung from a huge cedar tree (Figure 12.4).

The event was supported by local councillors and funded by the National Lottery. Giant, illuminated posters advertized the show, and audio work was broadcast on Resonance FM radio. For the first time, an evening event took place, with work by light- and sound-based artists Mayfly, Madarms and Harald Smykla. Music, food and drink were supplied. Over a thousand visitors flocked to the wood throughout the weekend.

CONCLUSION

Despite, or perhaps because of this success, *Upstaging Nature* was the last exhibition to be held at Sydenham Hill Wood. There was a danger of the exhibition outgrowing the wood. Should the popularity of the event continue to escalate, issues of public safety, public conveniences and licensing would have to be addressed. The requirements for street lighting, toilets and cafés posed too much of a threat to the very wilderness the exhibitions were celebrating. Furthermore, a prestigious event on such a scale requires a huge amount of work and commitment from all parties involved. Sadly, due to changes within the managerial structure of the LWT, Ian left, and the support and creative vision he had provided were no longer available. The importance of the right person in the right role should never be underestimated when it comes to utilizing the creative potential of an urban wildscape.

However, the Sydenham Hill Wood exhibitions left a legacy. The wildscape inspired 64 new artworks, seen by over 3,000 people in the original woodland

Figure 12.4
Painting the Roses,
Joanna Morse Palmer,
2005 (photograph: Helen
Morse Palmer and John
Deller)

setting. Variations of these works have since been shown in other exhibitions. The artists involved gained experience and insight into new ways of working, and many reported a change of direction in their practice as a result of the woodland show. Emerging artists benefited from a raised profile and a networking opportunity, whilst established artists enjoyed a new platform for their work. The individual nature of the event attracted substantial media attention, resulting in many articles, including a full-page spread in the prestigious *Artists Newsletter* magazine.

Failure to secure major funding meant that there were no artists' fees for *The Art of Permanence and Change* and *Eco Vandalism*. The fact that 95 per cent of selected artists chose to participate regardless speaks volumes for the draw of the urban wildscape. The LWT benefited from a significant increase in membership figures, representing a greater awareness and appreciation of the wood. The exhibitions raised the profile of Lookoutpost and expanded its database of practising artists.

Perhaps the people to benefit the most were the audience. Those familiar with the wood gained a fresh look at their surroundings through the medium of contemporary art. Those drawn by the art discovered a haven of natural tranquility peppered with a dash of adventure. Children, in particular, responded with innocent delight to the exhibitions and the wood, but it seems a wildscape coupled with creativity has the potential to make children of us all.

NOTES

1 www.lookoutpost.co.uk.
2 Artists involved in the *The Art of Permanence and Change*: Anna Pharaoh, Michelle Griffiths, Roger Nell, Jane Thurley, Magpie Seven, Joanna Morse Palmer, Kim Simons, Alex Zika, Eek Art, Darshana Vora, John Deller, Disinformation, Laura Cronin, David Brinkworth, Dumb Projects, Lee Campbell, Rita Evans and Helen Morse Palmer.
3 Quotes from comments book for *The Art of Permanence and Change*.
4 Artists involved in *Eco Vandalism*: Jonathan Aldous, Dave Ball, Weiyee Cheung, Verity Gwinnett, Paul Lewis, Giles Pritchard, Sara Heitlinger, John Deller, Etta Ermini, Andy Fung, Eliza Gilchrist, Bruce Ingram, Anne Marie Pena and James Steventon.
5 Artists involved in *Upstaging Nature*: Chris Baxter, Phillip Kennedy, Ami Clarke, Joanna Lathwood, John Deller, Madarms, Weiyee Cheung, Harald Smykla, Joanna Morse Palmer, Mayfly, Laura Travail, Megan Broadmeadow, Jack Brown, Bram Arnold, Sally Barker, Verity Gwinnett, Stuart Silver, Helen Morse Palmer, Tree Caruana, Kim Charnock, Anne Gutt, Bern Roche Farelly, Etta Ermini, Laura Holden, Christina Marie Guerrero, Caroline Kraabel, Joe Banks, Julius Murinde, Maria Laet, Doina Kraal, Jenna and Thomas Barry.

PART 3

IMPLICATIONS FOR LANDSCAPE PRACTICE

Chapter 13: Buried narratives

Catherine Heatherington

Growing up in small town England in the 1960s and 70s meant there was more freedom to play outside unsupervised than there is today, and my childhood was full of hidden places where adults rarely ventured; many of these were forgotten spaces – a ruined castle, rotting hulks of ships and the wild edges of railway tracks. Here we dreamed of exciting futures and played our make-believe games, yet somehow we were always intuitively aware of the buried narratives that connected these derelict spaces with the outside world. Gilles Tiberghien (2009: 156) sums this up when he writes: 'Landscape is a sedimentation of collective acts, the witness of usages that have often disappeared, the memory of a world that has sometimes lost its sense for those who inhabited it.'

Storytelling is not only a crucial part of childhood development; it also connects individuals and communities with their history and environment. Narratives may be formalized as rituals; bonfire night in Lewes brings the festival of Guy Fawkes up-to-date as current politicians and even traffic wardens join a long line of effigies of the despised and hated burnt over the centuries (Tucker 2009). Other stories are more personal; the family tradition of a weekend walk in the park includes memories of past outings which then become part of a shared connection with the landscape.

These cases describe how narrative is embedded in our understanding of place and how it contributes to local distinctiveness at both a community and a personal level. However, the twentieth century has brought with it an increased mobility that sometimes compromises this understanding of place. The 'modern' cult of the new has resulted in an increase in obsolescence of the built environment; derelict sites are abandoned or replaced by opportunist and homogeneous developments. Dirlik (2001: 42) explains the impact of capitalist economics on place making: 'a modernity driven by capitalism has rendered places into inconveniences in the path of progress to be dispensed with, either by erasure, or … by rendering them into commodities.'

Nostalgia for a past filled with meaningful landscapes must not be allowed to obscure the fact that narratives of place are often contested; the question of who controls the story and who is excluded from it are central to a discussion of the meaning and value of place. There is a move amongst some landscape designers, therefore, to seek ways of creating significant places that are open to multiple readings and interpretations. As Massey (2005: 140) suggests, an alternative 'event' of place is formed by negotiation between humans and the world around them: a 'here and now (itself drawing on a history and a geography of thens and theres)'. This understanding of place as flexible, with porous boundaries, influenced by layers of history and events, can inform the discussion of landscape and contemporary narrative theory. The landscape itself and the relationships between it, the people and the wider surroundings become the story to be read; always questioning who is writing the text and who is establishing meaning.

There is a perception that as the narratives of derelict industrial landscapes are often ones of hardship, pollution and exploitation they are of no value, as this comment by the son of a steelworker makes clear: '…preserve a steel mill. It killed my father, who wants to preserve that?' (Lowenthal 1995: 430). Connerton (2008: 61–2) formalizes this view, suggesting that 'prescriptive forgetting' can be seen as a positive action – a decision to erase the past, with the idea that it is in the best interests of everyone concerned. However, the erasure of a significant part of the history of a community can cause conflicting emotions; Binney et al. (1977: 25) describe how 'the dislocation and sense of loss can break down the pride and respect ordinary citizens may have in their hometown. What they identified as being their world ceases to be a part of them.' In derelict landscapes there are traces of these worlds to be found, read and valued. Roth et al. (1997: 17) refers to Marcel Proust's account of memories that can be stimulated by detours through and around unknown objects, prompting 'the past to emerge from the oblivion to which it seems to be consigned'. Edensor (2005: 126) writes of the multiple and varied memories conjured up in much the same way by small fragments of the past stumbled upon when exploring derelict industrial sites. Visual traces as well as textures, smells and even ways of moving through a space evoke strong reminders of past experiences. These will be different for each visitor and may be only fleeting but they add to the wealth of interpretations and understandings of a landscape.

There is also often a layer of plants writing a new history in the dereliction of the site; Gilbert (1992) explains how pioneer species specific to the region quickly colonize wasteland, and Anneliese and Peter Latz (2001: 74) describe the unusual plants found in the bunkers at Landscape Park Duisburg-Nord, introduced in the raw materials brought to this former steelworks from around the world.

Although storytelling may not be the primary aim of landscape architects working with these sites, it is often the traces left behind that influence the design and implicitly or explicitly contribute to new narratives. The most obvious use of such traces is the symbolic incorporation of relics, materials, buildings and infrastructure from the derelict site into the new landscape. This explicit use of traces as signs or symbols may go some way towards creating narratives and meaning but, as Treib (2002: 99) comments, 'significance lies with the beholder and not alone in the place. Meaning accrues over time … it is earned, not granted.' An alternative approach to the use of symbols examines, appropriates and subverts the processes inherent in the derelict site; the landscape remains a text to be read but it is one that is changing and unfinished, allowing the visitor the freedom to construct their own narratives. Potteiger and Purinton (1998: x) explain that the story may be an addition imposed on the existing landscape or alternatively the materials and processes within the landscape may implicitly reveal the narrative. Corner (2002: 148) explores the idea of the reader, arguing that a site can only be understood by the habitual experience of moving around and through the landscape: 'the experience of landscape *takes time*, and results from an accumulation of often distracted events and everyday encounters'. The idea of a somatic and perceptual relationship with a site prioritizes the individual but also, in describing events and encounters, Corner alludes to the importance of relationships. A direct comparison may be made between his ideas and Massey's event of place (2005: 140).

Thus, rather than a landscape literally telling a predetermined story, narrative is temporal. Visitors may 'read' the processes and historical traces within the site in multiple ways, depending on the experiences they bring, and they may also leave their own traces behind to be interpreted by others. Eventually some traces become buried, either intentionally by redevelopment or unintentionally by natural processes, thus creating new layers in the palimpsest of landscape. The concept of intertextuality in literary theory, conceived by Julia Kristiva who stated that 'every text is absorption and transformation of another text' (Kristiva, cited in Potteiger and Purinton 1998: 55), may also be applied to landscape narrative theory. Intertextuality here refers to the impact of the layers of history, or 'texts', on the understanding and reading of the site and to the possibilities of designing and interpreting the site in the context of the wider landscape.

In the discussion that follows, I explore the connections between the ways of writing and reading narratives in the landscape, and interventions made to derelict and post-industrial sites. Four different design approaches are considered with reference to their implicit or explicit narrative possibilities. The *tabula rasa* approach is outlined in the first section and this is followed by case studies of sites that incorporate traces of past use as symbols in the new landscapes. The concept of process when applied to derelict site regeneration is then discussed and the final section introduces a relational approach where visitors physically engage with elements of the historic and the new landscapes.

THE *TABULA RASA*

Until recently in England, developers of industrial sites have preferred to start from a blank canvas with a 'dig and dump' approach to contamination (English Partnerships 2006: 33). However it is now recognized that the removal of waste to landfill is not a viable long-term solution and new techniques have been developed to enable remediation to take place on site. Nevertheless the presumption remains that derelict and waste land is a problem that needs 'solutions' and prescriptive forgetting (Connerton 2008: 61–2), and erasure is often still the norm. The development of the 2012 Olympic site in London sums up this philosophy with the huge hoardings stating 'demolish, dig, design'; the designer is required to start from the point of erasure (Figure 13.1). Ling *et al.* (2007: 299), in describing a multifunctional approach[1] to landscape regeneration, suggest that this view of brownfield sites as the problem divorces them from the 'wider complex pattern and process operating in the area'. The lack of a multifunctional approach and the inability to value the changing narrative of the site is epitomized in the case of the former Grimethorpe Colliery, in South Yorkshire, UK (Rodwell 2009); the abandoned mine was becoming colonized by primary succession plants and over 10–15 years had started to develop as a scrubby woodland. It was then decided that its appearance was a disincentive to inward investment; the site was cleared, regraded with new topsoil and planted with, unsurprisingly, native plants to create ultimately – a woodland.

Many derelict sites on the edges of our towns and cities are developed only when it becomes economically viable; the resulting landscapes and buildings are often homogeneous and any elements of local distinctiveness are lost. A *tabula rasa* approach makes economic sense to developers, and sites where contamination or pollution has been treated or removed are usually a preferable alternative to those where reuse of materials may require a more costly or experimental approach to remediation. It is important to acknowledge the impact heavy industry has had on the environment and it would be impossible and undesirable to

Figure 13.1
'demolish, dig, design' –
the 2012 Olympic Site
(photograph: Catherine
Heatherington, 2009)

replicate Duisburg-Nord across the industrial sites of Britain (see below for more information about this project).[2] However, the British Government now acknowledges that some sites may have value in themselves. *Planning Policy Statement 9: Biodiversity and Geological Conservation* (Department for Communities and Local Government 2005) states that where sites have elements of biodiversity that are seen as important locally, the aim should be to preserve these elements within the new development.

SYMBOLS: NARRATIVE[3]

Easington in County Durham is an example of a landscape where almost all traces of former use have been erased and replaced by cliff-top meadows overlooking the North Sea. Heatherington (2006: 22) describes the mining village with two large pitheads and coal seams extending for eight miles under the sea. It was decommissioned in the 1990s, the topography resculpted and the site planted with wild flowers and grasses; there is little indication of the black, spoil-covered beaches of the recent past. This return of an industrial landscape to nature is a preferred option for regeneration when new buildings and infrastructure are not a viable proposition. However it is necessary to question which version of nature is being selected and when, if ever, the restored natural habitat was a part of this landscape; this form of restoration does not necessarily result in a landscape that connects with its history and context.

The large scale of the mining infrastructure and the extensive contamination around Easington meant that some form of restoration of the landscape was essential; 14 kilometres of coastline was covered with black slag, waste and other pollutants and 1.5 million tonnes of coal spoil were removed from the beaches as part of the clean-up process (Heatherington 2006: 23). If you know where to look there are fragments of the old mining infrastructure still to be found hidden in the undergrowth, and a memorial stands alone at the top of the cliff; a now static pitcage, once used for transporting miners down the shafts, symbolizes the finality of the demise of the mining industry. This acknowledgement of the history of the site is an attempt to bridge past and future narratives but as Heatherington (2006: 23) points out, at least one former miner has no appreciation of its value, commenting, 'I don't know what the bugger that's about!'.

In 2009, a new linear park opened to much acclaim in the meat-packing district of New York, USA; the High Line is an elevated landscape, about 10 metres above street level, designed by James Corner Field Operations with architects Diller, Scofidio + Renfro, on a disused and abandoned railway line (Figure 13.2). That the park has been constructed at all is due to the persistence of a community organization, Friends of the High Line, (Pearson *et al.* 2009: 84–95); their lobbying, and the support of famous and influential contacts, ensured financial backing. Photographs (Sternfeld 2000) commissioned of the abandoned railway show a landscape with 'an aesthetics of melancholy' (Bowring 2009: 128–9) and galvanized many into supporting the project to save the High Line.

Figure 13.2
Summer on the High Line
in New York
(photograph: Alex
Johnson, 2010)

The resulting design flows seamlessly from hard to soft landscape; benches rise out of the paving which, in turn, gradually blends into planting before emerging again and continuing on its linear path. Edgerton Martin (2009: 101) describes how the park 'calls attention to the time layers of the surrounding city landscape and not its own'. However Richardson (2005: 24) sees this as a problem with the design, pointing out that as well as having no internal architectural focus, the park also has no readable 'narrative or episodic quality'. Nevertheless, the lack of a sequential storyline is not necessarily a defect as the form of the park with its various access points allows visitors to dip in and out in an unstructured fashion and the absence of any programming also encourages a flexible approach to enjoying the space. There are unobtrusive references to the original use of the site; the linear nature of the paving and the park itself allude to the journey and sunbeds even roll along tracks. Pearson *et al.* (2009: 84–95) describe how the old railway tracks, which were numbered, removed and cleaned, now run through sections of the paved and planted areas, and the planting itself, designed by Piet Oudolf, is evocative of the wild colonies of herbaceous and shrubby plants which had colonized the old railway.[4]

Only a few months after the first phase opened, property values in the area began to rise, but the success of this new park will become apparent over time;

some question whether meeting the running costs of an estimated US$3.5–$4.5 million a year will be possible, and it has been suggested that planting and views of the city are not enough; that more programming will be required to retain public interest (Ulam *et al.* 2009: 96). Oudolf's planting follows a naturalistic planting aesthetic and will need careful and knowledgeable maintenance to keep the essence of spontaneity seen in Sternfeld's (2000) photographs. Some reviews have been less than enthusiastic; Bowring (2009: 128) writes that the symbolic elements of this elevated landscape are little more than 'representative fragments'. Nevertheless, retaining the railway as it was would have been unpopular with local property owners; campaigns since the 1980s had called for its demolition and it was viewed by many as a blight on the community, (Ulam *et al.* 2009). The excitement that greeted the opening of this park and its continuing popularity with visitors is testament to a beautiful and inspiring project – 'a place that is wild and cultivated, slow but animated, intimate and gregarious' (Gerdts 2009: 22). It is to be hoped that the calls for more structured activities will be resisted and that the openness and contemplative nature of the landscape will allow visitors to the High Line to discover their own narratives.

In contrast with the use of an elevated site to create a new landscape, in their proposal for the redevelopment of the Carlsberg breweries in Copenhagen, Entasis Design Architects have taken the floor plans of cellars under the breweries as the location of open spaces in a new multi-use urban development. Entasis' subtle use of trace as symbol sees the spatial structures of the cellars as the starting point for a two-dimensional plan. Layers of history are often revealed by digging down and uncovering (Riesto and Hauxner 2009), and this idea of exposing hidden stories has perhaps contributed to the interest and excitement this proposed scheme has generated. The cellars themselves were a subterranean world fundamental to the brewing process but unknown to the general public; the design imposes them onto the street-space (Riesto and Hauxner 2009), proposing a network of open squares and in one case, even a swimming pool (Figure 13.3).

These examples use traces as explicit symbols in the new landscape; at Easington and on the High Line signifiers are clear and unproblematic for the visitor to read. However, in both cases the implicit political and economic subtexts also make more controversial and pertinent narratives. The Carlsberg breweries proposal is not yet realized and it is to be hoped that a concept that has captured the public imagination can be retained as a meaningful narrative during the building of this large project.

PROCESS AS FRAMEWORK

Derelict sites in urban situations have been defined by Ignasi de Solà-Morales Rubió (1995: 118–123) as *terrain vague*; places with vague or uncertain meaning whose uncontrolled nature contrasts with the organization of the city. In order to retain these elements of uncertainty some designers prioritize process rather than

Figure 13.3
The Carlsberg Breweries
Proposal: a cellar
becomes a swimming
pool (image: Entasis
Design Architects)

finished product, creating landscapes which are always in flux. In such sites, focus is often on sustainability, water management, the recycling of elements and the management of change; the ecological narrative may be as simple as making visible the processes of decay and succession or a more complex reading of the slow production of soil on reclaimed landfill or the gradual cleaning of waterways through planting.

Kamvasinou (2006: 255–262) describes the vague park as one where the essence of the derelict site or the uses to which it was put are given form in the new landscape, citing as an example Michel Desvigne's masterplan for the river-banks of Bordeaux. Desvigne's proposal is simple and innovative; as the industrial lots along a six-kilometre stretch of the industrialized River Garonne become vacant, they will be planted with a tight grid of trees. The 30-year project retains elements of unpredictability: the local council will acquire the lots and release them for planting gradually, leaving derelict sites and roads interspersed in the developing forest (Kamvasinou 2006: 255–262). The new woodlands will be thinned out in a seemingly unplanned sequence and access to the site will be maintained throughout this period. Tiberghien (2009: 155–156), discussing Desvigne's work, explains that the form arises from the historical and geomorphological parameters of the site, and the resulting landscape 'involves a completion that is always deferred'. Corner (2009: 7) points out that Desvigne's designs are about 'cultivation, process and change over time'. On the riverbanks the natural processes of ruination and succession are made explicit; concrete becomes woodland. Desvigne (2009: 13) rejects the trace as symbol, saying; 'The showcasing of traces is not enough. To content oneself with that would be like doing restoration work. To commandeer these traces, to invert or distort them – therein lies the innovation.'

The nature reserve of Südgelände in Berlin was originally a shunting station, part of the German railway system. The division of Berlin after World War II left the site isolated by politics and separated by congested roads from its surroundings and the local community (Chapter 11 in this book). The landscape that developed as result of this lack of disturbance was of high biodiversity, and it is this mix of industrial relic and natural succession which the new park seeks to retain. Südgelände epitomizes the *terrain vague* and process is at the heart of the design. The visitor walks along a raised metal walkway above the natural vegetation thus making the site both accessible and valued. In addition to the ecological narrative there is also the more subtle and contested political narrative implicit in the site's development; the existence and structure of the park is a reflection of the political processes of Germany's division and reunification in the latter half of the last century (Figure 13.4).

One of the least interventionist approaches to site regeneration is the use of spontaneous vegetation as a basis for new planting designs. Norbert Kühn's research (2006: 46–53) on the public perception of such planting schemes indicates that some form of enhancement is necessary with, for example, the planting of conspicuous flowering plants amongst the colonizers. It is also important to select plants which form stable communities, and one of the dangers is the possibility of introducing invasive species (Kühn 2006: 46–53). Further research is needed to establish whether this approach could be used to maintain wastelands and derelict sites as they stand; the decaying of the industrial ruins gradually running hand in hand with the process of enhanced succession (Chapter 10 in this book).

EXTENDED RELATIONSHIPS: INTERTEXTUALITY

Julian Raxworthy (2008: 76) describes Peter Latz's design for the Landscape Park Duisburg-Nord as 'using engagement with the existing site materials as the organisational logic, with circulation putting people into different physical relationships with the industrial relics'. Raxworthy calls this the Relationship Approach to design.[5] I would go further and suggest that Latz not only structures the engagement with the materials on the site but also takes a multifunctional

approach, connecting people with the wider landscape – an extended relationship which parallels ideas of intertextuality in narrative theory.

Kamvasinou (2006: 255–262) describes the importance of local involvement in the planning and financial development of Duisburg-Nord, which took place at a time of growing appreciation for the industrial aesthetic. Latz integrated existing patterns of industrial use with decaying ruins and natural processes (Kamvasinou 2006: 255–262); he was aware of how people were already using the site – for tours of its history and plant life as well as for urban 'rock' climbing in the coal bunkers – and he worked with these ideas to create his master plan. Layers of history in the site are made visible in the new landscape, creating narratives which can be read by the visitor in multiple ways. The extended relationship approach is exemplified in Latz's use of the railway tracks; these stretch across the surrounding landscape towards the River Emscher and fan out in curves to the individual buildings on the site. In places they become cycle paths and walkways into and around the park and above the sintering and ore bunkers. Thus, the view of the railways from the top of the blast furnaces, whilst alluding to the developing post-industrial landscape, situates the site within the industrial history of the Ruhr, connecting it with the River Emscher, the waterway that brought raw materials to the area. Latz has specified that the vegetation along the sides of the railways should be cleared and mown, leaving the interconnectedness of these structural elements visible (Weilacher 2008: 122).

Figure 13.4
The ghostly traces of the railway tracks at the Nature-Park Südgelände in Berlin (photograph: Catherine Heatherington, 2007)

In Britain it is harder to find examples of the extended relationship approach to designing post-industrial landscapes. However, on the Thames Estuary, east of London, sandwiched between the Eurostar High Speed Rail Link and the River Thames and crossed by huge pylons, is the tiny RSPB[6] site of Rainham Marshes. This ancient wetland is one of the few remaining in the London area and throughout the twentieth century was used by the military as a firing range. Now a bird reserve with an award-winning visitors' centre, Rainham Marshes shows what can be achieved on a small scale with a derelict site. A simple raised board-walk, designed by the architectural practice Peter Beard Landroom, circumnavigates much of the site, allowing the visitor to walk through the marshland and yet, by constraining movement to the path it implicitly draws attention to the value and importance of the landscape (Figure 13.5). The path leads past bird hides and traces of military use; discrete information boards explain each ruined structure and the habitats and wildlife that now occupy it. There is no attempt to sanitize the ruins or the surrounding environment; with trains speeding past every few minutes and pylons, chimneys and wind turbines on the horizon, the visitor cannot help but be aware of the relationship between past, present and future in this site.

Figure 13.5
The RSPB Rainham Marshes with the Eurostar Rail Link in the background
(photograph: Catherine Heatherington, 2010)

Ballast Point Park, Sydney Harbour in Australia is designed by landscape architect team, McGregor Coxall[7]; the site was originally an oil depot, its sandstone escarpments blasted to make way for heavy machinery (Hawken 2009: 46).

Although much of the industrial architecture of the site was removed before the designers started work, the topography of the landscape has been distinctively shaped by its past uses. The design works with the existing spatial structures and access routes to expose the layers of sandstone and the concrete foundations (Hawken 2009: 47–8). Photos (McGregor Coxall 2010) show clearly the juxtapositions between the rough and textured materials, the industrial structures and the blue skies and water of Sydney Harbour; the design appears to lead the visitor through the layers of the once-despoiled site before dramatically revealing the links to the landscape beyond (Figure 13.6). McGregor Coxall consciously and deliberately break the cycle of exploitation by reusing crushed and broken bricks and rubble, installing wind turbines where an oil tank once stood and ensuring plants are sourced from local genetic stock (Hawken 2009: 46–51). If there is a

Figure 13.6
The layering of materials at Ballast Point Park, Sydney Harbour (photograph: Christian Borchert, McGregor Coxall Landscape Architects)

narrative written by the designers here it is one that talks of both environmental process and progress, drawing on the relationship between the past and present uses of the site and the wider landscape.

CONCLUSION

Consultation with the local community is a significant factor in determining the success of many of these projects; perceptions of sites as 'blighted' may be deeply embedded and the industrial past too recent for some to accept its incorporation into the new landscape. Structures are often too dangerous to save, and health and safety as well as economic priorities may dictate the direction of the redevelopment. Erasure is sometimes the only way forward for highly contaminated sites and developers may insist on starting with a blank canvas. However, in some cases there is the opportunity for a range of innovative and sustainable interventions; the reuse of materials, on-site remediation techniques, reduction in removal of waste and the enhancement of biodiversity.

Maintenance is an important consideration in any development, especially if an element of 'wild' or spontaneous planting is planned; self-seeding and re-colonizing by opportunist plants may eventually erase all traces of the industrial past, and the decay and ruination of buildings needs to be controlled for safety reasons. Natural succession begins with opportunist annuals and perennials giving way to taller herbs and grassland, before scrub and woodland takes over, and the decision must be made as to how far such succession is allowed to proceed.

Symbols as gestures to past use run the risk of becoming little more than static memorials; if meaning is prescribed there is always the danger that the visitor will merely say 'yes, I get it' and have no impetus to connect further with the site. Cultural background impacts understanding of both the derelict and the regenerated landscape and symbols may be overlooked or misread in this context. Regeneration projects have a tendency to refer to their industrial history in the use of a common palette of materials – rust, steel, Cor-Ten, concrete, gabions – which, whilst aesthetically interesting and sometimes challenging, create a generic narrative and may do little for site specificity.

Several of the projects discussed above draw on the history of the site in such a way as to enable new narratives and meanings to be read in a landscape that is flexible and open to change; often these designs use traces of the derelict in ways other than the overtly symbolic. The concept of process recognizes intertextuality in its reference to the historical texts within the site, whilst the unfinished nature of such schemes brings with it the possibility of multiple authors and varied interpretations. Such process-driven approaches imply that the old narratives become unrecognizable or are eventually lost, but the traces of past use may inform new meanings. However, designs driven primarily by an ecological ethic may need to include an element of education for the visitor who is unversed in an understanding of the underlying processes.

Intertextuality is also evident in the extended relationship approach; the new narrative is shaped by texts from within and beyond the site. These projects recognize the importance of such permeable boundaries for the development of a multifunctional landscape where the visitor participates in the unfolding of meaning within the wider context of the site and its surroundings.

Desvigne (2009: 13) writes of his work, 'we transform landscapes produced by society. We draw inspiration ... in the traces of society's activities ... we aim to help this society envision other ways of occupying and constituting the area'. These concepts could be said to encapsulate the thinking of many landscape architects working with derelict post-industrial sites; in recognizing landscape as a palimpsest of both human and natural processes and in bringing invention and innovation to the design, another layer is added to the narrative, traces and memories are valued and the scene is set for new relationships and interactions between nature and culture.

NOTES

1 Here multifunctionality does not refer to mixed-use development but to a whole landscape approach whereby different functions work within the wider landscape in an integrated fashion.
2 In 1923, (when coal mining in Britain was at its peak), there were around 300 mines in County Durham alone (Durham Mining Museum 1951).
3 The heritage approach to the regeneration of derelict landscapes is not dealt with here but it is the ultimate example of the use of past elements of the site; history is fixed at a point in time determined by the developers and is concerned with a definitive 'telling' of the story.
4 A survey of the original planting (Stalter 2004: 387–393) found 161 species of vascular flora and stated that the species richness of 38.8 species/ha may be one of the highest levels in urban environments in the region.
5 Raxworthy (2008: 68–83) describes the relationship approach taken in the design of McGregor Partners' BP Park, Waverton, Sydney Harbour. This park was completed in 2005 before construction of Ballast Point Park.
6 The RSPB, the Royal Society for the Protection of Birds, is a UK charity.
7 McGregor Coxall were called McGregor Partners when they carried out the work and they took over from a team who drew up the original version of the master plan; this first team consisted of Anton James Design, Context Landscape Design and CAB Consulting.

REFERENCES

Binney, M., Fitzgerald, R., Langenbach, R. and Powell, K. (1977) *Satanic Mills: Industrial Architecture in the Pennines*, London: SAVE Britain's Heritage.

Bowring, J. (2009) 'Lament for a lost landscape: the High Line is missing its melancholy beauty', *Landscape Architecture*, 99(10): 128–129.

Connerton, P. (2008) 'Seven types of forgetting', *Memory Studies*, 1(1): 59–71.

Corner, J. (2002) 'Representation and landscape', in S. Swaffield (ed.) *Theory in Landscape Architecture*, Philadelphia: University of Pennsylvania Press.

—— (2009) 'Agriculture, texture and the unfinished', in *Intermediate Natures: The Landscapes of Michel Desvigne*, Basel: Birkhauser.

de Solà-Morales Rubió, I. (1995) 'Terrain vague', in C. Davidson (ed.) *Anyplace*, Cambridge MA: MIT Press.

Department for Communities and Local Government (2005) *Planning Policy Statement 9 (PPS9) Biodiversity and Geological Conservation*, Norwich: TSO.

Desvigne, M. (2009) *Intermediate Natures: The Landscapes of Michel Desvigne*, trans. E. Kugler, Basel: Birkhauser.

Dirlik, A. (2001) 'Place-based imagination', in R. Praznaik and A. Dirlik (eds) *Places and Politics in an Age of Globalization*, USA: Rowman & Littlefield.

Durham Mining Museum (1951) *The Guide to the Coalfields (Colliery Guardian)*: Durham. Online: www.dmm-gallery.org.uk/maps/index.htm (accessed 8 January 2010).

Edensor, T. (2005) *Industrial Ruins*, Oxford: Berg.

Edgerton Martin, F. (2009) 'An old system made new', *Landscape Architecture*, 99(10): 101–102.

English Partnerships (2006) *The Brownfield Guide*. Online: www.englishpartnerships.co.uk/landsupplypublications.htm#brownfieldrecommendations (accessed 9 January 2010).

Gerdts, N. (2009) 'The High Line: New York City', *Topos*, 69: 16–23.

Gilbert, O. (1992) *The Flowering of the Cities: The Natural Flora of Urban Commons*, London: English Nature.

Hawken, S. (2009) 'Ballast Point Park in Sydney', *Topos*, 69: 46–51.

Heatherington, C. (2006) 'The negotiation of place', unpublished MA thesis, Middlesex University, London. Online: www.chdesigns.co.uk (accessed 8 January 2010).

Kamvasinou, K. (2006) 'Vague parks: the politics of the late twentieth century', *Architectural Research Quarterly*, 10 (3/4): 255–262.

Kühn, N. (2006) 'Intentions for the unintentional: spontaneous vegetation as the basis for innovative planting design in urban areas', *Journal of Landscape Architecture*, Autumn: 46–53.

Latz, P. and Latz, A. (2001) 'Imaginative landscapes out of industrial dereliction', in M. Echenique and A. Saint (eds) *Cities for the New Millenium*, London: Spon Press.

Ling, C., Handley, J. and Rodwell, J. (2007) 'Restructuring the post-industrial landscape: a multifunctional approach', *Landscape Research*, 32(3): 285–309.

Lowenthal, D. (1995) *The Past is a Foreign Country*, Cambridge: Cambridge University Press.

Massey, D. (2005) *For Space*, London: Sage Publications.

McGregor Coxall (2010) *Ballast Point Park*. Online: www.mcgregorcoxall.com (accessed 22 April 2010).

Pearson, L., Clifford, A. and Minutillo, J. (2009) 'Two projects that work hand in hand, the High Line and the Standard New York bring life to New York's West Side', *Architectural Record*, 197(10): 84–95.

Potteiger, M. and Purinton, J. (1998) *Landscape Narratives: Design Practices for Telling Stories*, New York: Wiley.

Raxworthy, J. (2008) 'Sandstone and rust: designing the qualities of Sydney Harbour', *Journal of Landscape Architecture*, Autumn: 68–83.

Richardson, T. (2005) 'Elevated landscapes: NY', *Domus*, 884: 20–29.

Riesto, S. and Hauxner, M. (2009) 'Digging for essence and myths: the role of the underground in the Carlsberg urban redevelopment', paper presented at European Council of Landscape Architecture Schools Conference entitled *Landscape and Ruins: Planning and Design for the Regeneration of Derelict Places*, at the University of Genova, September 2009.

Rodwell, J. (2009) 'Spirit of place', paper presented at conference on *Spirit of Place*, at the Garden Museum, London.

Roth, M., Lyons, C. and Merewether, C. (1997) *Irresistible Decay: Ruins Reclaimed*, USA: The Getty Research Institute Publications and Exhibitions Programme.

Stalter, R. (2004) 'The flora on the High Line, New York City, New York', *Journal of the Torrey Botanical Society*, 131(4): 387–393.

Sternfeld, J. (2000) *Walking the High Line*. Online: www.thehighline.org/galleries/images/joel-sternfeld (accessed 27 April 2010).

Tiberghien, G. (2009) 'A landscape deferred', in *Intermediate Natures: The Landscapes of Michel Desvigne*, Basel: Birkhauser.

Treib, M. (2002) 'Must landscapes mean?', in S. Swaffield (ed.) *Theory in Landscape Architecture*, Philadelphia: University of Pennsylvania Press.

Tucker, E. (2009) *Tonight's the Night: Bonfires and Fireworks*. Online: www.women.timesonline.co.uk/tol/life_and_style/women/the_way_we_live/article6903456.ece (accessed 7 July 2010).

Ulam, A., Cantor, S. L. and Martin, F. E. (2009) 'Back on track: bold design moves transform a defunct railroad into a 21st century park', *Landscape Architecture*, 99(10): 90–109.

Weilacher, U. (2008) *Syntax of Landscape: The Landscape Architecture of Peter Latz and Partners*, trans. M. Robinson, Berlin: Birkhauser.

Chapter 14: Taming the wild

Gyllin's Garden and the urbanization of a wildscape

Mattias Qviström

INTRODUCTION

> Once, when I came walking along this path with a pair of secateurs to prune a little, I met a women who had a pair of secateurs in her hand as well … and we said, 'Oh, it's you', and, 'I have always wondered, I noticed that someone else was cutting as well … you know, in order to be able to walk here…'

I am accompanying Birgitta and her dog along their usual route in Gyllin's Garden at the edge of the city of Malmö (Figure 14.1). For forty years, she has lived next to the former plant nursery, which soon after abandonment was appropriated as an informal area for recreation and play (Figure 14.2). 'This has been a paradise for kids!' she says as we enter the garden; 'They pick daffodils, as many as they can carry, build huts, and we pick nettles for nettle-soup, blackberries and dew-berries'. When describing the everyday use of the garden, she simultaneously

Figure 14.1
Gyllin's Garden
(photograph: Mattias
Qviström, 2005)

Figure 14.2
Birgitta's family in Gyllin's
Garden in 1976/77
(photograph: Birgitta
Geite)

demonstrates a moral responsibility for its management. The paths, she emphasizes, need to be managed: branches have to be pruned, and if a tree falls, the path has to be redirected. During snowy winters, the trails have to be trodden frequently, and over the past winter, with an unusually long period of snow, she cut branches for the rabbits to eat so they would not gnaw the stems of the trees. In a similar way, she cares for the strange flora originating from the former nursery. Some of the flowers now appear in her garden: 'As I see it, I have *saved* some of the plants', she argues. Birgitta is far from the only one who has entered Gyllin's Garden with spade or shears. Once, she encountered a man practising grafting. Others visit the garden to pick apples, blackberries, cherry plums, sloes, dewberries and elder flowers, or tulips, narcissus, lilac and forsythia. Advancing towards an impressive forsythia hedge in full bloom, she points out that the bushes would not be as beautiful if it were not for the people coming to cut branches every year, since that is the way to rejuvenate the shrub.

At the end of the walk, we enter the northern part of the area, which is undergoing rapid transformation (Figure 14.3). About 23 hectares of the garden were designated as a nature-park ten years ago, but the remaining 43 hectares will be the site of 700 residential apartments, housing about 2,000 new inhabitants with Gyllin's Garden as their backyard. With multi-storey buildings, the area will become a landmark in a neighbourhood of small villas and one-storey semi-detached houses. Bulldozers have levelled the fields and new tarmac roads and street lighting have been installed ahead of the main construction work. Alluding to the name of the place as well as its wild character, the area is being marketed using an image of a huge flowerpot and the slogan 'Live in the middle of the nature – a stone's throw from the city'.

Figure 14.3
Former windbreaks turned into scenery for new housing areas (photograph: Mattias Qviström, 2009)

Studies in urban development inevitably bring the entwined dynamics of cities and wildscapes to the fore (for example, Shoard 2000; Qviström 2007; Rink 2009). However, urban development consists of more than raising new houses or bulldozing land for highways and shopping malls – it is the process whereby our

conceptions of city and country, nature and culture, are renegotiated and realized. In capturing these renegotiations, studies of details concerning park management at the city edge can be as informative as analysis of discourses on large-scale land use transformations. It can be as fruitful to study the work of the lawnmower as that of the bulldozer. This chapter describes the gradual transformation of a 'nature-park' in order to illustrate the taming of a wildscape. Inspired by Ingold (2007; 2008), special attention is paid to the furnishing and framing of the place.

This case study is based on participatory observations of the planning process during spring 2010, a semi-structured interview with the project leader and another landscape architect at the Municipality of Malmö (in May 2010), the interview and walk with Birgitta described above (in April 2010), and repeated field studies (2004–2010), archive studies and an analysis of contemporary municipal planning documents.

FROM INDUSTRIAL LANDSCAPE TO WILDSCAPE

In the early 1930s, Knut Gyllin purchased the farm *Bäckagården* (which corresponds roughly to the area of the nature-park) in order to expand his nursery situated a few hundred metres to the north. Soon, it was transformed into an industrial landscape: when the enterprise reached its peak, the Gyllin greenhouses covered more than 100,000 m², together with 60 hectares of outdoor plantations (Qviström and Saltzman 2006) (Figure 14.4). The company was

Figure 14.4
Cultivation of carnations in Gyllin's Garden, 1965 (photograph: Malmö stadsarkiv: Fastighetsnämnden (Malmö Municipal Real Estate Office))

advertised as being the largest cultivator of gladioli in the Nordic countries, and the largest cultivator of peonies in the world (Vikberg 2003; Bengtsson 2007). Stories of the impressive establishment and of Gyllin himself (infamous for his rigorous discipline) are still abundant among the senior users of the place.

In the 1930s, *Bäckagården* was situated among vast arable fields in a rural landscape dominated by agriculture. Twenty years later, the expanding city had incorporated the municipality in which Gyllin's estates were situated, and ever since, municipal plans have designated the area for urban development. In the 1960s, the municipal authority purchased extensive land holdings at the city edge in order to control urban development (Qviström 2009). In 1965, Gyllin's Garden was an island of privately owned land in an agricultural and suburban landscape owned by the municipality, and plans were made to expropriate the garden and other real estate at the city edge owned by Gyllin (Stadsfullmäktige i Malmö 1965; Malmö stadsarkiv: Fastighetsnämnden) (Figure 14.5). Constrained by urban development and constant threats of expropriation, the business declined. In 1967, a storm devastated parts of the greenhouses in *Bäckagården*, but due to the uncertain future, repairs were delayed (Malmö stadsarkiv; Malmö tingsrätt). In 1976 the business went bankrupt and two years later the municipality finally gained access to the industrial site after years of fruitless negotiations (Stadsfull-mäktige i Malmö 1974; 1978).

Figure 14.5
Gyllin's Garden in 1965: an industrial landscape (photograph: Malmö stadsarkiv: Fastighetsnämnden (Malmö Municipal Real Estate Office)

Photographs taken in 1965 capture the property the municipal authority wanted to acquire, with an old-fashioned farm that had been turned into a stable, a sheep barn, a garage/smithy, various sheds, a pump house, oil storage tanks, a flower packing house, a number of wooden greenhouses, a furnace house with a gigantic smokestack, and the crown jewels of the estate: eleven huge greenhouses made of iron (see Figures 14.4 and 14.5, Malmö stadsarkiv: Stadsfullmäktige i Malmö 1978). The backgrounds of these pictures indicate a lush garden next to the farm, and high poplars beside the greenhouses and scrapyards. Ten years later, the documents relating to the bankruptcy tell another story; the farm was fire-damaged, the wooden greenhouses had collapsed, and the iron greenhouses were in very poor condition (Stadsfullmäktige i Malmö 1978). The buildings were accounted as being of no (or minor) value, and a year after the purchase, in 1978, it was decided that all the buildings would be torn down (Malmö stadsarkiv: Fastighetsnämnden). The main asset of the company was of another kind; a meticulous inventory in 1975 listed 1,500 metres of lilac hedges and almost as much of forsythia, approximately 1,600 peonies, 1.8 million daffodils, 225 m² of roses, a nursery for cypresses and *thuja*, 2,200 old beech trees, 2,500 old oaks, 170 buckets of asparagus and 4,000 buckets of maidenhair ferns, more than 2,000 lily bulbs, fields of cornflowers and ox-eye daisies, and so on (Malmö stadsarkiv; Malmö tingsrätt). Some of the green assets were sold, but windbreak plantations and other large trees, fruit trees, some of the hedges and scattered bulbs were left as a living ruin, echoing the former activities and structure of the business (Figure 14.6).

Figure 14.6
Thuja trees mingling with shrubbery. Gyllin's Garden is a living ruin from the site's industrial era (photograph: Mattias Qviström, 2010)

Comprehensive municipal plans drawn up in the 1980s and 1990s decreed that the abandoned area should be turned into a residential district, with the surrounding arable fields to the west and east designated for park and recreational purposes. While waiting for the development to be realized, Gyllin's Garden changed, as well as the appreciation of the place; despite extensive amounts of shattered window-glass, neighbours appropriated the garden for everyday recreation, and the garden species mingled with weed and brushwood into an urban wilderness suitable for play, picnics and walks. In a comprehensive plan produced in 2000, these qualities were finally recognized by the municipal authority and Gyllin's Garden was designated a 'nature-park' in which the wild character should be maintained, while the surrounding arable fields were to be turned into residential areas (Qviström and Saltzman 2006). The initial investigation carried out by the municipal authority acknowledges the ambiguous character of the place, although metaphors from the traditional cultural landscape were used in the characterization:

> Gyllin's Garden of today is neither nature nor park but a combination. It is culture recaptured by nature and run wild. Rows of trees and bushes divide the area, and in between grow grasses and herbs. The character and content of the different parts of the area vary substantially – open meadows, deciduous forests, groves, semi-open areas with solitary trees, which makes the area varied and interesting…
>
> (Malmö stadsbyggnadskontor 2001: 13)

However, vague categories are at odds with the spatial ordering of cartography and land use legislation. Notions of ambiguity (as well as of multifunctionality) are vulnerable within planning as they need to be explained and argued for at every step and in every document if they are not to be habitually replaced with conventional categories. When the initial ambitions were taken one step further, in a comprehensive design proposal, the ambiguous character was downplayed, and the nature-park was divided into nature *and* park (Malmö stad 2008). This division is maintained in the detailed development plan which is currently being developed (Malmö stad 2010a) (Figure 14.7). In the interview with the landscape architects involved, they explained that the option of labelling the garden as nature-park was discussed, but there was uncertainty as to whether a new classification could simply be invented, and what the consequences of such a classification would be. Before making a thorough investigation into the possibilities, it was decided that a divide between nature and park was useful and served the interests of the planners. For instance, the classification 'park' attracts more funding for management, while the classification 'nature' offers stronger protection for preservation of the site (as nature). The landscape architects involved also stressed that the actual line between nature and park will not be visible; nevertheless, the buildings allowed in the two parts will speak different languages: a bird-watching tower would be allowed in the nature reserve, a café and lavatories in the park. Even so, the plan only offers a loose framework for the actual development, so in order to understand the impacts of the urbanization, the actual design proposal and the planning process need closer examination.

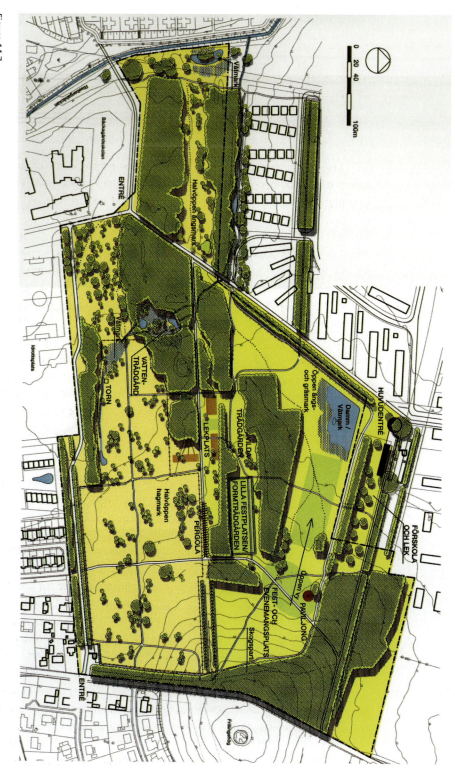

Figure 14.7
The detailed development plan. Whereas the divides between nature, park and areas for play are crystal clear on the legally binding map, the divisions are downplayed in the illustration: Nature = yellow, park = green (image: Malmö stad Gatukontoret und Tema (Malmö Municipal Highways Department))

CONTESTED IDEAS CONCERNING THE WILD NATURE OF THE GARDEN

A cautious step towards adjusting the garden into an urban context was taken in spring 2010, when the municipal authority launched an ambitious programme to inform the public about the plans and gather information. This programme included a public meeting, a dialogue with the schools in the neighbourhood, a walk in the garden (see below), and a questionnaire (submitted to 3,000 households and available on the internet) on the use and assets of the garden (Malmö stad 2010b).

The public meeting attracted twice as many people as the organizers had expected and 100 people gathered in a crowded room to watch the PowerPoint presentations. Initially, the design proposal roused heated feelings. A teacher from a school nearby argued: 'All we need is logs to sit on, not benches: then it becomes a park and we want nature.... Gyllin's is not a park, it is something else – will anything of Gyllin's Garden be left?' Another teacher emphasized the number of children who use the place. '[Today], the children can play anywhere, we don't need to tell them that there are places where they cannot go', she said. 'We are afraid the character of the place will disappear – we note how remnants from the time of Gyllin's are vanishing.'

The ready-made plan with specific sections and areas for certain activities was particularly provoking for the public, even though the planners emphasized that it was only an illustration (see Figure 14.7). An upset woman argued: '[In your plans], I see something which is ready-played [sic] where I want to be able to walk in my own footsteps. You have decided that there one should do this and there one should do that.' An elderly man continued; 'I would like to support these arguments. If you want to be on your own and philosophize, you go to Gyllin's.'

Another man raised the question of picking elderflowers and forsythia in the garden – would this be allowed in the future as well? The response was that in general such activities are not tolerated in parks, but the project team do realize that this is a quality of Gyllin's, and perhaps it could be allowed in one part of the garden in the future as well. 'Only, how are we going to arrange this for 2,000 visitors?' The challenge of adjusting the place for much more intensive use was emphasized several times by the representatives of the municipality.

The heated feelings were partly provoked by the use of maps and drawings, whereas photos of other places aiming to spur a discussion about the future use of the site were met with positive comments. The landscape architects were struck by what they saw as a sudden shift in attitude: first, the users were afraid that the site would lose its essential qualities, then suddenly they welcomed ideas of a café, art exhibitions, farmers' market, etc. I would argue for another interpretation, which reconciles these apparently contradictory audience reactions. No-one at the meeting argued for the protection of a *particular* site, or opposed a particular label; rather, it was the spatial representation and labelling *as such* that evoked protests. Furthermore, the philosophical or existential comments at the meeting illustrate that the lure of the wild character of Gyllin's relates to its qualities as a 'loose space', i.e. a place that is open for personal interpretations as much as for personal itineraries and actions (see Franck and Stevens 2007). With such an attitude, it is no surprise that new activities are welcome, whereas schemes designating the use of particular areas of the site are regarded as intrusions, threatening the wild and its openness to new interpretations.

FRAMING THE GARDEN

The spatial outline of the nature-park is based on an investigation by a consultant landscape architect in 2008 (Malmö stad 2008). In the report, the main idea for the design is expressed in the following way:

> Refine the spatial structure and utilize the landscape-architectonic qualities! The place should offer vast open spaces as well as large closed volumes. Additionally, small open rooms and small closed volumes…

(Malmö stad 2008: 10)

Throughout the report, abstract language governs the analysis and the proposals. The concepts used are conventional within landscape architecture, with *room* (or enclosure) a key term. The metaphor is based on a visual analysis of topography and vegetation, which facilitates an interpretation of outdoor environments in terms of rooms (which are classified as open or closed, etc.). Once the metaphor has been accepted, *edges* (walls) and *entrances* are easily added to the analysis and design. Next, *sequences* and *rhythm*, *hierarchies*, *contrasts* and sense of *direction* can be introduced. However, such a visual analysis emphasizes abstract space in a similar way to cartographic representations, and in combination with maps and drawings, it easily reduces an ambivalent place into discrete spaces and seamless relations into clearly defined objects (Söderström 1996; Qviström 2007; Ingold 2008).

The difference between abstract space (with boundaries, labels and directions) and the wild character of Gyllin's can be interpreted with the help of Ingold (2007). Exploring the concept of dwelling, he raises the question of what it means to be an *in*habitant of the world rather than an *ex*habitant, living *on* the world. The modern distinction between ground and earth, he argues, makes it difficult to conceptualize *in*habitation. In real life we do not encounter such divides:

> [A]nyone who has walked through the boreal forest in summer knows that the 'ground' is not really a coherent surface at all but a more or less impenetrable mass of tangled undergrowth, leaf litter and detritus, mosses and lichens, stones and boulders, split by cracks and crevasses, threaded by tree roots, and interspersed with swamps and marshes over-grown with rafts of vegetation that are liable to give way underfoot. Somewhere beneath it all is solid rock, and somewhere above the clear sky, but it is in this intermediate zone that life is lived, at depths depending upon the scale of the creature and its capacity to penetrate an environment that is ever more tightly packed.

(Ingold 2007: 33)

Ingold illustrates the absence of boundaries, not only between ground and earth, but between the forest and its inhabitants, or, more importantly, between humans and nature. In a similar way, the ground, edges and paths of Gyllin's Garden have seamless relationships to their surroundings, offering interfaces open for new interpretations. Like many other industrial ruins (for example Edensor 2005: 42ff), Gyllin's Garden transcends the orderly categories and concepts of a modern society, with the vague traces of a former order emphasizing this feeling.

The concepts in the design programme are not simply used analytically, but are *materialized* in the design; they are, so to say, added to the place. Whereas the former fields of Gyllin's had no definite boundaries between grass, bushes, clumps of trees and fringes, the recent introduction of the lawnmower (in one part of the garden) not only created a 'floor', but also made the edges of the 'room' visible. However delicate a transformation, it illustrates the domestication of the wild through the introduction of a spatial framework, echoing well-known guidelines within landscape design as well as a cartographic way of seeing. The discussion at the public meeting was concerned with the furniture of the garden, such as the introduction of benches, but no mention was made of the general furnishings shown in the plan, such as rooms, walls, solitary trees, and clearly defined entrances and paths.

The intricate web of paths in the garden holds the key to understanding its character. The history and nature of the paths differ, with the widest and straightest being remnants of old dirt roads. Other paths are temporal and individual, for instance trails made into the thorny bushes when picking berries. The paths of children playing in the forest seem to be even more ephemeral, since they are constantly searching for new ways instead of treading the old ones. Other routes have been established by people in the neighbourhood, who cut back the vegetation to keep the path alive. Being able to tread one's own path is part of the basic experience of the place. Ingold argues:

> Literally, an environment is that which surrounds. For inhabitants, however, the environment does not consist of the surroundings of a bounded place but of a zone in which their pathways are thoroughly entangled. In this zone of entanglement – this meshwork of interwoven lines – there are no insides or outsides, only openings and ways through. An ecology of life, in short, must be one of threads and traces...
>
> (Ingold 2008: 103)

The municipal plan offers another perspective on the paths, stating: 'The system of paths should have a clear hierarchy: it should be obvious how adventurous one wants to be when choosing a path' (Malmö stad 2008: 14). In the document, the *historical* and *temporal* differences are turned into *spatial* categories. Furthermore, according to the report a path has to be chosen, not trodden, let alone managed or redirected. With the spatial and a-historical representations, the users are transformed from inhabitants to exhabitants.

ANOTHER WALK

On a chilly day in May, about 60 people gathered in Gyllin's Garden for a walk with the municipal planners. 'Plans have been made', the landscape architect began, 'but now we would like to take a step back in the process, in order to let you in. We would like to make space for your notions of your favourite places. Please...', she waved a large map of the area, 'mark your favourite places on the maps which have been handed out, and try to describe their character'. I accompanied the crowd on the walk, the route for which has been decided in advance, with the landscape architect as guide, only to meet a third lady who used to bring her pair of secateurs to the garden in order to manage her paths.

At the meeting and during the walk, the development of the garden was referred to as a slow process with no final date. In the interview with the two landscape architects, they argued that the public meetings have made them even more convinced of the necessity for slow development of the area, with no final date when the design should be finalized. They believed the ideal outcome would be if the users formed an organization ('Friends of Gyllin's', perhaps), with which the municipal authority could communicate. In some respects, such an organization could even take on the responsibility for some of the activities in the garden. One of the most important lessons learned so far, according to one of the landscape architects, is that

> there is so much engagement and love for this place: if only we could, like, work together with it [sic], and get together in order to improve the communication between us, it would be at least as important as the actual design of [for instance] this little entrance area, right?

Even though the public walk was combined with an ambition to map the garden, it could offer a seed for another way of thinking, beyond the spatial framing. With the current emphasis on the open process and public involvement, it could even be argued that the management is at a crossroads, with two possible ways forward, as discussed below.

CONCLUSION

Like many other wildscapes, Gyllin's Garden is important not only for everyday life and the maintenance of urban biodiversity, but also for the cultural heritage of Malmö city. The recognition of the informal use and green values of Gyllin's Garden as a nature-park, 'culture recaptured and run wild' as the report from 2001 has it, defies the nature–culture divide and will hopefully inspire planners elsewhere (Malmö stadsbyggnadskontor 2001). Ironically, the municipal authority played a major role in the initial phase of the wildscape as well, since municipal planning (in a bid for land ownership) contributed to the bankruptcy of the company, which in turn was the starting point for establishment of the nature-park.

Despite the promising ambitions in 2001, the current process illustrates the difficulties in handling the qualities of urban wilderness in the urbanization process. There are two diverging options for the future development of the garden. On the one hand, abstract space manifested in representations, professionalism (i.e. the language of landscape architects), administrative divides (including for instance allocation of funds for management), maps and legal documents threaten to order, label and furnish the garden. This is described by Qviström (2007) as the taming of the disordered fringe into an ordered city within modern planning. This process threatens to recreate the divides between nature and culture which the ruin and everyday use of the place managed to break down. On the other hand, the open process promises a close dialogue with the users and a slow transformation where the process is more important than the plan. Whereas formal documents, maps and drawings fail to recognize the ambiguity of the place and the assets of disorderliness, such qualities could probably be dealt with in an open and continuing dialogue with the users. This tension, between a design emphasizing abstract space, containment and furnishing, and generic development of the place, characterize the project of today. However, in order to fully capture the qualities of an urban wilderness, it needs to be understood *historically*, as a generative process, rather than *spatially*. If only the planners could step into the paths of the users, and follow the story lines of the place as a base for the design, the inhabited natureculture of the garden could be partly preserved and work as a model for other projects.

A historical investigation could further encourage such an understanding of the site as a process. In the case of Gyllin's Garden, a historical analysis would probably reveal the importance of the everyday management of the place, which contradicts the current historiography that the garden has been 'untouched' and 'abandoned' for decades (Malmö stad 2008). The latter description emphasizes the naturalization rather than the inhabitation of the place, opening the way for further scientific arguments and investigations concerning the garden as *nature* (cf. Asikainen and Jokinen 2009).

Furthermore, a historical study would reveal that Gyllin's Garden is a ruin of a garden industry, which is an entirely different thing from an ordinary garden (or a romantic old-fashioned garden shop). In addition, the phase as a ruin has been as long as the industrial phase and its history needs to be acknowledged on its own; gathering fruit, picking flowers or even digging up plants have been frequent activities in the area. In a way, the ruin has more to do with small-scale gardening than Knut Gyllin ever had. Even so, Gyllin's Garden should not be regarded a garden, or as a park or nature. It is a living ruin and it needs to be treated as such; what needs to be developed is a way to garden an industrial heritage.

Due to urban development, adjustments to Gyllin's Garden are inevitable. The more visitors, the greater the need for conventional management, so the hybrid character is likely to fade eventually. However, the success in acknowledging an urban wilderness can be measured in another way; even if ephemeral or transitory, in the process of integrating its assets and qualities in the city, such urban

wildernesses can transform the idea of urban nature. In the process of urbanization, new concepts could be brought into the legal and administrative frameworks,
and new management regimes could be developed. If a concept such as nature-
park were to be brought into the legal realm of detailed development plans due to
Gyllin's garden, the project would have made a contribution to urban nature
beyond the actual site at a national level. If every project on urban wilderness
showed as much interest in transforming administrative divides as in issues regard-
ing design and management, urban nature would soon start to change.

REFERENCES

The archive of Malmö stads fastighetsnämnd (Malmö municipal real estate office): protocols
1979, photographs.
The archive of Malmö tingsrätt (the district court): diary of bankruptcies 1975, bankruptcy
files 1975.

Asikainen, E. and Jokinen, A. (2009) 'Future natures in the making: implementing biodiversity
in suburban land-use planning', *Planning Theory and Practice*, 10: 351–368.
Bengtsson, N. (2007) 'Impopulär rosodlare förslås få egen gata', *Expressen*, 4 July.
Edensor, T. (2005) *Industrial Ruins: Space, Aesthetics and Materiality*, Oxford: Berg.
Franck, K. and Stevens, Q. (eds) (2007) *Loose Space, Possibility and Diversity in Urban Life*,
New York: Routledge.
Ingold, T. (2007) 'Earth, sky, wind and weather', *Journal of the Royal Anthropological
Institute*, 13: S19–S38.
—— (2008) *Lines: A Brief History*. London: Routledge.
Malmö stad (2008) *Program för naturpark Gyllins trädgård*.
—— (2010a) *Samrådshandling tillhörande detaljplan för del av Gyllins trädgård(naturparken)
i Husie i Malmö*.
—— (2010b) Online: www.malmo.se/gyllinsnaturpark (accessed 24 May 2010).
Malmö stadsarkiv (The City Archive of Malmö).
Malmö stadsbyggnadskontor (2001) *Program för detaljplan för Gyllins trädgård*, Husie
172:123 m.fl., i Husie och Sallerup, Malmö, Skåne län.
Qviström, M. (2007) 'Landscapes out of order: studying the inner urban fringe beyond the
rural – urban divide', *Geografiska annaler series*, 89B: 269–282.
—— (2009) 'Nära på stad: framtidsdrömmar och mellanrum i stadens utkant', in
K. Saltzman (ed.) *Mellanrummens möjligheter: studier av stadens efemära
landskap*, Göteborg: Makadam.
Qviström, M. and Saltzman, K. (2006) 'Exploring landscape dynamics at the edge of the
city: spatial plans and everyday places at the inner urban fringe of Malmö,
Sweden', *Landscape Research*, 31: 21–41.
Rink, D. (2009) 'Wilderness: the nature of urban shrinkage? The debate on urban
restructuring and restoration in eastern Germany', *Nature and Culture*, 4:
275–292.
Shoard, M. (2000) 'Edgelands of promise', *Landscapes*, 2: 74–93.
Söderström, O. (1996) 'Paper cities: visual thinking in urban planning', *Ecumene*, 3: 249–281.
Stadsfullmäktige i Malmö (1965) *Protokoll med bihang*.
—— (1974) *Protokoll med bihang*.
—— (1978) *Protokoll med bihang*.
Vikberg, J. (2003) 'Han började på torgen och slutade som godsägare', *Skånska dagbladet*,
10 November.

Chapter 15: Disordering public space

Urban wildscape processes in practice

Dougal Sheridan

INTRODUCTION

'Urban wildscape' both as a term and landscape condition can potentially appropriate many of the spaces described by a host of names in urban design and architectural discourse, including badlands, brownfields, derelict areas, no man's lands; and the characteristics of these areas can be as diverse as the terminology that attempts to define them. In previous studies I have found it useful to understand them as any area, space, or building where the city's normal forces of control have not shaped how we perceive, use, and occupy them (Sheridan 2007: 98). This is an interpretation of urban wildscapes that concentrates on the social and cultural dimensions of these spaces and their significance to cities and the public realm. These wildscapes have a set of social processes and dynamics, which metaphorically parallel the environmental processes occurring there. They become places in which particular activities, events, initiatives, and subcultures are able to take hold and develop.

The unique qualities of these spaces are increasingly recognized for their environmental, social, and cultural value. The fact that they have emerged outside official urban development mechanisms raises the question of whether practice can learn from such spaces and the processes at work in them. Can these qualities and processes inform not only how we preserve and intervene in existing wildscapes, but also how we operate within the normal mechanisms of practice and approach the making of places generally?

To investigate this question I would firstly like to revisit some previous research investigating these spaces in the specific historical, cultural, and sociological context of Berlin, where the existence of such indeterminate territories has significantly affected the cultural life of the city. This will allow us to establish, analyze, and abstract the underlying processes and properties of these spaces and to understand how they are dealt with in local development and regulatory frameworks. I would then like to explore how these processes and properties can be transposed onto the production of space through the mechanism of conventional practice by landscape architects, architects and urban designers. I propose to do this by examining three projects through the lens of these processes and properties. Although the projects have evolved out of our work as architectural and urban design practitioners, they have been informed both intuitively and self-consciously by the formative experiences of the diverse and innovative appropriation of urban wildscapes.[1]

THE BERLIN CONDITION

In Berlin, urban wildscapes have been a pervasive condition due to significant historical forces beyond the usual processes of spatial obsolescence resulting from post-industrialization. Wartime destruction, the succession of fascist, communist, and capitalist regimes and ideologies, and both the erection of the wall in 1961, and its removal in 1989, have produced spatial gaps within the city as well as gaps within the city's regulatory forces. The resulting indeterminate territories have taken the form of empty or abandoned buildings and vacant terrains, which have been occupied and appropriated in the absence of the deterministic forces of capital, ownership and institutionalization which, to a large degree, govern people's relationship to the built environment. In particular, in the vacuum of control and responsibility in East Berlin following the removal of the wall, all kinds of self-generated activities and projects sprang up as 'the alternative scene' shifted from the west to the eastern side of the city. These activities and projects have been described as a 'dense network of subcultures and alternative practices, encompassing around 200,000 people' (Katz and Mayer 1983: 37).

Abandoned buildings offered the potential for reuse and adaptation in ways limited only by the structures themselves and the means and imagination of the occupier. Frequently, a building's potential permeability was exploited in contrast to the cellular separation of tenancies and territories characteristic of conventional building occupancy. These situations offered the opportunity for new uses and forms of living not possible within the normal tenancy subdivisions. This enabled the easy insertion of many self-initiated programs including theatres, cinema, venues, galleries, cafés, clubs, and community spaces, with the result that these locations took on public, cultural, and political roles.

Vacant sites were settled by mobile and temporary structures and were used for various transient activities including markets, circuses, outdoor theatres, parties, and even farming. Their occupants ranged widely in nature from the 'homeless' to utopian semi-agrarian communities playing public roles as providers of places of entertainment and carnival. The large open spaces remaining where the Berlin Wall had been, allowed many of these *Wagendorfer* – literally 'wagon villages' – to be centrally located on highly prominent sites. With the Reichstag or other Berlin institutions as a backdrop, these surreal landscapes appeared to critique conventional monumentality and static urban architecture by visually confronting them with open, un-institutionalized and implied nomadic space (Figure 15.1).

Indeterminacy provides a space for the self-determination of the occupant and allows them a less mediated and more direct relationship with the specific

Figure 15.1
Wagendorf and farm
animals with the
Reichstag in the
background
(photograph: Dougal
Sheridan, 1995)

qualities of a place. A study of how subcultural groups are exploiting the spatial opportunities offered by these spaces, in a *Besetztes Haus*,[2] revealed fluid and changing patterns of usage compared to the stratified and permanent division of space found in regulated urban environments (Sheridan 2007: 112) (Figure 15.2). The tasks of repairing and intervening in these spaces also necessitate a large degree of collective action and decision-making. Because the division and distribution of space and facilities are not predetermined, normal assumptions about spatial organization and use may well be questioned and alternatives developed. Such situations allow the occupant to interact with the built fabric as though it were a landscape that is settled rather than a structure where the rules of occupancy are pervasive. The absence of those conditions that usually predetermine our perception of such places makes our encounter with their specific qualities all the more intense. For example, a canal bank is used for floating structures, existing waste vegetation becomes a garden, a roofless ruin becomes a terrace, an industrial shed a covered market, and a bank vault a club. Observations made in the case study of this increased mutual influence between the urban fabric and those occupying it revealed the formative effects of these indeterminate territories on subcultures (Sheridan 2007:117). These urban wildscapes simultaneously contain traces of the past, reveal the processes of change occurring there, and imply alternative concepts and utopian futures in their open-ended appropriation.

The occupation and reinvention of disused or indeterminate areas of Berlin has recently been termed the activity of 'urban pioneers' and recognized and championed by Berlin's Department of City Development (Senatsverwaltung für Stadtentwicklung Berlin) in its publication of the same name (2007). The shift in position from youth cultures/subcultures at loggerheads with the municipal authorities, to their legitimization as 'urban pioneers' has paralleled realization of

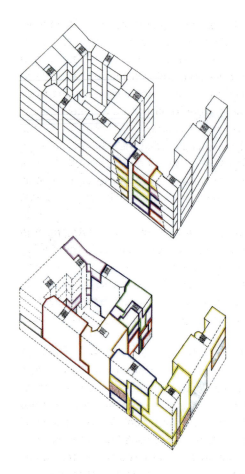

the pragmatic potentials such modes of urban activism have for the city's economic and cultural development; namely, the benefits for property owners in relation to re-activating vacant and abandoned buildings and properties, and secondly, the opportunity to incorporate the creative work occurring in these spaces into the capitalization process as 'creative industries'. The sociological interpretation of such a 'culturepreneur' is 'an urban protagonist who possesses the ability to mediate between and interpret the areas of culture and of service provision', who 'closes gaps in the urban with new social, entrepreneurial and spatial practices' (Lange 2006: 145,146).

Such perceptions romanticize the image of a 'self-reliant, pioneer-like entrepreneurship in the adventure playground of the city' (Lange 2006: 151). Continuing the adventure playground analogy of a non-risk-averse attitude to urban wildscapes, the financial and operational risks of culturepreneurs are not seen as existential threats, but instead as opportunities for innovation and for developing personal knowledge and skills for future ventures.

Indeterminate spaces in Berlin have become breeding grounds for new forms of art, music, and pop culture, as well as for technological inventions or

Figure 15.2
Case Study of a *Besetztes Haus* (a squatted house), Brunnenstrasse 6 and 7, Berlin, 1995 – comparison of the spatial arrangement to the conventional occupancy arrangement of a similar courtyard building. Areas are colour coded to indicate different occupant groups; and appropriation of courtyard space (Sheridan 2007:116)

start-ups. These spaces give financially weak protagonists the possibility to grow in an unrestricted but unsubsidized environment and become active participants in the shaping of their city (Misselwitz *et al.* 2003: 2). Traditional planning and market-driven development models have been criticized for both a failure to deal with the boom and gentrification that leads to social exclusion and to an increasingly divided urban society, and failure to adapt to the context of economic collapse that leads to urban stagnation and neglect (Studio Urban Catalyst 2003). Research in this context has proposed that the informal modes of urbanism evident in Berlin offer alternative models of development that find a way between these two extremes, and provide an opportunity to critically examine and question existing planning procedures (Studio Urban Catalyst 2003).

This discourse has led the Senate Department of Urban Development in Berlin to recognize the importance of temporary use, commissioning a study focusing on the 'informal' actors leading the process of informal urbanism, *Raumpioniere (Land Pioneers of Berlin)* (2004). Subsequently, the term *Zwischennutzung* (interim use) has been introduced into the German planning system and a dedicated Agency for the Temporary Use of Property has been established.

Although outside the scope of this study, the significant change in outlook and policy by the Berlin and German national development authorities, could inform how these urban wildscapes are approached in the regulatory contexts of other countries. For example, German federal building legislation was reformed in 2004 to allow 'Planning Permission for a Limited Period', facilitating approval of projects on temporary or conditional terms, and Berlin's Building Regulations were revised in 2005 to reduce the number of mandatory state inspections and licensing procedures and to increase the type of works that do not require planning permission (Senatsverwaltung für Stadtentwicklung Berlin 2007: 163). In addition, new municipal tools have been developed to allow local authorities to facilitate this new mode of informal urbanism. These include Temporary Use and Relinquishment Contracts, which hand over sites to temporary users free of charge subject to Maintenance Contracts; and Urban Development Contracts from district councils, which allow a more flexible approach to planning permission, licences, and the exemption of rates (Senatsverwaltung für Stadtentwicklung Berlin 2007: 160).

PROCESSES AND PROPERTIES OF URBAN WILDSCAPES

The processes and properties summarized below are conditions observed at play in the urban wildscapes of Berlin. In these studies I have interpreted 'urban wildscapes' or indeterminate territories to include not only vacant or un-built areas but also, where relevant, built structures. Understanding these areas as landscapes is useful because of the social, performative, changing, and 'found' nature of these spaces. It is these landscape conceptions of time, change, and experiential and performative potentials, rather than the more formal ideas of composition and permanence often associated with Architecture and Urban Design, that are the basis of the strategies described below.

Registration of change

Urban wildscapes allow an unmediated experience of the physical traces of the past that they often contain. These traces or fragments, including structures, surfaces, industrial artefacts, landforms, and vegetation, are not maintained in a fixed condition, either physically or representationally, or interpreted from a fixed perspective. Urban wildscapes are in a state of flux (growing, weathering, transforming, etc.) as are the forms of human appropriation they host, and these changes and processes of transformation are by their nature clearly legible. The juxtaposition of past and present layers of occupation are not framed or presented but are discoverable in raw form. This is because these spaces exist outside the frame of urban identity, which usually presents an image of historical continuity, and thus they are not presented as being complete from a fixed perspective and point in time: by existing as gaps or cracks in the hegemonic forces of the city, these indeterminate spaces escape the processes of identification and incorporation that tend to locate objects, events, and our understanding of them within the dominant structures of the present (Sheridan 2007: 108). The encounter with this underlying condition, rather than their picturesque form, is the potential of such ruins.

Indeterminacy and ambiguity

Lack of classification and identification leaves a space of interpretation and ambiguity, which is integral to artistic practice and stimulation of the intellect. Indeterminate spaces ask questions rather than deliver fixed answers, and allow a space for the subjectivity, appropriation, development, adaptation, and expression of those occupying these indeterminate environments. The spatial ambiguities of wildscapes – inside or outside, public or private, building or landscape – create stimulating environments that encourage appropriation. However, ambiguity in the normative professional and regulatory processes of producing the built environment (planning applications, building control, health and safety) is generally incompatible with the dictates of classification and compliance on which these frameworks are based.

Temporal and temporary interventions: architecture on probation

Incremental and temporary strategies allow structures, uses, and interventions to occur outside the more stringent regulatory requirements of permanent architectural and urban design projects. Temporary structures and uses are reversible, in contrast to many planning and development strategies that assume permanence, and do not allow for removing or revising an unsuccessful development. Indeed, our cities are left with the legacy of planning and development decisions, which from their moment of completion are recognized as being misjudged.

Incremental growth and development in urban terms closely mirrors the organic process perceivable in urban wildscapes, allowing uses and programmes to evolve through experiment and 'probation'.

Mobility: roving subjectivities

A temporal approach may also necessitate a strategy of mobility. As the conditions or opportunities in a context expire or change, the activities and inhabitants that have flourished there will in some cases migrate to a new location of opportunity. Mobile subjectivities, by their nature tend to be highly adaptive and capable of reconfiguration to suit new environments. Mobile strategies also allow the creation of spaces, places, and programs while avoiding the rigid regulatory frameworks of fixed architecture and building code that may not be applicable or enforceable in such instances. Berlin's Development Authorities recognize such structures as *Fliegende Bauten* or 'Flying Buildings', which can be granted licences for up to five years.

Quality of incompleteness

Related to both temporal and transient approaches to spaces is the perception that they have not reached a final state of completion. This open-ended approach allows projects and spaces to grow and evolve over time. It also implies that there is space for further participation and contribution, and therefore the project remains alive. In practice this may involve dividing the implementation of projects up into incremental steps, so that interventions can be tested and subsequent steps can adapt and evolve in response to the success or failure of earlier interventions.

Performative properties

The unmediated relationship to the specific potentials and physical attributes of wildscapes results in them being understood and utilized in a highly performative manner. In comparison, more regulated conventional spaces come with a pervasive set of assumptions and expectations that often predetermine and in this way limit usage, often in favour of organizational and visual order.

Participatory processes

It is evident from examples like Berlin, that it is often self-initiated projects and activities that emerge out of the space and opportunities offered by wildscapes. Such bottom-up interventions, driven as they are by local communities and protagonists will involve the social processes of negotiation and participation. Such projects are usually interventions into existing spaces or structures with distinctive qualities and potentials and therefore require consideration and discussion of how to intervene. In contrast *tabula rasa* approaches to sites and contexts are not conducive to dialogue.

Diversity

Successful participatory processes result in the interests, expression, or activities of multiple groups being retained within a project. The structures documented in the Berlin *Besetztes Haus* case study (1995) contained 14 different (sub-)cultural groups, and 11 different shared, semi-public, or public programs (Sheridan 2007: 112). A more recent case study of the 65 temporary uses unofficially residing on the land of Berlin's former *Reichsbahnausbesserungswerk* (National Railroad repair factory) or 'RAW-site' concluded that 'the strong social and cultural inclusiveness demonstrated on the RAW-site has provided space for the co-existence of multiple and diverse activities and encounters' (Zagami 2009: 11, 21).

INFORMING PRACTICE

The following projects have presented opportunities to explore how these properties and processes can inform practice at three different levels of intervention in the public realm, ranging from strategies of minimal intervention in an existing 'urban wildscape', through alternative regeneration processes for a city park, to the design of a public square within the conventional procurement apparatus.

Portable Art Space: urban camping

The Portable Art Space has been completed as part of a 'Regenerate' arts programme for the Craigavon area in Northern Ireland. It involved artists using a wide range of art forms to engage with diverse groups of people to tackle local social, community, and environmental issues across a wide geographic area.[3] Spanning five borough councils Craigavon was planned and constructed as a 'New City' in the 1960s. It is similar in concept to Milton Keynes in England and was conceived as a linear city linking the adjacent towns of Lurgan and Portadown to create a single urban area and identity. It was planned with an almost complete separation of motor vehicles, pedestrians, and cyclists, and implemented under a single use zoning strategy separating commercial, civic, and residential functions into mono-use zones amid a landscape of roundabouts and oversized road infrastructure.

Sub-standard and untested building techniques and the closure of local industry resulted in approximately 50 per cent of what was planned not being built, and large swathes of what was constructed being vacated and falling into dereliction. In some cases, the urban fabric has been demolished, leaving only a residue of foundations and forlorn street lighting along the empty suburban streets. This deserted infrastructure has been re-claimed by vegetation and wildlife, and in some cases re-inhabited in a more transient manner by the Travelling Community who have been able to utilize the existing infrastructure with their mobile homes and vehicles.

A desire to engage with the qualities and social reality of this context, and to facilitate the work of artists across this broad and varied landscape were the driving conceptual parameters of the Portable Art Space. As we have seen, the quality of these wildscapes and how they are perceived and experienced results largely from their unmediated, unmanaged, and autonomous position within the city's spatial and regulatory structures. However, as we have also seen in the literature and case studies, some degree of intervention is often needed to sustain and make these spaces accessible.

In the Portable Art Space project we explored a strategy of intervention into such spaces without disrupting the specific qualities and 'wildness' of the spaces themselves. This approach of non-threatening or minimal interventions into existing environments is synonymous with the desire to engage with social contexts in a non-imposing, uninstitutionalized manner. Two differing strategies were simultaneously adopted (Figure 15.3).

First was the creation of a mobile object that would provide the minimum temporary infrastructure required to accommodate an artist (or other agent) and to facilitate their engagement with the context of their location. The Art Space was designed to be highly distinctive and visually autonomous so that it quite clearly does not belong specifically to the spaces it occupies and therefore inversely the spaces it occupies do not belong to it. It clearly registers the change it makes as a new element co-existing with the diversity of the existing context without disrupting the incompleteness and sense of freedom of the location it temporarily occupies.

Secondly, the Art Space was designed with a built-in capacity to adapt to its context, which is a condition of successful nomadic subjectivities. Exterior walls flip up to form shelter, and inner walls pivot to extend out into the surroundings. These pivoting walls act physically, extending into the surrounding context, and visually, by orienting the occupant's field of view and drawing their gaze outwards to the surrounding landscape. These walls, in addition to offering spatial enclosure, shelter the adjacent outdoor space, allowing it to be used as a gathering space for discussions, talks, performances, or film. The wall surfaces can also be used for digital projections and hanging artwork. A ramp folds down to connect the floor surface of the Art Space with the surrounding ground plane.

The moveable adaptive elements of the flip-up roofs, pivoting walls, and fold-down ramp provide a series of different configurations that allow the mobile art space to tune itself to its context and its performative role in that context. In many cases this role is to enable dialogue and participatory processes relating to the context it occupies within a neutral but facilitating environment. This ranges from completely open to its more enclosed configurations suitable for hosting meetings and workshops in a heated, serviced, comfortable interior environment. The mobile nature of the space allows it to travel into highly specific and varied social, urban, and landscape contexts. This enables direct engagement between artist and context and provides a studio/workspace for this work 'on location'.

Woodvale HUB: negotiating the social topography

Negotiation and participation are social processes that define the self-initiated projects and activities that emerge out of the space and opportunities offered by

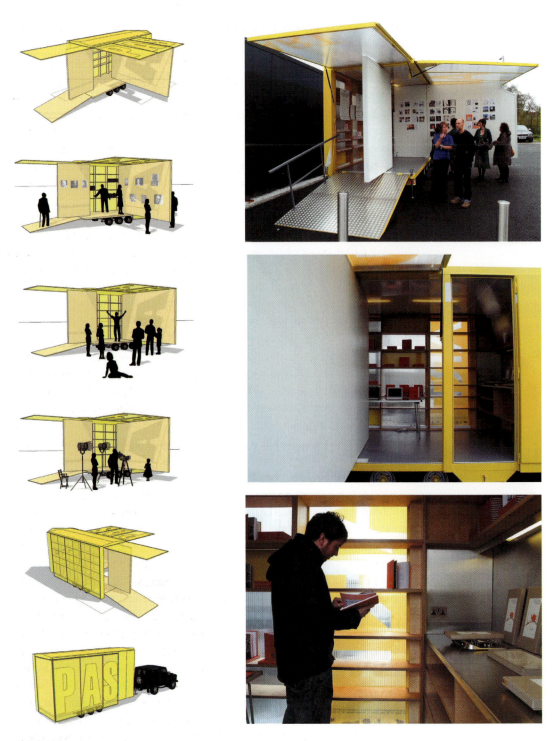

Figure 15.3
Portable Art Space: design-stage images showing different configurations and uses; launch of the Portable Art Space, April 2010, Craigavon (images: Deirdre McMenamin, Dougal Sheridan, Sarah Allen, Ryan Ward – LiD Architecture)

urban wildscapes. Although the context of this project was an existing park rather than an indeterminate urban landscape, the 'bottom-up' initiative of people wishing to reuse and re-imagine this space, the participatory processes of realizing a project of this nature, and the questions of managing and negotiating people's expectations of possible and compatible activities for an urban landscape without over-restricting the park's pattern of usage, are all issues relevant to this theme.

In our capacity as members of 'Building Initiative'[4] we were approached directly by a citizens' group wishing to initiate a project and to improve a local under-utilized and negatively perceived public space, Woodvale Park, which is located in the socially and economically deprived area of the Upper Shankill in west Belfast. The lack of action from the City Council's Parks Department, despite ongoing campaigning and lobbying by local residents, located proposals to intervene in the park within the realm of citizen-led initiatives. This raised the question of how it was possible as practitioners to act as agents of this alternative action outside the institutional and developer-driven mechanisms that often shape the public spaces of cities like Belfast.

Local residents described their wish to improve a corner of the park in order to 'make the park equally welcoming to users including those traditionally at odds (for example, young adults and pensioners, racial minorities and long-term white residents, etc.) all of whom feel a sense of "ownership" of the place'. This area of the park contained an abandoned cinder football pitch and surrounding trees and undergrowth that were being informally appropriated by young people, and had some of the properties and perceptions associated with urban wildscapes in the form of less restricted activities including riding dirt motorcycles, hitting golf balls, drinking alcohol, hanging out after nightfall, and minor vandalism to physical structures and vegetation.

The polarized thinking that grew out of the civil conflict in Northern Ireland is reflected in equally polarized perceptions of acceptable and unacceptable behaviour in the public realm. For example, young people gathering and socializing in the park is readily categorized as 'anti-social behaviour'. It was hoped that questioning and discussing these perceptions with all parties and age groups could lead to less predetermined ideas of public space, where acceptable behaviour could be negotiated in the context of each situation. To build consensus, confidence, and capacity within this fragmented social context it was necessary to establish and facilitate a forum of discussion and negotiation with local residents including young people, city authorities, local business, and other stakeholders. This involved establishing a program of workshops and events, and developing a number of methodologies and tools in support of these. These included running the project as a student design project, making temporary site interventions and performances in the park, engaging television media, developing a board game and interactive mobile exhibition model, and publishing several issues of a locally-distributed newspaper about the project (Sheridan 2009: 157–161) (Figure 15.4).

Figure 15.4
Woodvale HUB: methods and strategies developed to facilitate the participatory design process, including (a) Board Game, where pieces represented different conditions and functions ranging from landscape surfaces to buildings, each with corresponding construction and maintenance costs, thus allowing participants to prioritize proposals against different budget scenarios; (b) *Yellow Press* newspaper, each issue of which had a print run of 10,000 and proved invaluable in disseminating information about the project to the local and wider population; and (c) Mobile Interactive Model – used for workshops and discussion as well as for exhibition in various venues throughout the locality (images: Deirdre McMenamin, Dougal Sheridan, Sarah Allen, Ryan Ward – LiD Architecture)

The micro-politics of this participatory process, of engaging the social, cultural, and economic spheres that form public space were reflected in the eventual outcome. The proposal that emerged was called the 'Plug-in-Path', a strategy that allows these spheres to overlap and reconfigure themselves according to changing needs. The Plug-in-Path would provide a new route connecting the park with the adjacent shopping centre, increasing the movement of people through this cut-off corner of the park and thereby improving the feeling of safety. The performative properties of this path were emphasized in its role as programmed surface containing lighting, tiered seating, electricity, and water supplies. Events organizers and participants could 'plug in' to these services to support activities like outdoor cinema, concerts, markets, and festivals.

Therefore, rather than a formal architectural proposal, the outcome was a temporal strategy to allow the incremental development of a set of programmes, which had been identified, negotiated, located, and set in an order of priority. In this way the evident diversity that had emerged during the participation process came to be reflected in the proposal. The diverse elements included community gardens, a kiosk that could move between different locations on the path, a large translucent roof over the tiered seating area that would create a space where young people could gather, and where outdoor cinema and performance could occur. This area would also overlook a multi-purpose games area which could be added next, followed by a semi-enclosed toddlers' play space and finally a pavilion containing flexible gathering and meeting spaces (Figure 15.5).

This strategic programmatic staging plan could adapt and reconfigure itself around the organizing principle of the Plug-in-Path, which would be the unifying surface, shared by all age groups and park users. This incremental strategy was also a response to the likelihood that funding would need to be sought from different sources for the various programmatic elements, and would therefore become available at different times. In addition, this strategy of incompleteness allows trust in the project to develop gradually and for it to adapt and respond to changing social·dynamics. For example, the first step is likely to be the community garden with an integrated art project developed by an artist who participated in the workshop process.[5] The proposal is to construct scarecrows to protect the community garden with local young people, based on images of themselves. In this role reversal, those perceived to be the source of vandalism would become the symbolic guardians of the gardens.

Although the participants had originally proposed a 'building' containing facilities that would aim to address the park's inadequacies and social problems, it clearly emerged through the process that a landscape strategy was more appropriate and could 'activate the space without the weighty apparatus of traditional space-making' (Allen 2001: 37). The decision to work with the condition of uncertainty rather than resisting it resulted in a strategy of deliberate programmatic indeterminacy, allowing the proposal to respond to temporal change, transformation and adaptation.

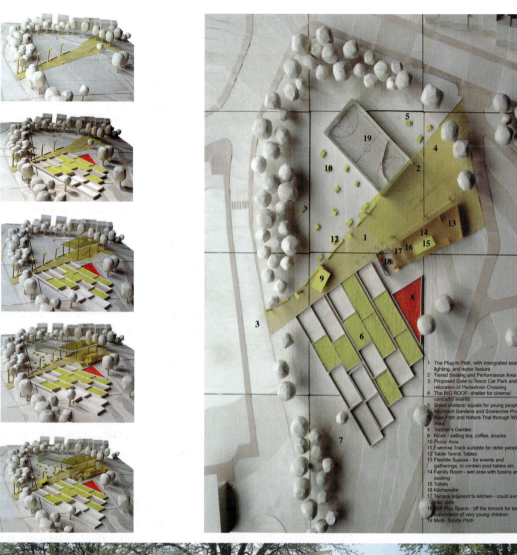

1 The Plug-In Path, with intergrated seating, lighting, and water feature
2 Tiered Seating and Performance Area
3 Proposed Gate to Tesco Car Park and relocation of Pedestrian Crossing
4 The BIG ROOF- shelter for cinema/ concerts/ events
5 Small shelters/ squats for young people
6 Allotment Gardens and Scarecrow Project
7 New Path and Nature Trail through Wild Area
8 Toddler's Garden
9 Kiosk - selling tea, coffee, snacks
10 Picnic Area
11 Exercise Track suitable for older people
12 Table-Tennis Tables
13 Flexible Spaces - for events and gatherings, to contain pool tables etc.
14 Family Room - wet area with basins and seating
15 Toilets
16 Kitchenette
17 Terrace adjacent to kitchen - could evolve into cafe
18 Soft Play Space - off the terrace for easy supervision of very young children
19 Multi- Sports Pitch

Figure 15.5
Woodvale HUB: plan view of model showing the temporal design strategy proposed, called the Plug-in-Path; the incremental 'plugging-in' of different programmes over time; and view of the path showing diversity of uses and users (images: Deirdre McMenamin, Dougal Sheridan, Sarah Allen, Ryan Ward – LiD Architecture)

Dublin Parlour: post-boom wasteland

This project deals with the conditions created by the recent economic crisis, particularly extreme in Ireland, which has seen valuable real estate and development sites transform into un-lettable, un-marketable empty buildings and unviable, incomplete construction sites. In comparison to Berlin, where wildscapes were the product of a vacuum of power, ownership and control, in Dublin unfinished commercial wastelands have resulted from a financial vacuum. However, unlike the bottom-up processes that flourished in Berlin in the 1990s, the Dublin Parlour project has resulted from a top-down desire to deal with this phenomenon.

The site is located at what was to be the focal point of the new Dublin Docklands redevelopment area, adjacent to the terminus station of a new light rail line and between the recently constructed 20,000 m^2 untenanted District Centre and a former dockland warehouse converted into a major concert arena. The site was to contain Ireland's tallest building and an adjacent marble-clad civic square with glass canopies and high-specification street furniture of matching corporate character. The demise of the speculative construction industry resulted in the office tower construction stalling at basement level and the associated civic square remaining unrealized. As an innovative contingency plan, an architectural competition was held by the City Council in partnership with the site's developer to find a design strategy to activate this space. The scheme presented here is the competition-winning proposal that our practice developed for a temporary-use response to this urban condition.

The proposal is for a public space which is highly flexible, adaptable, and robust in nature to enable a diverse programme of arts, culture and leisure events to occur, ranging from outdoor concerts, performances, and cinema, to markets and art exhibitions. In addition to this emphasis on performative attributes the proposal is intended to relate to the activity and energy of the adjacent working port and celebrate the temporary nature of the project. The shipping container, symbol of global trade and exchange, will be utilized as a building element to solve all the pragmatic design issues and to open up further possibilities and appropriations. A strategy of incompleteness was adopted whereby these highly flexible adaptable elements are only supplied with basic services (water and electricity) to allow appropriation and programmatic functioning to grow and evolve over time. The adaptability and small scale of individual containers was intended to allow diversity to develop in the operation and perception of these elements. For example, the ground level containers can be used as kiosks or market stalls and access is given to the upper levels of the containers allowing them to act as a continuous viewing gallery for watching events, or as linear semi-outdoor art galleries or individual studios (Figure 15.6).

The shipping containers will be stacked to form a permeable enclosure, and provide spatial definition to the square while creating dynamic variations of solid and void and light and shadow to visually animate the space and offer the potential integration of various art forms. At night, the open-ended containers act as

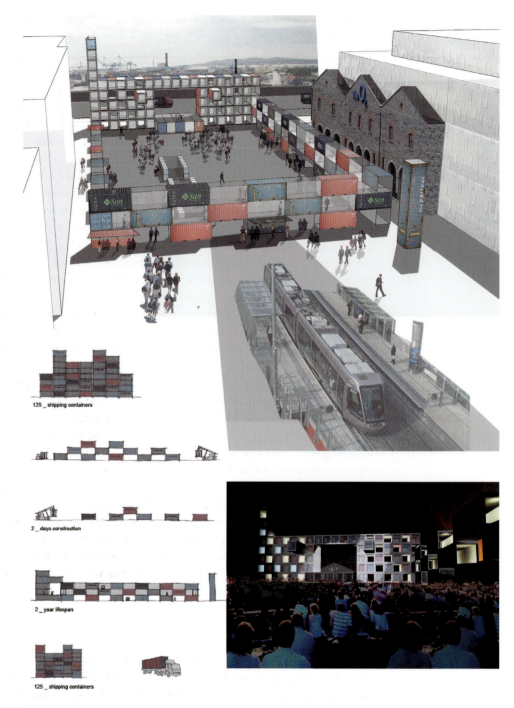

Figure 15.6
Dublin Parlour: the competition-winning scheme showing relationship to context; concept of 'borrowing' shipping containers for the project and returning to use as shipping containers when the temporary life of the project is over; night-view showing containers used for lighting, to create enclosure, and to build a stage (images: Deirdre McMenamin, Dougal Sheridan, Sarah Allen, Ryan Ward – LiD Architecture)

urban-scale light fittings, containing dynamic lighting that fluctuates and flickers in response to the intensity and direction of the winds blowing in from the sea. Easy to assemble, disassemble, transport, and re-use, as well as being locally sourced from the port, the shipping container, in this context, is the ideal sustainable building element.

Evoking the derelict piles of empty containers in the adjacent port, the proposal registers change and appears like a ruin of stalled global trade in juxtaposition with the empty commercial space of the adjacent speculative developments. This ruin-like quality is further intensified by dislodging and liberating the containers from their usual expectations and functions, allowing them to be interpreted in ways that provide scope for imaginative improvization and exploration. The spatial re-contextualization of the containers in this new use draws attention to their material qualities and potentials. The robust texture and materiality of shipping containers invites appropriation including tagging or graffiti art. This, in turn, provokes awareness of our sensual alienation from the surrounding sterile/corporate urban realm, where the smoothness of surface and constant maintenance of space restricts such material agencies.[6]

Asphalt, that ubiquitous material of the urban landscape, was chosen for the surface of the square because of its performative characteristics, as 'no other material has been found to be so flexible and so adaptable, capable of absorbing so many functions, enabling so many uses, and producing so many effects' (Bélanger 2006: 242). Not only is the seamlessness and durability of the surface functional and accessible but it can also be used as an urban scale graphic surface; In a collaborative work with a graffiti artist, the graphics and technology of road markings are to be applied to the surface and reinterpreted not only to satisfy pragmatic requirements of signage, etc., but also to allow the animation of the surface by populating it with the abstracted shadows of people.

Although this urban landscape project is not composed of organic, planted elements, it is informed by the processes and potentials found in urban wildscapes. Ruin-like registration of change, use of temporary programmes and structures, an emphasis on flexibility, adaptability and performative qualities, and an open-ended indeterminate attitude to the programmatic functioning of the space, allowing its appropriation to grow and evolve organically over time, are all traits and attributes informed by urban wildscapes.

CONCLUSION

The question of how practice in the broadest sense can engage with urban wildscapes and the processes at work in them has revealed three relevant areas – policy and legislation, alternative forms of practice, and design processes and strategies.

Urban wildscapes raise the question, in relation to planning and urban development policy, of the degree to which it is possible to leave public and environmental spaces to their own internal dynamic forces of evolution. As discussed, the significant change in outlook and policy by development authorities, which has occurred in Berlin to post-legitimize and harness the cultural and social capital generated by the informal urbanism of its wildscapes, could inform how these spaces are approached in the regulatory contexts of other countries. Until legislation and policy adapt to these alternative processes of urban development, practitioners who wish to act as urban protagonists in this area will look to find undefined areas in the regulatory matrix, and deploy strategies to maintain architectural, artistic, and environmental ambiguity within systems geared to regulatory certainty.

This leads to the challenge and potential of alternative and evolving forms of Architectural, Landscape, and Urban Design Practice. The spontaneous appropriation of space seen in the urban wildscapes of Berlin will probably continue to remain outside the sphere of conventional practice. However definitions and forms of practice are evolving to better engage with the social and environmental contexts of urban wildscapes. This includes not only the re-orientating of 'professional' practice but also recognizing the agency of diverse existing urban protagonists as valuable and effective forms of practice. Urban wildscapes often require and stimulate a proactive and interdisciplinary and participatory approach to practice where the roles of designer, user, developer, environmentalist, builder, business person overlap or converge. Working within existing urban wildscapes requires working in continuity with the existing social and environmental dynamics while facilitating a framework to allow continued appropriation and involvement of diverse interests.

Implications for policy and alternative forms of practice are issues related largely to the treatment of existing urban wildscapes and we have touched on some of the existing discourses relevant to these topics. However the question that has been the primary focus of the projects we have examined is how the informal appropriation processes observed in urban wildscapes can inform design processes and strategies for the making of public spaces generally. These strategies of registering change, temporal interventions, indeterminacy, ambiguity, mobility, incompleteness, diversity and participation, and an emphasis on the performative properties of public space have significantly informed the design and conceptual phases of the projects examined. However, it would be premature to attempt to assess the success of these strategies as implemented projects because they are still in the initial stages of occupancy or realization. Such assessment will require the critical distance of time and occupant/user experiences.

In these projects, we found that the potential for urban wildscapes to inform the production of public space within the conventional mechanisms of practice was not found in the superficial replication of their material or formal qualities. By definition, wildscapes grow outside of these conventional mechanisms and their visual constructions. Instead, understanding the underlying processes at play in wildscapes and transposing these onto the production of public space may offer a more meaningful opportunity to learn from urban wildscapes.

NOTES

1 'We' refers to LiD Architecture (Landscape in Design) www.lid-architecture.net, an architectural, urban design, and landscape practice engaged in both practice and research, founded by Deirdre McMenamin and Dougal Sheridan. One of the projects examined here was undertaken in collaboration with 'Building Initiative.'
2 A squatted house, directly translated as an 'occupied house'.
3 The 'Regenerate' Project is an Arts Council of Northern Ireland-funded project, co-ordinated by Craigavon Council and surrounding local councils. www.regenerateprojects.com/carbondesign.htm.
4 'Building Initiative' is the name adopted by a collaborative group of Architects, Urbanists and Artists, who also use the term to describe the 'mode of agency' they have chosen to inform and realize citizen-led urban regeneration. www.buildinginitiative.org (Sheridan 2009).
5 'Scarecrow Sketches' by Tom Hallifax in *Yellow Press* Issue no. 3 (McMenamin and Sheridan 2008).
6 Tim Edensor describes these attributes in relation to industrial ruins (Edensor 2005).

REFERENCES

Allen, S. (2001) 'Mat urbanism: the thick 2D', in H. Sarkis (ed.) *Case: Le Corbusier's Venice Hospital*, Munich: Prestel.

Building Initiative (2007) *Yellow Space Belfast: Negotiations for an Open City*. Online: www.buildinginitiative.org (accessed 28 June 2010).

—— (2006) Online: www.buildinginitiative.org (accessed 28 June 2010).

Bélanger, P. (2006) 'Synthetic surfaces', in C. Waldheim (ed.) *The Landscape Urbanism Reader*, New York: Princeton Architectural Press.

Craigavon Borough Council Arts Development Department (2009) *Regenerate Projects*. Online: www.regenerateprojects.com/carbondesign.htm (accessed 20 March 2010).

Edensor, T. (2005) *Industrial Ruins: Space, Aesthetics and Materiality*, Oxford: Berg.

Katz, S. and Mayer, M. (1983) 'Gimme shelter: self-help housing struggles within and against the state in New York City and West Berlin', *International Journal of Urban and Regional Research*, 9, 1: 15–45.

Lange, B. (2006) 'From Cool Britannia to Generation Berlin? Geographies of culturepreneurs and their creative milieus in Berlin', in C. Eisenberg, R. Gerlach and C. Handke (eds) *Cultural Industries: The British Experience in International Perspective*, 145–172. Online: http://edoc.hu-berlin.de/docviews/abstract.php?lang=ger&id=27716 (accessed 1 April 2010).

McMenamin, D. and Sheridan, D. (2006) LiD Architecture. Online: www.lid-architecture.net (accessed 28 June 2010).

—— (2008) *Yellow Press* August. Online: www.buildinginitiative.org/yellowpress.html (accessed 28 June 2010).

Misselwitz, P., Oswalt, P. and Overmeyer, K. (2003) *Strategies for Temporary Uses – Potential for Development of Urban Residual Areas in European Metropolises: Final Report (Extract)*. Online: www.studio-uc.de/downloads/suc_urbancatalyst.pdf (accessed 20 March 2010).

Senatsverwaltung für Stadtentwicklung Berlin (Senate Department of Urban Development Berlin) (2004) *Raumpioniere (Land Pioneers of Berlin)*.

—— (2007) *Urban Pioneers: Temporary Use and Urban Development in Berlin*, Berlin: Jovis Verlag.

Sheridan, D. (2007) 'Berlin's indeterminate territories: the space of subculture in the city', *Field Journal*, 1: 97–119. Online: www.fieldjournal.org/index.php?page=2007-volume-1 (accessed 1 May 2010).

—— (2009) 'Building initiative in Belfast', *Architectural Research Quarterly*, 13, 2: 151–162.

Studio Urban Catalyst (2003) *Urban Catalysts: Strategies for Temporary Uses, Berlin: Studio Urban Catalyst.* Online: www.templace.com/think-pool/attach/download/1_UC_finalR_synthesis007b.pdf?object_id=4272&attachment_id=4276 (accessed 1 July 2011).

Zagami, B. (2009) 'Indeterminate spaces: an investigation into temporary uses in Berlin and the implications for urban design and the high street in the UK', unpublished M. Urban Design Thesis, University of Westminster.

Chapter 16: Anti-planning, anti-design?

Exploring alternative ways of making future urban landscapes

Anna Jorgensen and Lilli Lička

INTRODUCTION

The aim of this chapter is show how the characteristics of urban wildscapes can be used to inform planning and design strategies for the urban environment more generally, and to contrast these strategies with some contemporary approaches to the planning and design of urban public open space. It is divided into four sections. This introduction outlines the overall structure and content of the chapter and defines urban wildscapes. Section two critiques some contemporary approaches to the planning and design of urban public space, especially ideas concerning the creation of local distinctiveness and place identity, and proposes that alternative strategies may be derived from the properties of urban wildscapes. In section three, these properties are examined in more detail, and six key characteristics are explored: multiplicity, ambiguity, polyvalence, communality, dynamism, mutability and process. Placed alongside this theoretical commentary are a series of illustrated case studies of completed landscape projects,[1] which demonstrate how these characteristics may inform the planning and design of urban public space.

The final section explores the implications of these characteristics for the planning and design of urban public spaces. A central idea running through this chapter is that there is no dichotomy of regulated versus wild (or unregulated) urban spaces; rather, there is shifting dialectic existing at multiple different scales. Places need not be (and are not) either regulated or wild, but may be shades of both, and it is the tension between these states that gives rise to creative possibilities in urban public space.

For the purposes of this chapter, urban wildscapes are defined as spaces 'between or on the margins of more programmed and controlled urban spaces … characterized by the opportunities they provide for a diverse range of human and non-human activities and processes' (Jorgensen 2009).[2] Many of these spaces have developed incrementally over time, as the result of the interactions between officially sanctioned planning and design interventions, more informal changes made by the users and maintainers of these spaces, and natural processes including the aging and degeneration of materials and structures and the overgrowth of vegetation.

RECENT TRENDS IN THE PLANNING AND DESIGN OF
URBAN PUBLIC OPEN SPACES

A post-modern dilemma confronting urban planners and designers globally concerns the purposes and forms of city morphologies and spaces, now that they are becoming so far removed from the processes that originally shaped them. Urbanization first occurred to facilitate commercial exchange in specific locations dictated by geographical expedience but as changes in transport and communications have enabled industrial production to move away from urban centres, and commercial transactions are relocating from the market place to the virtual spaces of information and communications technology (Lyster 2006), the functions and meanings of urban spaces have changed. Nowadays, the urban centres of 'developed' countries are given over to leisure activities; especially the consumption of globally-produced goods and cultures, and the flows of people needed to fuel the local economies that depend on these activities.

Whereas once the form and fabric of buildings and spaces were shaped by local resources, crafts and ideologies; great changes in architectural and building technologies, and the global movement of materials, expertise and ideas, mean that the forms, functions and meanings of urban spaces are no longer constrained by their locality. However, this has not generally resulted in greater diversity of urban public spaces. Instead, alongside the dedication of urban centres to consumption and leisure, an approach to urban planning and design has developed that has resulted in an erosion of local identity.

Within these new urban spaces, land uses or activities that compete with or detract from the prescribed ones, such as unlicensed performance or vending, organized gatherings or political demonstrations, children's play, young people hanging out (Worpole 2003), skateboarding and rough sleeping, are generally prohibited. External and internal spaces that facilitate or enable the sanctioned land uses are preferred. In the case of retail, these spaces must provide unambiguously positive experiences that are free from confusion, risk or discomfort; and visitors must be able to move 'seamlessly' from one locality to the next (Edensor 2005).

The city of Sheffield, UK typifies these trends. Faced with the progressive collapse of its steel industry, the erosion of the city centre by decades of car-centred planning and competition from its regional rivals (the cities of Leeds and Manchester), Sheffield City Council's new masterplan envisages a renaissance based on developing the city's retail and cultural provision (Sheffield City Council 2008).

Along with the goods and services that may be purchased there, the city itself is becoming a 'product' to be consumed; thus the fabric of the city, its buildings, streets and open spaces, have to be packaged and commodified (Kwon 1997). As part of its own branding exercise, Sheffield city centre has been divided up into twelve 'quarters', with their own names and distinguishing characteristics, linked by various routes, including the 'gold' and 'steel' routes.

Local identity must be enhanced to offer visitors something distinctive. Attempts to bolster or create local identity include preserving historic fabric and structures, adding fresh material to maintain the 'look' of a particular historical period (especially paving and street furniture), and creating new landscapes alluding to notable aspects of local history and culture. Sheffield is well-known for its historic role as a centre for the manufacture of steel and cutlery. Hence, Sheaf Square, the new public space that welcomes visitors leaving the railway station, is bounded by the 90-metre long *Cutting Edge* stainless steel sculpture *cum* water feature (Sheffield City Council 2007) (Figure 16.1). This sculpture also exemplifies an approach to the design of urban public space that consists of the assembly of significant objects, rather than the manipulation of landscape elements to make coherent spaces. The presence of objects as symbols of place stands in for the experience of being in place (Baudrillard 1983).

The pre-eminence of physical structures as the preferred manifestation of local identity and 'placeness' necessarily limits the number of ways in which those places can be used and interpreted. A particular historical period or cultural perspective is privileged, and differences smoothed over (Hellström 2006). It also privileges tangible objects over less tangible components of place, including space, time, movement, flux, absence, and natural process. Thus, in Sheaf Square, the River Sheaf runs underground in a culvert nearby, whilst the open space is structured around an enormous, artificially powered, water feature that stands in for its namesake.[3] Both the scale and form of this water feature typify the use of a rather florid, baroque design language to articulate spaces and functions (Lund 1997).

Furthermore, although manuals of urban design practice purport to celebrate local culture (CABE 2000), social and environmental processes are generally eschewed in favour of static, fixed representations of place. In her critique of the regeneration of UK industrial ruins, Heatherington (2006) refers to Doreen Massey's (1993; 2005) interpretations of place as a temporary crystallization of diverse narratives, ideologies and human and non-human entities in space, rather than a collection of objects with fixed meanings.

Figure 16.1
The Cutting Edge sculpture and water feature in Sheaf Square (2007), designed by Si Applied and Keiko Mukaide (photograph: Anna Jorgensen, 2009)

QUALITIES OF URBAN WILDSCAPES

This section explores how urban wildscapes exhibit certain qualities that can be used to highlight a more rounded conception of place and local identity. The case studies that accompany the text show how these characteristics may be promoted through particular approaches to urban planning and design in urban public open space more generally.

There is a developing literature concerned with the characteristics and meanings of urban wildscapes, though terminology and definitions vary (see Edensor 2005; Doron 2007; Franck and Stevens 2007 for some recent texts). They include derelict sites and indeterminate spaces of all kinds ranging from wilderness-like places such as woodlands, disused post-successional sites (and buildings) and linear sites such as railways, rivers and canals, to more incidental 'loose spaces' (Franck and Stevens 2007) that are close to and sometimes part of more regulated urban spaces such as gap sites, 'leftover' spaces, underpasses, and small liminal spaces around the entrances and exits to buildings (Stevens 2007) (Figure 16.2).

The 'Good Fairy', 15th district of Vienna

The 'Good Fairy' project was implemented by koselička in the context of a commission by the City of Vienna to enhance the 'playable city' in 1992. In a prototypical area the urban open spaces, consisting of the streetscape and small parks and squares, were analyzed for their potential to form a network of spaces for children to use. Low-key interventions made use of existing physical structures, such as railings, unknown passages and wider pavements as well as the social capital of the area. The aim was to improve children's autonomous mobility in order to impart spatial and social competences.

'Good fairies' were owners of shops or workshops on the ground floor who committed themselves to helping children by sticking a magic wand on to their shopfront window. Children on their way to school or the playground could pop in to make an urgent phone call home, or get a glass of water or a plaster.

Workshop owners could also express their invitation to children to watch them working by sticking an eye-sticker on their window facing the pavement. Children – as well as adults – could then observe the production going on in the basements or on the ground floor as 'spies' on their way to school. An unexpected variety of handicrafts counted for lost were part of the 'spy' community. The scheme revealed the diversity of activities behind the walls: engravers, glass-chasers, manufacturers of radiator grills for old-timer cars, carpenters, just to name a few. Now, many small creative firms look for shopfront workshops or studios to stay in contact with the city. They enrich the streetscapes; however, production very often stays hidden behind the walls or blinded windows.

Figure 16.2
(Clockwise from top left) The 'Good Fairy': the good fairy sticker at the entrance to a tailor's premises; the good fairy and spy stickers displayed together at another small business; 'I spy a carpenter's workshop'; spy sticker at the entrance to a Landscape Architect's office – all in the 15th district of Vienna (photographs: Ursula Kose and Lilli Lička – koselička, 1992)

Many factors help create the physical and social conditions that enable a diverse range of activities to take place in urban wildscapes, ranging from large-scale informal occupation and trading (Hellström 2006; Sheridan 2007, Mörtenböck and Mooshammer 2007) to activities involving intimate and sometimes challenging engagements with their natural and built surroundings (Edensor 2005). These activities are the result of what Manolopoulou (2007: 63) calls 'the modest simplicity of chance'. This capacity to accommodate diverse activities and experiences is often referred to as multifunctionality, seen as a desirable objective in urban planning and design (CABE 2000), but often incorrectly interpreted as mixed-use. Mixed-use developments are not multifunctional, as each unit of development only has one sanctioned land use (Ling *et al.* 2007). Multifunctionality should also not be confused with flexibility or adaptability, which either risks redundancy, or attempts to control the way in which an environment should change to accommodate anticipated future uses (Manolopoulou 2007). 'Multifunctionality' also privileges function, at the expense of less-instrumental forms of activity. 'Multiplicity', though rather open-ended, seems to be embrace a wider range of interactions with place (Figure 16.3).

Schule Rieden (the school car park), Bregenz

Building on previous work on the site by koselička, an open space of 3,500 m² was redesigned in order to provide more than a car-parking function. Two local secondary schools adjacent to a commercial academy took part in the commissioning process for the new design, instigated by the City Council of Bregenz, a provincial capital in Austria. The project was completed in 2010.

Situated next to the main cycle and pedestrian route leading from the railway station to the school complex and the surrounding neighbourhood, the intention is that this open space will fullfil several functions simultaneously: it will provide a little neighbourhood park as well as acting as the school-yard for the secondary schools, and it will serve as the car park for the sports hall of a successful local handball team.

Existing spatial qualities will be used more effectively including the relationships between open spaces and building facades and a stunning old tree. As part of the previous intervention the canopy of the old *Sophora* tree became a natural roof for the open-air classroom. The rows of benches underneath it also protect the roots of the tree.

The several functions of this small public open space are not expressed by explicit design tools but are offered by making its elements available to everyone. The way of use is decided by the people passing by or by the schoolchildren.

Figure 16.3
Schule Rieden (the school car park), Bregenz (photographs – from top: Gisela Erlacher, Lilli Lička, 2009)

The uses of a place are closely related to its meaning (Blundell Jones 2007), emphasizing that meaning is not something to be passively absorbed from one's surroundings, but is part of an active and individual engagement with place. In contrast to the partial, simplified and sanitized meanings encoded in so many of today's urban public spaces, urban wildscapes contain multiple, often contradictory, meanings, including insecurity, disorder, decay, waste, confusion, freedom, possibility, discovery, adventure and enchantment (Jorgensen and Tylecote 2007). Grappling with the ambiguity and 'polyvalence' (Hellström 2006) of these spaces involves intellectual effort, which is in itself an act of engagement with place.

As Heatherington (Chapter 13 in this book) demonstrates, the overt use of symbol as an expression of local identity renders urban landscapes into riddles that are easily solved. Alternative approaches range from using abstraction in the manipulation of form to capture the essential qualities of a site or its context (Dee 2010), to using physical or cultural traces within the site as a starting point for the introduction of fresh layers or interventions (Figure 16.4).

Tschavoll-Park: a narrow park with garden-pearls, Feldkirch

Adjacent to the medieval centre of Feldkirch, a small town in the west of Austria, a narrow triangular piece of land had been left over by the street and some industrial buildings making use of the stream in the gorge. The city of Feldkirch held a competition to solve the problem of this rather uncanny degenerated space, where drug abuse and other unwanted behaviour occurred. The enclosed location between the steep sides of the gorge makes the park of 5,000 m² look smaller.

koselička's competition entry involved the creation of a bright 'surface' by allowing more natural light to enter the space, providing good views into and out of the space and allowing for a multiplicity of crossings. The idea was that the number of pedestrians would increase, and deserted corners would disappear, resulting in a change of image for the space. Referencing the medieval *hortus conclusus*, round-hedged enclosures were dropped onto the plain surface. These grassy garden pearls provided a soft quality, whilst still enabling informal supervision of the space. The retention of the mature existing trees would also provide changes in the atmosphere through variations in colour and light. The space would become a soft square with a number of garden elements in it, rather than a park with areas of hard surface.

The design responded to the constraints of the situation in two ways: the space was opened for general use and the sight lines into and over the space to the impressive rocks of the gorge were re-established. Though this radical interpretation of a park achieved some recognition by the competition judges, another entry was chosen for realization.

Figure 16.4
Tschavoll-Park: a narrow park with garden-pearls, Feldkirch. (From top) existing trees; the garden-pearls; views in and out of the site; existing paths; the site in context including surrounding buildings and river (plans: Ursula Kose and Lilli Lička – koselička)

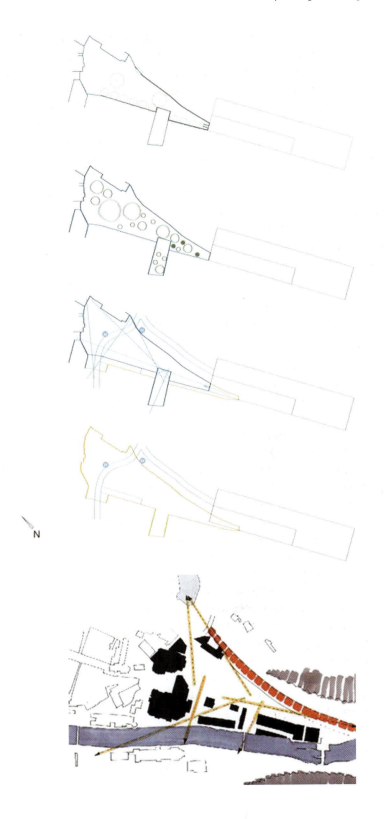

N

Human engagements with urban wildscapes often involve the temporary or permanent modification of their physical fabric in ways that are impossible in more closely regulated urban environments. Fruits and objects may be harvested, acquired or discarded, structures built or destroyed (Edensor 2005). Such spaces are communal in the sense that anyone seems entitled to appropriate them, provided they still remain open to appropriation by others. By contrast, in many contemporary urban spaces, unauthorized modifications are prohibited, and even temporary signs of use or occupation are positively discouraged. The detritus generated by users is routinely removed, and worn or damaged landscape components are replaced in order to maintain these places in their pristine condition. However, where less intensively regulated and maintained urban landscapes are permitted to evolve, the results are arguably more interesting, and more expressive of their locality.

Urban regeneration strategies frequently call for the wholesale renewal of urban spaces; but there are numerous low-intervention landscape architectural approaches that utilize existing landscape layers within a site. These include revealing what is already present – whether that be established trees and plants or hard landscape structures – or reframing, by placing such elements within a new spatial or material context, as well as editing an existing landscape by removing elements that are deemed to have lost their value or purpose (Figure 16.5).

Augustinplatz: a small public open space, Vienna

In a narrow intersection two small triangular open spaces are formed by two residential blocks set back from the street. Sunlight in the square of 1,300 m² is reduced by the high facades dating from the turn of the last century. Over recent decades this space has been filled up with a statue of Augustin, a character from a Viennese folk song, a fountain, shrub planting, benches, a service road, and bus shelters. The City of Vienna commissioned the redesign of this small public space in order to establish a pleasant place to linger in or to pass through. In a public consultation process pursuant to Agenda 21 the requirements for the renovation of the space were defined.

Rather than radically reconfiguring and renewing the space the new design followed a simple strategy of providing space for multiple functions by renovating and simplifying the space, reducing traffic by removing the service road, connecting different areas and providing more generous seating options. The result is a space which feels lighter and more open but still contains its historical elements as reminders of the past in the new landscape.

Figure 16.5
Augustinplatz: the small public open space, Vienna (photographs: Martina Kremmel, 2010)

Urban wildscapes are dynamic: continually changing as part of larger social and environmental cycles and processes. Langer (Chapter 11 in this book) has demonstrated how the Nature-Park Südgelände in Berlin owes its whole existence and ecology to a coalescence of natural, social, political and economic forces. They are also mutable: liable to sudden, unplanned or unexpected change. A tree falls, a building is demolished, or a development elsewhere alters public access to a site, setting off a whole new chain of landscape consequences.

Urban spaces that are susceptible to appropriation, adaptation or change are likely to be more usable by a greater diversity of users, and by extension, more durable in the long term. If additions or adaptations can be made to an existing scheme to meet changing user needs, then wholesale renewal will not be necessary (Figure 16.6).

Bruno Kreisky Park: an old park in Vienna

This park of 10,300 m² has existed at Vienna's 'outer ring' since the city's fortification was built in the eighteenth century. It had been changed and adapted over time and was due for refurbishment in 2000. The City Council of Vienna, encouraged by its own Department of Gender-Sensitive Planning and Building and Quality of Everyday Life to promote gender equality in its public open spaces, announced a competition for a gender sensitive redesign of the park. koselička's winning competition entry was based on the aim of reducing the definition of spaces as much as possible, in order to allow for everyone to do everything in the park.

In addition to removing the soccer cage, a simple structure was introduced into the space as a whole by placing wooden platforms of 4 × 2 metres on the grass. These platforms create islands of appropriation, and by situating them carefully between the existing mature trees they also define centres for spatial units within the park. These units may change in size and shape depending on how the platforms and surrounding spaces are used. Apart from these crystallization points the park is kept rather open, since it contains an important path connection from the residential quarter to the underground station. In 2009, Michael Kienzer, a Vienna-based artist, added a large number of red hammocks as an art installation. These proved so popular with park users that the Garden Department re-installed the hammocks the following year.

Urban wildscapes have not had 'local identity' imposed on them, they are just themselves: the palpable result of a set of interactions and processes over a period of time, though an appreciation of their qualities requires a radical redefinition of our values and aesthetics.

IMPLICATIONS FOR URBAN PLANNING AND DESIGN

Figure 16.6
The hammocks in Bruno
Kreisky Park, an old park
in Vienna (photograph:
Anna Jorgensen, 2010)

This brief review of the failings of some current approaches to urban planning and design and the corresponding qualities of urban wildscapes reveals six key characteristics that can be used to inform urban planning and design: multiplicity, ambiguity and polyvalence, communality, dynamism, mutability and process. The case studies that form part of this chapter demonstrate that these characteristics do not need to be restricted to extreme or challenging urban localities but can inform the planning and design of accessible, inclusive and usable urban public open spaces. What are the implications for the planning and design of urban areas more generally?

First, the values and meanings underpinning planning and design decisions and aesthetics need to be subject to more rigorous examination. Where do they come from, what do they signify and whom do they benefit? Landscape architectural practice and education needs to become more aware of, and more critical of the aesthetic, cultural, social and political assumptions on which they are based. The core purposes and values of urban planning and design need to be re-examined. Urban planners and designers need to have a wider remit, beyond making places profitable, which embraces a wider range of objectives, including social justice and environmental equity. This has many implications, including the need to find new ways of funding urban development projects that do not place so much reliance on private finance. Urban public open space should be seen as a form of indispensable public infrastructure, and should be publicly funded. Landscape interventions should not have the imposition of meaning as their primary objective (Hallal 2006). Treib (2002) has suggested that facilitating pleasure is an end in itself, though it is questionable as to whether 'pleasure' includes a wide-enough range of responses to landscape. Does it, for example, include the exigencies of negotiating risk in landscape (CABE Space 2005)?

Next, these characteristics imply an acceptance and even a celebration of the materiality of the existing fabric of the city in all its diversity and imperfection. Critiquing the idea of masterplanning the perfect, sustainable city, the architect Alexandre Chemetoff (2009: 82) asserts:

> This purist ecology, that of oblivion and segregation, leads to a mode of production of our cities which would thus escape from their history, their necessary filth, their diversity and their ambiguity, all of which are fundamentally necessary. I rather like diversity, I like impurity and like the popular side to the production of cities and territories.

They also reassert the value of the everyday 'make do and mend' landscapes that have been shaped by numerous different makers over time: planners, designers, the people who maintain these sites, and last but not least, their users. They demonstrate that all human actors have a role to play in making the spaces of the city either by means of physical interventions, what Chemetoff calls 'the popular side to the production of cities and territories', or by the usage and experience that renders urban space meaningful.

Next, they reaffirm that urban areas are the product of numerous processes, globalizing forces that make buildings and structures redundant or useful, human activities stimulated by the available opportunities and non-human, natural processes responding to the flux of human occupation, and challenge us to find ways of working more creatively with these processes. Urban design and planning strategies will need to integrate these processes and ecologies (Mostafavi and Najle 2003; Waldheim 2006); which necessitates finding methodologies sophisticated enough to take account of the complexities of all the data involved (Corner 2006); and may also require a widening of the scope of landscape architectural practice.

Thus, they suggest that change is inevitable, that attempts to create stasis are mostly if not always doomed to failure and that instead of aiming for the steady state we should aim to create urban spaces that accommodate change.

Finally, the idea that regeneration necessitates wholesale renewal should be challenged. If landscapes that have evolved incrementally through time are more expressive of local identity, then 'small scale interventions that have the potential for large scale impact' should always be considered (Corbin 2003); an approach to landscape design informed by what Dee (2010) has called 'the aesthetics of thrift'. Urban planning and landscape architecture needs to learn when to stand back: doing nothing, or doing as little as possible may often be preferable to a *tabula rasa* approach.

NOTES

1 The landscape projects that are used to illustrate this chapter are the work of the landscape architectural practice koselička in Vienna, www.koselicka.at.

2 This chapter is based on a paper given at the *Landscape – Great Idea!* conference, University of Natural Resources and Applied Life Sciences, Vienna, April 2009.

3 The authors are indebted to Catherine Dee, Senior Lecturer at the Department of Landscape at the University of Sheffield, for these observations, and for her generous advice, and the time devoted to many discussions that have helped shape the ideas expressed in this paper.

REFERENCES

Baudrillard, J. (1983) *Simulations*, New York: Semiotext.

Blundell Jones, P. (2007) 'The meaning of use and the use of meaning', *Field*, 1: 4–9. Online: www.field-journal.org (accessed 5 January 2009).

CABE (Commission for Architecture and the Built Environment) (2000) *By Design: Urban Design in the Planning System: Towards Better Practice*, London: CABE.

CABE Space (2005) *What Are We Scared Of? The Value of Risk in Designing Public Space*, London: CABE Space.

Chemetoff, A. (2009) 'The projects of Grenoble and Allonnes or the economy of means', *Journal of Landscape Architecture*, Autumn: 82–89.

Corbin, C. (2003) 'Vacancy and the landscape: cultural context and design response', *Landscape Journal*, 22(1): 12–24.

Corner, J. (2006) 'Terra fluxus', in C. Waldheim (ed.) *The Landscape Urbanism Reader*, New York: Princeton Architectural Press.

Dee, C. (2010) 'Form, utility and the aesthetics of thrift in landscape education', *Landscape Journal*, 29: 1–10.

Doron, G. M. (2007) 'badlands, blank space...' *Field*, 1: 10–23. Online: www.field-journal. org (accessed 5 January 2009).

Edensor, T. (2005) *Industrial Ruins: Space, Aesthetics and Materiality*, Oxford: Berg.

Franck, K. A. and Stevens, Q. (2007) *Loose Space: Possibility and Diversity in Urban Life*, London: Routledge.

Hallal, A. M. (2006) 'Barcelona's Fossar de les Moreres: disinterring the heterotopic', *Journal of Landscape Architecture*, Autumn: 6–15.

Heatherington, C. (2006) 'The negotiation of place', unpublished MA dissertation, Middlesex University. Online: www.chdesigns.co.uk (accessed 8 January 2009).

Hellström, M. (2006) 'Steal this place: the aesthetics of tactical formlessness and "the Free Town of Christiania"', unpublished doctoral thesis, Swedish University of Agricultural Sciences: Alnarp.

Jorgensen, A. (2009) 'Anti-planning, anti-design? Exploring alternative ways of making future urban landscapes', paper presented at *Landscape – Great Idea!* conference, University of Natural Resources and Applied Life Sciences, Vienna, April 2009.

Jorgensen, A. and Tylecote, M. (2007) 'Ambivalent landscapes: wilderness in the urban interstices', *Landscape Research*, 32(4): 443–462.

Kwon, M. (1997) 'One place after another: notes on site specificity', *October*, 80: 85–110.

Lund, A. (1997) *Guide to Danish Landscape Architecture*, Copenhagen: Arkitekten's Forlag.

Ling, C., Handley, J. and Rodwell, J. (2007) 'Restructuring the post-industrial landscape: a multifunctional approach', *Landscape Research*, 32: 285–309.

Lyster, C. (2006) 'Landscapes of exchange', in C. Waldheim (ed.) *The Landscape Urbanism Reader*, New York: Princeton Architectural Press.

Manolopoulou, Y. (2007) 'The active voice of architecture: an introduction to the idea of chance', *Field*, 1: 62–72. Online: www.field-journal.org (accessed 5 January 2009).

Massey, D. (1993) 'Power geometry and a progressive sense of place', in J. Bird, B. Curtis, T. Putman, G. Robertson, and L. Tickner (eds) *Mapping the Futures: Local Cultures, Global Change*, London: Routledge.

—— (2005) *For Space*, London: Sage.

Mörtenböck, P. and Mooshammer, H. (2007) 'Trading indeterminacy: informal markets in Europe', *Field*, 1: 73–87. Online: www.field-journal.org (accessed 5 January 2009).

Mostafavi, M. and Najle, C. (eds) (2003) *Landscape Urbanism: A Manual for the Machinic Landscape*, London: AA Publications.

Sheffield City Council (2007) *Cutting Edge Sculpture: More Information.* Online: www.sheffield.gov.uk/out–about/city-centre/public-spaces/sheaf-square/cutting-edge-sculpture (accessed 3 January 2011).

—— (2008) *Sheffield City Centre Masterplan and Roll Forward.* Online: www.creativesheffield. co.uk/DevelopInSheffield/CityCentreMasterplan (accessed 30 December 2008).

Sheridan, D. (2007): 'The space of subculture in the city: getting specific about Berlin's indeterminate territories', *Field*, 1: 97–119. Online: www.field-journal.org (accessed 5 January 2009).

Stevens, Q. (2007) 'Betwixt and between: building thresholds, liminality and public space', in K. A. Franck and Q. Stevens (eds) *Loose Space: Possibility and Diversity in Urban Life*, London: Routledge.

Treib, M. (2002) 'Must landscapes mean?', in S. Swaffield (ed.) *Theory in Landscape Architecture: A Reader*, Philadelphia: University of Pennsylvania Press.

Waldheim, C. (ed.) (2006) *The Landscape Urbanism Reader*, New York: Princeton Architectural Press.

Worpole, K. (2003) *No Particular Place to Go? Children, Young People and Public Space*, Birmingham: Groundwork UK.

Illustration credits

Figure F.1 © Richard Keenan
Figure I.1 © Marian Tylecote
Figure I.2 © Anna Jorgensen
Figure I.3 © Marian Tylecote
Figures I.4–I.6 © Anna Jorgensen
Figures 1.1–1.6 © Christopher Woodward
Figure 2.1 © Chicago Park District
Figures 2.2–2.4 © Paul H. Gobster
Figure 2.5 © US Forest Service
Figure 3.1 *Vauxhall Fete:* engraving by George Cruikshank, reproduced by kind permission of Lambeth Archives Department; © Lambeth Archives Department
Figure 3.2 © Anna Jorgensen
Figure 3.3 © Marian Tylecote
Figure 3.4 © Anna Jorgensen
Figure 3.5 © Marian Tylecote
Figures 3.6–3.7 © Anna Jorgensen
Figures 4.1–4.2 © Tim Edensor
Figure 4.3 © Ian Biscoe
Figures 4.4–4.5 © Tim Edensor
Figures 5.1–5.4 © James Sebright
Figure 6.1 © Henning Seidler, nothofagus.de
Figure 6.2 © Rianne Knoot
Figure 6.3 © Renée de Waal
Figure 6.4 © Frank Döring
Figure 6.5 Archiscape/bgmr; © IBA Fürst-Pückler-Land GmbH
Figure 7.1 © Shanghai Urban Planning and Design Institute
Figure 7.3 © Turenscape Design Institute
Figure 7.4 © Yichen Li
Figure 7.5 © Shanghai Urban Planning and Design Institute
Figure 8.1 (from top) © Udviklingsselskabet By og Havn (The City and Port Development Association); © Nils Vest
Figure 8.2 © Anna Jorgensen

Figure 8.3 Plan of Christiania © Slots – og Ejendomsstyrelsen (The Palaces and Properties Agency) and printed with their kind permission

Figure 8.4 © Maria Hellström Reimer

Figure 9.1 Plan based on OS and UKBORDERS 2001 Census boundary data; © Crown copyright Ordnance Survey, All rights reserved.

Figure 9.3 Reproduced with the kind permission of Sheffield City Council

Figures 9.2, 9.4 and 9.5 © Richard Keenan

Figures 10.1–10.2 © Nigel Dunnett

Figure 10.3 (from top) © Marian Tylecote; © Nigel Dunnett

Figures 10.4–10.6 © Marian Tylecote

Figure 11.1 (lower photograph) © Grün Berlin GmbH

Figure 11.2 Plan of the Nature-Park Südgelände © planland Planungsgruppe Landschaftsentwicklung

Figure 11.3 Section of the Nature-Park Südgelände © planland Planungsgruppe Landschaftsentwicklung

Figures 11.4–11.5 © Laura Silva Alvarado

Figures 12.1–12.4 © Helen Morse Palmer and John Deller

Figure 13.1 © Catherine Heatherington

Figure 13.2 © Alex Johnson

Figure 13.3 © Entasis Design Architects

Figures 13.4–13.5 © Catherine Heatherington

Figure 13.6 © Christian Borchert, McGregor Coxall Landscape Architects

Figure 14.1 © Mattias Qviström

Figure 14.2 © Birgitta Geite

Figure 14.3 © Mattias Qviström

Figures 14.4–14.5 © Malmö stadsarkiv: Fastighetsnämnden (Malmö Municipal Real Estate Office)

Figure 14.6 © Mattias Qviström

Figure 14.7 © Malmö stad Gatukontoret and Tema (Malmö Municipal Highways Department)

Figures 15.1–15.2 © Dougal Sheridan

Figures 15.3–15.6 © Deirdre McMenamin, Dougal Sheridan, Sarah Allen, Ryan Ward – LiD Architecture

Figure 16.1 © Anna Jorgensen

Figure 16.2 © Ursula Kose and Lilli Lička – koselička

Figure 16.3 (from top) © Gisela Erlacher; © Lilli Lička

Figure 16.4 © Ursula Kose and Lilli Lička – koselička

Figure 16.5 © Martina Kremmel

Figure 16.6 © Anna Jorgensen

Index